PRENTICE-HALL
CONTEMPORARY COMPARATIVE POLITICS SERIES
JOSEPH LaPALOMBARA, Editor

published

forthcoming

ROBERT D. PUTNAM

University of Michigan

Prentice-Hall, Inc.

Englewood Cliffs, N.J.

THE
COMPARATIVE
STUDY
OF
POLITICAL
ELITES

Library of Congress Cataloging in Publication Data

PUTNAM, ROBERT D
The comparative study of political elites.

(Contemporary comparative politics series)
Bibliography: p.
Includes index.
1. Elite (Social sciences) 2. Power (Social
sciences) I. Title.
JC330.P88   301.44'92   75-43604
ISBN 0-13-154195-1

for L.P., J.P., and R.W.P.

THE COMPARATIVE STUDY OF POLITICAL ELITES
Robert D. Putnam

© 1976 by Prentice-Hall, Inc., Englewood Cliffs, New Jersey

Printed in the United States of America

10 9 8 7 6 5 4 3 2 1

PRENTICE-HALL INTERNATIONAL, INC., London
PRENTICE-HALL OF AUSTRALIA, PTY. LTD., Sydney
PRENTICE-HALL OF CANADA, LTD., Toronto
PRENTICE-HALL OF INDIA PRIVATE LIMITED, New Delhi
PRENTICE-HALL OF JAPAN, INC., Tokyo
PRENTICE-HALL OF SOUTHEAST ASIA (PTE.) LTD., Singapore

CONTENTS

v

FOREWORD

The series in Contemporary Comparative Politics is unabashedly committed to several goals. We assume that the undergraduate student is by and large not interested in becoming a political scientist but is planning to follow other pursuits. This being so, we aim to expose these students to aspects of politics that will be salient to them throughout their lives. In order to make this point stick though, we believe it is necessary to avoid using the so-called "grand theories" of political science as organizing frameworks. Such "theories" are subtle forms of misinformation; they mislead students—and sometimes others—into believing that we know more about political systems and processes than is actually the case.

It is also our assumption that only the rare undergraduate wishes to master the workings of any single political system. Even where such interest may be present, the study of single countries rarely leads to anything resembling systematic comparative analysis. Therefore, we have sought to focus on a wide range of interesting and important aspects of politics that individual volumes in this series treat comparatively.

We also believe that those aspects of politics included in this series should be treated from both an institutional and a behavioral perspective. Political science will remain a hobbled discipline as long as those who write or consume it elect one of these orientations or the other. Political science will become or remain an arid discipline if we neglect to treat the normative side of politics. The authors of this series are neither bare-facts empiricists nor "cloud-ninety" political moralists. They are prepared to use whatever forms of comparative analysis are available to permit us better to understand the relationships between political institutions, behavior, values, and man's condition. The range of understanding we seek to achieve is reflected in the core of the series (Joseph LaPalombara, *Politics within Nations*) and in the titles of individual series volumes.

Because no series can encompass all areas of politics, we have had to make choices. Some of these choices will introduce the reader to aspects of politics not often treated on a comparative basis. Our published volumes on political violence, political corruption, and legal culture, and a forthcoming book on the military and politics, fall into this category. Other choices will expose the reader to more traditional aspects of government and politics treated in a fresh comparative perspective. Series volumes on national legislatures, bureaucracies, and elections fall into this category.

This volume by Robert Putnam encompasses both of these categories. Political leadership and the role of strategic elites in the political process are an enduring facet of what fascinates and engages students of politics. Nevertheless, these subjects have rarely received the central attention they deserve. Even more rarely have they been accorded the kind of tightly reasoned theoretical and comparative attention that Putnam displays in the pages ahead.

Putnam brings to this enterprise his own extensive research experience in the comparative analysis of legislative, bureaucratic, and military elites in many countries. His published works represent striking additions to our knowledge as well as important, often ingenious, innovations in the questions we ask about political elites and how we go about providing good answers to these questions. Beyond these efforts, however, is the remarkable synthesis this book achieves regarding what several of the social sciences have to tell us on the subject. These two dimensions of the book, taken together, make of it an extraordinary contribution to students and teachers alike, and to the profession of political science as a whole.

In providing us with this rich array of information, theory, and analytical approaches and insights, Putnam has raised the study of political elites to the level of attention it deserves. Beyond the inputs into the processes of government that we associate with elections, interest group behavior, political communication, public opinion, and the like, we need to know more about the role of elites in the formulation, enactment, and execution of public policies. We must know more about who these elites are, where they come from, how they are recruited, what values they hold, how they relate to the electorate and general public, how they orient to their tasks and interact among themselves—and what difference variations in and among these (and other) factors seem to make here and there.

It is precisely because issues of this nature are frankly addressed and clearly and rewardingly discussed that this is an important book. Whatever else may be said of it, it will surely be recognized as a beacon to guide us down the complicated path to clearer understanding of politics and government.

JOSEPH LaPalombara

New Haven

PREFACE

Insofar as political decisions matter, political decision makers do, too. This book is written with two audiences in mind: students wishing to learn more about those whose decisions shape our world, and scholars seeking an introduction to the rapidly expanding professional literature of elite analysis. In crafting a volume that might speak to the diverse interests of these audiences, I have had several broad objectives.

First, I have tried to bridge the gap—unusually large in this field of scholarship—between abstract, general theories and masses of unorganized empirical evidence. As the selective bibliography at the end of this volume indicates, scholars have investigated many elites in this country and around the world. I have tried to integrate their copious, but disparate, findings in such a way that cumulative answers emerge to the grand questions posed by classical elite theories. (In some cases I have included illustrative evidence from my own research; unattributed data throughout the book are drawn from the projects reported in Putnam [1973a and 1973b].)

Because our knowledge of elites is still evolving, I have offered some generalizations that seem well substantiated by numerous studies, some generalizations that are supported by limited, but reasonably reliable evidence, and some that are for the moment merely plausible hunches. Often I have raised questions for which we still lack conclusive answers, for like James Thurber, I believe that it is less important to know all the answers than to know some of the questions. Ten years hence, some propositions tendered here will have been modified by further research, but it is doubtful that the underlying questions will have disappeared, for they involve some of the most enduring concerns of political and social science.

In a book of limited compass, it is impossible to consider all the issues relevant to an understanding of social power and political involvement. Decision makers always operate within institutions—legislatures, armies, bureaucracies, parties, firms, and so on. Moreover, they must often adjust their actions to the immediate political and socioeconomic circumstances. Hence, a rounded explanation of a leader's behavior must take account of both his institutional context and his tactical calculus. But to have discussed such factors in general, comparative terms would have transformed this volume into an encyclopedia of politics. Similar considerations lead me to concentrate primarily on national political leaders, to devote less attention to socioeconomic elites, and to ignore almost entirely such topics as the social psychology of small group leadership, the nature of political activism at the mass level, and the patterns of power characteristic of local communities and preliterate societies.

A common weakness of much research on political elites is insufficient attention to the "so what?" issue. I have tried to address this question systematically and to speculate on the broader political and social implications of the empirical patterns that are documented here. I have not discussed explicitly and at length the link between elites and public policy, primarily because this is a topic about which we have much "common knowledge" but remarkably little rigorous evidence. But throughout the book I have tried to lay out what is known, as well as what is suspected, about the more distant consequences of elite characteristics and behavior.

Beyond the roster of fellow researchers recorded in the footnotes and bibliography, I have had indispensable help from many colleagues, students, and friends in the preparation of this book. I want particularly to thank—and absolve—Joel Aberbach, Gabriel Almond, Robert Axelrod, John Campbell, Martha Dean, Giuseppe DiPalma, Fritz Gaenslen, Alexander George, Zvi Gitelman, Kai Hildebrandt, Arnold Kanter, Heather Maclean, Nelson Polsby, Kenneth Prewitt, Austin Ranney, Helena Smith, Ezra Suleiman, Victoria Van Dyke, Jack Walker, Aaron Wildavsky, Philip Wion, and William Zimmerman. Uniquely useful contributions were made by Joseph La Palombara and Rosemary Putnam.

ROBERT D. PUTNAM

INTRODUCTION

1

"Who rules?" has a fair claim to be the central question of empirical political science, just as its normative counterpart, "Who should rule?" is perhaps the central question of political philosophy. Like any truly fundamental question about social relations, "Who rules?" has generated a long history of speculative answers and a rich store of "common knowledge." Sage commentators, from Plato and Aristotle to our nightly television newscasters, tell us much about power and leadership, but their profundities, when carefully examined, often turn out to be incomplete and ambiguous. Recently, however, systematic research has begun to produce a modest store of knowledge about political elites that is both reliable and reasonably coherent. To summarize and assess our evolving understanding of those who rule is the purpose of this book.

THE CLASSICAL ELITE THEORISTS

That rulers are fewer in number than ruled might seem an unexceptionable first step toward answering our fundamental query. For many centuries, in fact, it was an unquestioned axiom of political thought that power in society is distributed unequally. In eighteenth-century Europe, however, a contrary view began to gain credence among philosophers and men of affairs: that all citizens—or at least all men—might share power equally. The age of the democratic revolutions had dawned. During the nineteenth century radical critics of bourgeois society decried the persistence of oligarchy but insisted that in the long run a society without rulers was desirable and possible—perhaps even inevitable.

At the close of the nineteenth century, however, this democratic optimism began to be questioned by more pessimistic students of society, who argued that behind the diverse facades of government, power was always confined to a ruling few. As Gaetano Mosca phrased the argument:

> *In all societies . . . two classes of people appear—a class that rules and a class that is ruled. The first class, always the less numerous, performs all political functions, monopolizes power and enjoys the advantages that power brings, whereas the second, the more numerous class, is directed and controlled by the first.*[1]

From the outset the dispute between the elitists and their opponents has been bedeviled by confusions among what *is*, what *could be*, and what *ought to be*. The radical democrats argued that power should be shared equally and, by implication, that it could be. The elitists replied not merely that in fact power was monopolized by the few, but that as a practical matter things neither could nor should be otherwise. Thus, ideologically the elitists seemed merely conservative defenders of the established order.[2] Nevertheless, their writings contained some insights that deserve attention even from their adversaries.

Most prominent among these turn-of-the-century elitists, in addition to Mosca, were Vilfredo Pareto and Robert Michels. Later in this book we shall examine some of their specific arguments about the structure and circulation of elites. For the moment, however, we can concentrate on the general principles shared by all three.

1. *Political power, like other social goods, is distributed unequally.* Pareto was the most elegant in his formulation of this initial point.

> *Let us suppose that in every branch of human activity an index or grade can be assigned to each individual as an indication of his capacity, in much the same way that marks are awarded for the various subjects in a school examination. . . . To the man who has earned millions—no matter what means he has employed therein, fair or foul—we will . . . give 10. To the earner of thousands we will give 6, assigning 1 to the man who just manages to keep body and soul together, and zero to him who ends up in the workhouse. . . . The clever swindler who can pull the wool over people's eyes without falling foul of the law will be rated at 8, 9, or 10 according to the number of dupes he catches in his net and the amount of money he squeezes out of them. The wretched pilferer who snaffles the cutlery in a restaurant and bumps redhanded into the nearest policeman will be rated at 1. . . . Let us therefore make a class for those people who have the highest indices in their branch of activity, and give to this class the name of elite. It will help in our investigations into the social equilibrium if we distinguish two further classes within this main class of the elite: the governing elite and the non-governing elite. The first elite class includes those who directly or indirectly play a significant part in government and political life; the second comprises the rest of the elite personnel, those who have no significant role in government and politics.*[3]

---

[1] Mosca, 1939, p. 50.

[2] For useful summaries of the classical elite theories, see Bottomore, 1964, pp. 1–41, and G. Parry, 1969, pp. 15–50.

[3] Pareto, 1966, p. 248.

Already Pareto has introduced a number of complications; we might wonder, for example, about the relations between governing and nongoverning elites. But the fundamental idea is simple and persuasive: people can be ranked by their share of any good—wealth, skill, or political power.

2. *Essentially, people fall into only two groups: those who have "significant" political power and those who have none.* This second point is not logically implied by the first; Pareto's scheme, for example, could encompass intermediate positions on the scales of wealth, skill, and (presumably) power. But the classical elitists generally argued that for most purposes the distribution of power can be conceived in dichotomous terms.

3. *The elite is internally homogeneous, unified, and self-conscious.* This proposition, too, adds a new twist. The elite is not a collection of isolated individuals—a mere statistical artifact. Instead, like the members of some exclusive club, individuals in the elite know each other well, have similar backgrounds, and (though they may have occasional differences of opinion) share similar values, loyalties, and interests. James Meisel has summed up this proposition in his mnemonic "three C's"—group consciousness, coherence, and conspiracy (in the sense of common intentions).[4]

4. *The elite is largely self-perpetuating and is drawn from a very exclusive segment of society.* The classical theorists gave much attention to the long-term rise and fall of elites, but in the short run, they argued, successful leaders select their own successors from among the privileged few. The powerful are the scions and the representatives of the wealthy and the prestigious.

5. Finally and for all these reasons, *the elite is essentially autonomous,* answerable to no one else for its decisions. All important political questions are settled according to the interests or whims of this group.

This, then, is the portrait of society painted by the classical elite theorists: a socially isolated, self-seeking leadership caste that cleverly dominates the abject masses. Theorists have differed on the question of *why* societies were always so organized. Some, like Michels, stressed that the division of labor necessary in any organization implies that some people acquire the skills and perquisites of leadership, while others become accustomed to being led. Others, like Pareto, argued that oligarchy flows from the unequal distribution of innate personal qualities. And some more recent theorists, like Suzanne Keller, have proclaimed elite rule a functional requisite that must be satisfied if society is not to disintegrate. But all agreed that oligarchy is, as Michels put it, an "iron law."[5]

---

[4] Meisel, 1962, p. 4.

[5] Michels, 1959, pp. 32–36, 377; Keller, 1963, pp. 88–106. Keller does not endorse all the elements of classical elite theory.

Does a small, cohesive, unresponsive group actually run everything? This deceptively simple question has no single answer, for it is not a single question. The empirical complexities of elite analysis have often been compounded by a tendency to disguise issues of fact as issues of definition. For example, many social scientists have defined "elite" in terms of Meisel's three C's and have referred to the set of propositions outlined above as "the" elite theory of politics.

As Humpty Dumpty explained to Alice, words can mean anything we want. But we must beware of building dubious empirical assumptions into definitions, for, as Alice discovered, if the assumptions are false, the definitions will be very confusing. One well-known study, for example, defined the political elite as "the leadership [of a body politic] and the social formations from which leaders typically come, and to which accountability is maintained, during a given generation."[6] But whether leaders do in fact remain accountable to the groups from which they come is a matter for investigation, not stipulation. The leader who becomes "a traitor to his class" should not be ruled out simply by definition.

There is little consensus among social scientists about the definition of elite, but I propose to define the term broadly, leaving questions of size, composition, and autonomy for later empirical investigation. Let us begin with the first postulate of classical elite theory: some people have more political power than others; they are the political elite. This proposition is hardly profound, but definitions should open questions, not close them.

If we are to define our subject in terms of the distribution of power, we must consider the controversial concept of power itself.[7] Two distinct conceptions of power appear in both social science and common parlance: (1) power as the ability to influence other individuals and (2) power as the ability to influence collective decision making. We often say that one person has power over another, meaning that the first can make the second act in ways the second would not otherwise choose. On the other hand, when we speak of the political power of farmers, for example, we are really referring, not to their ability to change the behavior of other individuals, but to their ability to affect the government's agricultural policies. Of course, power over people is often a means to achieve power over outcomes. But in the practical analysis of politics it is often useful to keep these concepts separate.

For studying political elites, it is most useful to think in terms of power over

---

[6] Lasswell, Lerner, and Rothwell, 1952, p. 13.

[7] For useful introductions to the literature on power, influence, and related concepts, see Dahl, 1968, and Kadushin, 1968.

outcomes. The president of General Motors, the general secretary of the Soviet Communist party, the prime minister of Tanzania, or the chairman of the Swedish Labor Federation is a member of the political elite, not by virtue of his ability to issue binding orders to subordinates, but rather because of his influence on national policy. Hence, by *power* here I shall mean *the probability of influencing the policies and activities of the state,* or (in the language of systems theory) *the probability of influencing the authoritative allocation of values.*

Several important kinds of power relations are excluded by this definition. First of all, power over persons that does not affect government policy is omitted. The power of a Chilean general over his men, or of an English mill owner over his workers, or of a wife over her husband will be neglected unless it becomes a factor affecting affairs of state. Secondly, the ability to affect the well-being of others without using the mediating agency of government is also excluded from view. The decision of Henry Ford II to locate a new plant, or of a British union leader to call a strike, or of the pope to proscribe the pill—each has important consequences for many ordinary citizens, but these are not exercises of political power as I define that term.[8] On the other hand, power of these diverse sorts is often convertible into power over public policy and thus may become indirectly relevant to our study of political elites.

Several other distinctions are important here. First, we must carefully specify the *scope* of power—that is, the range of activities over which it extends. Military leaders may have much influence on defense policy, but little on agricultural matters. The chairman of a congressional committee may be quite powerful within a limited domain, whereas the director of the president's Office of Management and Budget probably has less intense influence over a broader range of issues. For some purposes it may be convenient to consider an actor's "average" power across the whole panoply of government activities, but caution is required, because in specific cases this average may be quite misleading.

Even among the very powerful, few people directly decide public policy. Hence, we must distinguish direct, indirect, and spurious influence. Figure 1–1 sorts out these possibilities. Actor A has *direct influence* when he participates himself in the final decision. Actor A has *indirect influence* when he influences actor B, who in turn decides policy. For example, the head of a central bank has indirect influence when he persuades the government to modify its fiscal policy. Actor A has *both* direct and indirect influence when he participates himself in the policy-making process and also influences other participants. This case is illustrated when the president successfully urges Congress to pass legislation originally drafted by the White House. Finally, in the case of *spurious influence,* actor B himself directly influences policy and at the same time determines the stand taken by actor A, who has no independent influence on the outcome. Here the

---

[8] The relative importance of government and politics (as opposed to, say, religion or the marketplace) in affecting the lives of ordinary men and women doubtless varies across time and space, but I shall not here discuss this broader question of the social significance of political power.

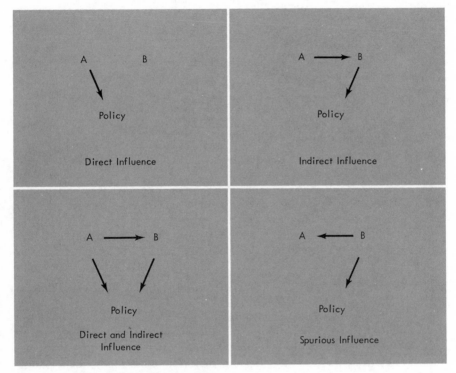

Figure 1–1   Direct, Indirect, and Spurious Influence

policy seems to coincide with actor A's preferences, but his apparent influence is spurious. This possibility is exemplified when a foreign minister merely announces a decision actually taken by the chief executive; the influence of the foreign minister is spurious. Our definition of power (and hence of elite) must allow for both direct and indirect influence, but it must exclude spurious influence.

Many years ago Carl J. Friedrich called attention to a troublesome aspect of power relations. Frequently, even a very powerful decision maker will take into account the possible reactions of other actors. In 1971 the British decision to enter the Common Market was made by the Conservative cabinet; probably they could have carried either a positive or a negative decision. Yet in reaching their final decision they doubtless considered the probable reactions of many other actors—their rank and file in Parliament, the Labour opposition, leading bankers, industrialists, and trade unionists, prominent journalists and commentators, and even the electorate. Friedrich termed this phenomenon "the rule of anticipated reactions."[9]

[9] Friedrich, 1937, pp. 16–18.

This rule plays havoc with any simple analysis of power, because the very real power of those whose reactions are anticipated need not be manifested by any action on their part. Power of this sort—let us call it *implicit power*—is elusive, but it can be detected. For example, if the ultimate decision maker fails to anticipate the reactions of some powerful actor, that actor may reveal his power by direct action. Indeed, holders of implicit power from time to time have to revalidate their claim to power by acting against some objectionable decision. The power of the U.S. Senate over Supreme Court nominations is normally only implicit, for the president usually tries to anticipate senatorial reactions. In 1970 and 1971, however, the senators' power was made explicit, when they rejected two of President Nixon's nominees.

Most important actors in a political system soon learn whose reactions they must anticipate; slow learners quickly become unimportant. Hence, we can often gain valuable clues to the distribution of implicit power by discovering the rules of thumb used by decision makers. Of course, information of this sort must be matched against other evidence, too, for reputation does not always reflect reality.

Implicit power must not be confused with *potential power*. Occasionally, an actor who seems to have the ability to influence policy forbears from exerting that influence. Many scholars, for example, believe that Dwight D. Eisenhower did not fully use the powers inherent in the U.S. presidency. His power, we might say, was in part only potential. Potential power sometimes generates implicit power, as others try to anticipate the reactions of the potentially powerful actor. But for our purposes, consistently unused potential power is much less significant than actual power. We are interested in those who actually influence policy, not in those who could, but never do.

POLITICAL STRATIFICATION

That some people have more power than others is, strictly speaking, axiomatic; I shall treat this proposition as largely self-evident, though I shall offer some collateral evidence shortly. Certainly no national political system displays a distribution of power at all approaching equality. Whether in some sense this *must be* so is irrelevant here; in the case of all political systems we know, it *is* so. And its empirical universality makes this a particularly useful axiom on which to base political analysis. To describe directly the distribution of power in any national political system would require an exhaustive and very difficult investigation. But just as physicists infer the shape of subatomic or extragalactic objects that they cannot directly observe, so too we can estimate the contours of the distribution of political power by relying on indirect evidence about the nature of political participation.

In all societies yet studied there is a high correlation among the following variables: interest in politics, political knowledge and sophistication, political skill and resources (particularly education), political participation, political position, and—here the evidence is less direct—political power. Citizens who are unusually interested in politics tend to be more knowledgeable about public affairs; those who have more political resources, such as education, wealth, and social prestige, are both more interested and more knowledgeable; and those who are interested, knowledgeable, and blessed with resources are more likely to participate actively. Furthermore, as we shall see in subsequent chapters, positions of political prominence are held disproportionately by people of exceptional political motivation and sophistication who have unusually abundant access to socioeconomic and political resources. Few generalizations in political science are so firmly grounded in rigorous research as these.[10]

None of this is very surprising. Nor can there be much doubt that political power itself—the ability to influence public policy—is also highly (though not perfectly) correlated with these variables. Those at the top of these several scales have the desire, the resources, the skill, and the occasion to exert influence. There is no reason to doubt that by and large they use these opportunities, nor that their fellow citizens who lack desire, resources, skill, and occasion are normally much less likely to affect the course of public affairs.

We can thus conceive political systems as stratified, much as sociologists speak of social stratification. Individuals toward the bottom of the political stratification system lack nearly all the prerequisites for exercising political power, whereas those toward the top have these characteristics in abundance. The empirical correlations that underlie this notion of political stratification are so strong and so universal that it offers a uniquely valuable key to the study of politics, more susceptible to cross-national comparison than, for example, elections or legislatures or political parties.[11]

To suggest the general outlines of political stratification systems, Figure 1–2 presents data from several nations on the proportion of their citizens involved in politics in varying degrees. Our interest here is less in the subtle and complex cross-national differences than in one striking cross-national uniformity: only a tiny proportion of the citizens in any of these countries has more than an infinitesimal chance of directly influencing national policy. We can use this

---

[10] For illustrative evidence, see Milbrath, 1965; Verba, Nie, and Kim, 1971; Verba and Nie, 1972, pp. 25–94, 127–129. Verba and his colleagues show that political participation is multidimensional; that is, some people engage in "harder" activities, like writing to officials, but fail to perform "easier" acts, like voting. Nevertheless, for the dominant modes of participation they confirm the propositions reported in the text.

[11] See Michels, 1959, pp. 52–53, and Key, 1961, pp. 182–202. Because the intercorrelations among the components of political stratification, though high, are not perfect, some people may rank high on one dimension, such as motivation or education, and low on others, such as participation or power. These discrepancies are themselves of considerable interest, because, as we shall discuss in Chapter 7, they may be a source of potential instability in a political system. For a discussion of status inconsistency, the analogous phenomenon in social stratification, see Lenski, 1966, pp. 85–88, 288–289.

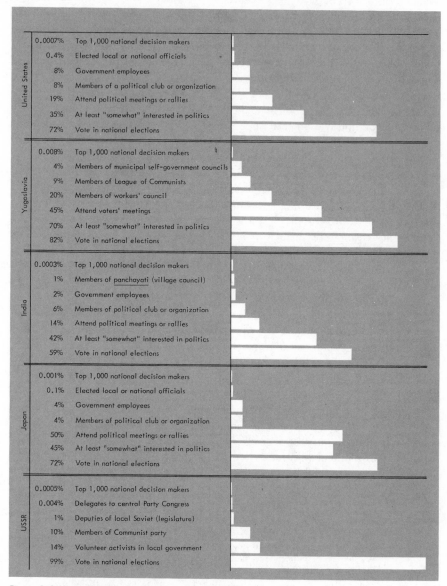

Figure 1–2   Several Pyramids of Participation
Sources: Verba, Nie, and Kim, 1971; Verba et al., 1973; Barton, Denitch, and Kadushin, 1973, p. 113; Russett et al., 1964, p. 70; Barghoorn, 1972, p. 245; Mickiewicz, 1973, pp. 163, 173; LaPalombara, 1974, p. 484; and various national statistical yearbooks.

indirect evidence to construct a general model of political stratification, distinguishing for convenience six broad strata, as illustrated in Figure 1–3.

At the top of the pyramid are those individuals directly involved in national policy making, the *proximate decision makers*. Incumbents in key official posts normally comprise most of this stratum, though as we shall discuss in a moment, it need not be limited to them.

Just below come the *influentials*—individuals with substantial indirect or implicit influence, those to whom the decision makers look for advice, whose interests and opinions they take into account, or from whom they fear sanctions. This stratum may include such figures as high-level bureaucrats, large landowners, industrialists, and financiers, interest-group leaders, and official and unofficial consultants. Of particular interest here are national opinion makers, "those who actively try to influence the opinions either of the national decision makers, the public as a whole or large parts of it, or the other opinion makers."[12] On many major issues the opinion makers set the terms within which policy is debated and decisions are framed. The history of American involvement in Indochina illustrates that over the long run opinion makers may be even more influential than official decision makers, although this case also shows that in the short run decision makers may have considerable autonomy.

The third stratum consists of the much larger number of citizens who take some active part in politics and government, perhaps as party members,

---

[12] Barton, 1969, pp. 1–2.

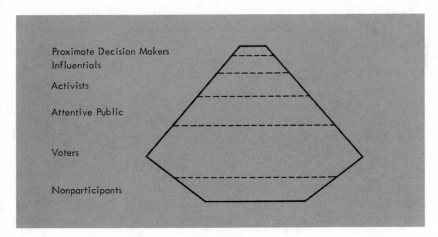

Proximate Decision Makers
Influentials

Activists

Attentive Public

Voters

Nonparticipants

Figure 1–3   A Schematic Model of Political Stratification

middle-level bureaucrats, or local editors, perhaps in some more private way, such as by writing to national legislators. This stratum we can term the *activists*. Below them are those for whom politics is a spectator sport. These men and women—the *attentive public*—are distinguished from most citizens by the unusual amount of attention they pay to public affairs. They recognize many of the leading players in the political game, perhaps even without consulting a scorecard, and they may discuss plays and strategy, but they rarely move onto the field themselves.

Next in the political stratification systems of representative democracies come the masses of ordinary citizens whose only impact on national politics comes in the polling booth. As we shall see in Chapter 6, *voters* have one important collective political resource—numbers—but as individuals they have, for all practical purposes, no political influence. Finally, at the bottom stand those men and women who are, in political terms, objects, not actors. Sometimes by choice, sometimes as a result of deliberate exclusion by the authorities, these *nonparticipants* are politically powerless. (Because in most modern political systems nonvoters constitute a minority of the adult population, Figure 1–3 shows this stratum as smaller than the one above it.)

To say that all political systems are stratified is not to say that all stratification systems are identical, either across countries or across time. The shape of the pyramid of participation—and by implication, the shape of the pyramid of power—is a matter of empirical investigation. Indeed, Harold Lasswell pointed out years ago that "nothing inherent in the geometry of power restricts power to the pyramid. . . . The significant point is that elite patterns are to be discovered by research and not settled by arbitrary definition."[13]

Empirically, distributions of power (pyramidal or not) differ in *height, profile,* and *stability.* In some countries differences in power between the top strata and lower layers—the height of the pyramid—may be very great, whereas in other times and places activists, the attentive public, and even voters may have relatively more influence. Profile refers to the varying proportions of the population that fall in particular strata. In most countries, for example, the pyramids of participation and power are more spike-shaped—fewer people have much power—for foreign policy than for domestic issues. Finally, although the contours of some political stratification systems seem to be quite stable, elsewhere patterns of participation and power vary greatly across time. For example, differences in the size (and hence in the composition) of the electoral stratum between primary and general elections help explain the ill-fated presidential nominations of Barry Goldwater and George McGovern.[14] The possibility of historical change is nicely illustrated by the finding that since the end of the

[13] Lasswell, Lerner, and Rothwell, 1952, p. 13.

[14] Ranney, 1972.

nineteenth century "the shape of the American political universe" has been drastically altered by declining rates of citizen participation.[15]

Unless interpreted carefully, the image of a pyramid may be misleading in several important respects. In the first place, we must make no a priori assumption about the cohesion, consciousness, or autonomy of particular strata. In some countries the top echelon may be a closed, cohesive cabal, unconstrained by circumstance or opposition, while elsewhere it may be open and competitive.

Nor should we assume that the political stratification system is organized hierarchically like an army. Members of higher strata cannot necessarily issue orders to members of lower strata, for power as defined here involves influence over policy, not over people. To be sure, people at the top may use their influence over policy to acquire power over other individuals. For example, the head of the secret police may assume special powers of search and imprisonment. Logically, however, it is equally possible for a decision maker to be divested of power over persons, without in any way limiting his power over policy. The development of the rule of law in Western constitutional history to some extent exemplifies this possibility.

In fact, a stratification model of politics highlights the importance of linkages between strata. Friedrich's rule of anticipated reactions points to the possibility of reciprocal influence. By definition, final decisions are taken by proximate decision makers, but they in turn may be subject to indirect or implicit influence from lower strata. On the other hand, the various strata may be mutually isolated, creating a so-called "elite-mass gap." Linkages between elites and nonelites will be examined in Chapter 6.

In many organizations some subordinates have more influence over policy than do their nominal superiors. The ability to control the flow of information, to preformulate decisions for formal ratification, to modify policy while seeming to implement it—all give rise to what Pahl and Winkler term "power from below."[16] This phenomenon appears a contradiction in terms only if one falsely assumes that distributions of power perfectly mirror organization charts.

Just as sociologists debate the number of social classes, political scientists do not agree on how to slice the pyramid of power. The classical elite theorists usually spoke as if there were only two classes, the powerful and the powerless. Others have instead proposed a three-class theory, including an intermediate stratum of leaders who transmit information and opinion between the top elite and the citizenry, help to implement the elite's decisions, and provide new recruits for the upper stratum.[17]

It is sometimes convenient to refer to specific layers in the political stratifi-

---

[15] Burnham, 1965, 1974.

[16] Pahl and Winkler, 1974, pp. 109–120.

[17] Mosca, 1939, pp. 404–410. See also Giddens, 1972, pp. 360–362, and Deutsch, 1966, pp. 154–155.

cation system. For example, Figure 1–3 distinguished six different strata, and later in this book I shall frequently speak of "the elite," in referring generically to people at or near the top of the pyramid of power. But in the absence of detailed information about the profile of a particular system, indicating natural points of demarcation, this terminology is merely rhetorical shorthand.

This ambiguity is not a major problem, so long as we keep clearly in mind that the underlying variable of participation and power is a matter of more-or-less, not all-or-nothing. For some purposes, we may confine our attention, say, to the top ten decision makers in a country, while for other purposes, we will want to define the elite more broadly to include several thousand individuals who occasionally influence national policy. However, we must not generalize our findings from the narrower to the broader group, or vice versa, without supporting evidence. Similarly, we must beware of comparing incomparable slices of different stratification systems, particularly because the heights and profiles of the systems may be quite different. But these complexities are best addressed in the context of particular research rather than in terms of general theory.

In addition to the horizontal divisions we have been considering, there may be vertical divisions—that is, distinctive groups within the same political stratum. In most modern societies there is considerable division of labor within the elite. Suzanne Keller suggests the term "strategic elites" for these functionally differentiated groups at the top of the pyramid of power.[18]

For our present purposes the most significant of these strategic elites is comprised of the full-time professional politicians—legislators, cabinet ministers, party officials, and their immediate advisors. Most research on political elites has dealt with only this category. However, other politically significant strategic elites include the following: senior civil servants; managers of important economic enterprises, public and private; leaders of mass organizations, such as labor unions, farm groups, and civic associations; high military officials; leading professionals, such as lawyers, doctors, and economists; prominent intellectuals, journalists, and religious leaders.

An elite defined in terms of influence over public policy need not be confined to "establishment" figures. As G. Lowell Field and John Higley point out, this conception "subsumes persons who are often labeled 'counter elite' because these persons quite clearly have the power, although perhaps only through negation, to affect political outcomes individually, regularly, and seriously."[19]

The relative importance of strategic elites varies from country to country and from time to time. For example, businessmen are reputed to play a more significant political role in America and Japan than they do in Western Europe, whereas intellectuals have traditionally been more influential in European poli-

---

[18] Keller, 1963.

[19] Field and Higley, 1973, p. 8.

tics. In Chapter 7 we shall examine the political power of managers and technocrats in postindustrial society as an example of how the standing of strategic elites may change over time.

Elite specialization in particular policy areas may produce another set of vertical distinctions. Policy subelites focus on such areas as military affairs, agricultural policy, education, social welfare, or economic planning. As I have already noted, influence in one policy area does not necessarily bring with it influence in others. Sometimes it is crucial to distinguish among separate policy subelites, but for other purposes we shall find it appropriate to group together all individuals and groups having influence in national politics, regardless of their areas of maximum impact.

FINDING THE POWERFUL   I have suggested that political systems consist of various strata, some more powerful than others, and that the most powerful stratum includes a number of functionally differentiated groupings. For empirical investigation, however, it is not enough to know that the powerful exist in any political system; we must be able to find them. Broadly speaking, social scientists have used three strategies for identifying elites: positional analysis, reputational analysis, and decisional analysis.[20]

Like most of us most of the time, political scientists using *positional analysis* assume that the formal institutions of government provide a useful map of power relations, and thus that incumbents of high positions in those institutions are likely to be politically powerful. In part this assumption is grounded in the fact that people derive power itself from institutional roles. As C. Wright Mills argued:

> *If we took the one hundred most powerful men in America, the one hundred wealthiest, and the one hundred most celebrated away from the institutional positions they now occupy, away from their resources of men and women and money, away from the media of mass communication that are now focused upon them—then they would be powerless and poor and uncelebrated. . . . To be celebrated, to be wealthy, to have power requires access to major institutions, for the institutional positions men occupy determine in large part their chances to have and to hold these valued experiences.*[21]

In a slightly different way, membership in some political organizations, such as European parliaments and Communist central committees, is a significant indicator of elite stature, less because these institutions confer power themselves

---

[20] On the problem of finding the powerful, see Frey, 1970, and Hough, 1975.

[21] Mills, 1956, pp. 10–11.

than because membership is mostly confined to persons who derive power from other sources.

Because formal institutions usually keep good records, positional analysis is the easiest and most common technique for finding the powerful. Most of the empirical studies I shall discuss in later chapters are based on the analysis of members of parliaments, cabinets, central committees, boards of directors, and other formal institutions. But cogent critics of positional analysis have denied that power is perfectly correlated with institutional position. One recent study of power within business organizations concluded soberingly that "Positional defin-itions distort organizational reality because organizations are more complex than authority hierarchies. Power is more than role structure. Men with power in organizations exist in various subdivisions, at various levels, and in staff positions outside the normal hierarchy."[22] History is replete with *eminences grises,* men and women of power whispering instructions from the shadows behind the throne.

Moreover, positional analysis assumes that we know which institutions are politically significant and which are shams, and it risks equating institutions that are formally similar, but functionally different. For example, members of the U.S. Congress, the British Parliament, and the Supreme Soviet surely do not hold comparable positions in their respective elites, although formally all are national legislators. We may be misled by positional analysis in two ways: (1) we may include among our elite, figureheads who simply rubber-stamp decisions reached elsewhere, and (2) we may fail to include informal opinion makers who influence the proximate decision makers. Positional analysis tends to overem-phasize spurious influence and to underemphasize indirect influence.

Reputational analysis relies, not on formal organization charts, but on informal reputations for power. Some researchers set out to discover who has power by querying informants who are presumed to have observed political machinations from close up. For example, one student of the American elite asked officials in several national organizations (such as the Chamber of Com-merce and the National Federation of Business and Professional Women's Clubs) for "the names of persons known to [them] who might be considered top policy makers at the national level." These nominees were then polled "to get their own choices of those whom they consider[ed] to be their peers."[23]

This technique is founded on the assumption that participants in a system will know who is powerful and who is not. It does allow the analyst to discover powerful figures whose influence is only indirect or implicit. However, reputa-tional analysis also has grave weaknesses, for a researcher using this method must decide whom to ask and what to ask. Errors in choosing informants may irrepara-

---

[22] Pahl and Winkler, 1974, p. 121.

[23] Hunter, 1959, pp. 16, 195.

bly bias the results. If the informants have no access to inside information, or if their knowledge is limited to a particular sphere of public affairs, they may innocently purvey a distorted picture of power relations. Moreover, informants are often even more confused than social scientists about what power is and who has it. More cautious reputational analysts ask their informants only about influence relations they have personally witnessed, but the reconstruction of overall patterns of power from a myriad of such individual reports remains a terrifically complex task.

This last variant of the reputation approach is closely related to the third main technique for identifying the powerful—*decisional analysis*. This method—sometimes also called event analysis—is based on the assumption that if political power is defined in terms of influence over government activities, we can detect it by studying how specific decisions are reached and, in particular, by noting who successfully initiates or vetoes proposals. In the best-known application of decisional analysis, Robert A. Dahl studied decisions in New Haven, Connecticut, on three topics: urban redevelopment, public education, and nominations for public office.[24]

This technique comes closer than either of the other two to capturing the realities of power as I have defined it. Critics, however, have discovered several significant flaws. First, as a practical matter, only a few important decisions can be studied in detail, and the analyst must infer the broader structure of power from his small sample of cases. Yet patterns of power may vary systematically from issue to issue.[25] Bias in the selection of the decisions to be studied may be nearly as damaging for this approach as bias in the selection of informants is for the reputational method.

A second weakness of decisional analysis is that it is best suited for studying matters that have already become recognized public issues. Yet controlling what gets on the agenda for decision is itself clearly an exercise of political power. If the powerful are able to keep certain controversies off the public agenda, their power is harder to detect by the decisional method.[26]

Because none of these methods for finding the powerful is without defects, some sophisticated analysts have merged several different approaches. For example, in a pair of pioneering studies of Yugoslav and American elites, Allen Barton and his collaborators combined positional and reputational analysis in the so-called "snowball" technique. In each country, incumbents of key formal positions constituted the initial elite, as defined operationally. Respondents from these positions were then asked for the names of others to whom they looked for advice or who they thought to be generally influential. People receiving at least

[24] Dahl, 1961, pp. 104–162.

[25] Lowi, 1964*b*.

[26] Bachrach and Baratz, 1962.

five such nominations were themselves added to the elite sample, and they in turn were asked for further nominations.[27]

The vigorous debate among social scientists over methods for identifying the political elite has often proceeded at too abstract a level. Too little attention has been paid to whether, when, and how our conclusions might be affected by our methods. Some have argued that reputational analysis overestimates the power and cohesiveness of elites, while decisional analysis underestimates these factors. But there is no systematic evidence that this is so. More to the point here, Barton and his colleagues found that in both small, one-party Yugoslavia and large, multiparty America power-as-reputation overlapped almost completely with power-as-position. Virtually everyone whose name appeared on the reputational lists was already in the positional sample. Moreover, the overlap between position and reputation was greatest in the governmental and (in Yugoslavia) party sectors, precisely the sectors of greatest centrality in terms of both reputation and political interaction.[28] Where it matters most, it seems, the differences among the three techniques matter least. Why should this be so?

In complex systems, formal and informal relations of power and coordination are likely to converge at the top. Organization theory suggests that even in small groups inefficiency increases sharply when formal and informal structures are discrepant.[29] The conduct of national affairs in the United States or the Soviet Union would be extremely difficult if institutionally designated leaders did not normally also possess effective power to make and enforce decisions. If petitions from Detroit or Dnepropetrovsk to the president or the party secretary had to be referred to an obscure, but all-powerful chestnut vendor in Lafayette Park or Red Square, organizational imperatives would soon require that the chestnut vendor's informal power be institutionalized. To be sure, institutional analysis must not be blindly legalistic; both the president of the Supreme Soviet and the queen of England are constitutionally prominent and politically impotent. Prudent students of power must be self-skeptical.

Scholars need to investigate the circumstances under which differing research techniques are most likely to be misleading. For instance, decisional, reputational, and positional power are probably more likely to converge in stable political systems than during periods of rapid change. Another example: it is no accident that the hottest methodological debate has centered on studies of local communities, for the divergence between formal and informal structures is likely to be greater in smaller, simpler social systems. We must keep these methodological problems in mind as we examine specific studies in the chapters that follow. But for the national elites we shall be discussing, methodological difficulties in finding the powerful should not be exaggerated.

---

[27] Barton, Denitch, and Kadushin, 1973; Bellisfield, 1973.

[28] Barton, Denitch, and Kadushin, 1973, pp. 24, 166–167; Bellisfield, 1973.

[29] Kadushin and Abrams, 1973, p. 189.

Students of politics and society sometimes assume that definitions and theories are logically prior to empirical investigation. This image of the scientific enterprise is correct insofar as it highlights how concepts guide research. But the relationship between concepts and data is dialectical. Answers to one set of questions invariably raise further questions and suggest conceptual and even definitional innovations. Hence, the concepts and definitions discussed in this chapter must remain tentative, open to correction as our grasp of the realities of power and politics evolves. In the chapters that follow we examine some of the many questions left open by these provisional theoretical formulations.

ELITES AND THE SOCIAL STRUCTURE

2

On November 29, 1917, shortly after the Bolsheviks' seizure of power in the name of the workers and peasants of Russia, a delegation of revolutionary intellectuals and military experts prepared to depart for crucial peace negotiations with the Germans at Brest-Litovsk. A young worker had been named to the delegation for appearance's sake, but as the envoys sped through the Petrograd evening toward their train, they realized in consternation that the group still included no peasant. Spotting an old muzhik trudging through the snow, they persuaded him to accompany them. The historic delegation was complete.

In the hot Miami summer of 1972 the Democratic party convened to nominate a presidential candidate. Television commentators noted how different the delegates appeared from their predecessors four years earlier, for new party rules now required each delegation to mirror its constituency in race, age, and gender. George McGovern, white, fifty, male, and the convention's choice, exulted that "my nomination is all the more precious in that it is the gift of the most open political process in our national history."

These episodes, otherwise unrelated, illustrate two fundamental points about the links between political elites and the social structure. First, many people in the modern world think it important that leadership be demographically representative. But, second and more important, extraordinary efforts are required even to approach this goal. Normal political processes rarely produce an elite drawn proportionately from all segments of society. In this chapter we shall examine how this is so, why it is so, and what difference it makes.

SOCIOECONOMIC STRATIFICATION AND POLITICAL STRATIFICATION

To understand how socioeconomic and political stratification might be related, consider two contrasting models of elite composition. In the first—let us call it the *independence* model—the correlation between political status and socioeconomic status is negligible. Any citizen's chance of entry into the elite is independent of his or her occupation, education, family background, age, sex, religion, ethnicity, and so on. Every social category is proportionately represented within the elite.

The opposite model posits a perfect correlation between an individual's place in the political stratification system and his place in the social hierarchy, so that a socioeconomically privileged caste monopolizes political leadership. Following Harold Lasswell, let us term this the *agglutination* model, for it assumes that the several value rankings in society are fused together.[1] The powerful are also the healthy, wealthy, prestigious, and (presumably) wise.

Reality rarely fits either of these simple models. But the classical elite theorists saw clearly that the truth lies closer to the second than to the first. As Mosca put it:

> *Ruling minorities are usually so constituted that the individuals who make them up are distinguished from the mass of the governed by qualities that give them a certain material, intellectual, or even moral superiority; or else they are the heirs of individuals who possessed such qualities. In other words, members of a ruling minority regularly have some attribute, real or apparent, which is highly esteemed and very influential in the society in which they live.*[2]

Mosca's insight has been confirmed by innumerable studies of the social backgrounds of political elites. The following generalizations are supported by virtually all the existing evidence.

1. *Political leaders are drawn disproportionately from upper-status occupations and privileged family backgrounds.* Table 2–1 shows the personal occupational backgrounds of national legislators in four Western democracies, together with a rough estimate of the composition of the work force in these countries. In each nation, higher-status occupations are vastly overrepresented and lower-status occupations vastly underrepresented; the evidence does not accord with our independence model.

Table 2–1   **Personal Occupational Backgrounds of Four Western Legislative Elites**

Occupational Category	United States	Great Britain	Italy	West Germany	National Population (estimated)
Higher managerial/professional	74%	78%	57%	82%	5%
Other nonmanual	25	20	40	17	30–35
Manual	1	2	3	1	60–65
	100	100	100	100	100

[1] Lasswell, 1965, p. 9.

[2] Mosca, 1939, p. 53.

Of course, this correlation between occupational and political status might simply reflect upward social mobility. Perhaps elites are comprised mainly of self-made men and women. The evidence in Table 2–2 on these politicians' social origins, however, argues strongly against this hypothesis. Although their family backgrounds tend to be more modest than their present circumstances, the overwhelming majority come from middle- and upper-middle-class families, even though during their childhood such families comprised barely a quarter of the population. By contrast, children from the working class constitute less than one-third of the elite, although they make up more than two-thirds of the population. In other words, in all these countries upper- and middle-class children have between five and ten times as good a chance of entering the political elite as do children of working class families.

Table 2–2   Family Occupational Backgrounds of Four Western Legislative Elites

Occupational Category	United States	Great Britain	Italy	West Germany	National Population (estimated)
Higher managerial/ professional	44%	58%	28%	35%	5%
Other nonmanual	38	20	36	35	20–25
Manual	18	22	36	30	70–75
	100	100	100	100	100

Despite the American "log-cabin" myth, the evidence in Table 2–2 suggests that far from having more upward mobility into the political elite than other nations, the United States in fact has somewhat less. Indeed, since the birth of the Republic American leaders have been drawn from upper social strata. "The 55 men who met in the summer of 1787 to establish a new national government were the most prestigious, wealthy, educated, and skillful group of 'notables' ever to be assembled in America for a political meeting."[3] As we shall see in more detail in Chapter 7, deviation from the independence model has persisted throughout American history. For example, of all U.S. presidents, vice-presidents, and cabinet members in the century and a half after 1789 only 2 percent were manual laborers or small farmers by occupation, and barely 25 percent were the sons of such workers.[4]

Upward mobility is apparently higher among the postrevolutionary elites

[3] Dye and Zeigler, 1972, p. 34.

[4] Anderson, 1935, pp. 516–517.

of Communist Eastern Europe. It has been estimated, for example, that more than four-fifths of the Soviet Central Committee are children of workers or peasants. More rigorous evidence from Yugoslavia indicates that 38 percent of the party and legislative leaders come from proletarian families and another 31 percent from the peasantry. Yet for children of white-collar Yugoslavs, the odds of entering the political elite are 15 percent better than for urban working-class children and more than twice as high as for children of peasants.[5]

The plebeian parentage of Communist elites is in one respect misleading. Many upwardly mobile Soviet leaders, for example, claim peasant origins, but in fact "only an extremely small fraction of them could be called peasants by the time they turned twenty, much less by the time they joined the party."[6] Members of the Communist party, comprising the top 10 percent of the Soviet political stratification system, are drawn disproportionately from middle-class occupations. As of 1968, "the chances of a worker entering the party were about twice those of a collective farmer, while the chances of a white-collar worker were six or seven times as great."[7] The Central Committee is virtually monopolized by members of the white-collar strata. More than 95 percent of the members of the 1966 Central Committee had been white-collar workers for at least thirteen years. The overwhelming majority were employed as senior officials in the party or state bureaucracy.[8]

Evidence of the universality of the correlation between social status and political power comes also from the developing countries of the Third World. A study of 269 prominent political leaders in Asia, Africa, and Latin America found that their parents were generally in the middle or upper middle classes. Most were the sons of teachers, merchants, civil servants, or traditional elites. Another researcher reports that the revolutionary agrarian movements of Latin America are led disproportionately by men of above-average social background. Indeed, from the American and French revolutions of the eighteenth century to the Russian and Asian revolutions of this century most successful rebel leaders have come from the middle and upper middle classes.[9] Apparently no significant political movement—revolutionary, reactionary, or establishmentarian— entirely escapes agglutination.

2. *The social backgrounds of administrative elites are at least as exclusive as those of political leaders.* In the contemporary West, senior civil servants are solidly middle class in origin. Table 2–3 shows the family backgrounds of high-level officials in four industrialized democracies. Like the data on legislative elites in Table 2–2, these figures diverge considerably from the independence

---

[5] Brzezinski and Huntington, 1964, p. 135; Barton, Denitch, and Kadushin, 1973, p. 125.

[6] Hodnett, 1965, p. 643n.

[7] Rigby, 1968, pp. 414–415.

[8] Gehlen and McBride, 1968, p. 1234.

[9] Von der Mehden, 1969, pp. 72–90; Obregon, 1967, pp. 325–326; Rejai, 1973, pp. 31–32.

Table 2–3   Family Occupational Backgrounds
of Four Western Administrative Elites

Occupational Category	United States	Great Britain	Italy	West Germany	National Population (estimated)
Higher managerial/ professional	47%	35%	42%	42%	5%
Other nonmanual	35	47	49	50	20–25
Manual	18	18	9	8	70–75
	100	100	100	100	100

model of elite composition. Scattered evidence on bureaucratic elites elsewhere in the world confirms this finding. In Turkey, for example, only one fourth of a 1964 sample of senior officials came from the middle and lower classes, which comprise perhaps nine-tenths of the Turkish population. The Yugoslav administrative elite have distinctly more privileged social origins than their party and legislative colleagues. Children of the white-collar strata in Yugoslavia have more than twice as good a chance of entering the administrative elite as do children of manual workers, and more than four times as good a chance as do children of peasant families.[10]

3. *Economic and other subelites are usually drawn from even more privileged backgrounds than are political and administrative elites.* This is particularly true of business leaders in capitalist economies. Based on current occupation and income, of course, big business executives invariably rank near the top of the social hierarchy, but they are also very likely to have been raised in middle- and upper-class homes. Self-made tycoons risen from humble origins are exceedingly rare. For example, 71 percent of a sample of leading U.S. businessmen were children of professional or managerial personnel, 20 percent were children of other white-collar employees, and only 9 percent were children of manual workers. Similarly high-status origins are reported for economic elites in such countries as West Germany, Japan, Canada, Venezuela, and Great Britain.[11]

Less is known of the social backgrounds of economic managers in Communist countries. The Yugoslav economic elite comes from relatively modest origins, certainly in comparison with Western business leaders and even in comparison with Yugoslav political and administrative elites. Only 22 percent of the economic leaders came from white-collar families, as contrasted to 26 per-

[10] Dodd, 1965; Barton, Denitch, and Kadushin, 1973, p. 125.

[11] Newcomer, 1965, pp. 30–31; Wildenmann, 1968, p. 10; Abegglen and Mannari, 1960, pp. 112–116; Porter, 1965, pp. 291–295, 394; Bonilla, 1970, pp. 79–84; Stanworth and Giddens, 1974, pp. 82–83.

cent of the Yugoslav party and legislative elites and 40 percent of the administrators. In the Russian case, however, Brzezinski and Huntington conclude on
the basis of indirect evidence that "it seems probable that the social origins of the
Soviet industrial manager today are considerably higher than those of the Soviet
political leader."[12]

Scattered evidence suggests that other strategic elites, such as the military,
the diplomatic corps, intellectuals, journalists, and religious leaders all come
from backgrounds at least as exclusive as those of economic elites. This is true, for
example, in West Germany, Yugoslavia, Japan, and the United States. In
particular, the military elite comes typically from higher origins than does any
other subelite; this is true even in Communist regimes, where all elites (including the military) come from relatively modest backgrounds. Alone among the
elites of modern societies, labor union leaders have distinctively lower social
origins, although in comparison with their membership even they do not completely match the independence model.[13]

**EDUCATION
AND
POLITICAL
STRATIFICATION**

Education is another important dimension of social
stratification that is highly correlated with political
status. Statistically speaking, the bias against the uneducated is even greater than the bias against those
from lower socioeconomic classes. Because education
and social class are themselves intercorrelated, we will
need to examine their joint relationship to political
status, but let us begin with some simple evidence on the educational backgrounds of political and governmental leaders.

Among Western legislative and administrative elites rates of university
education range from 59 to 100 percent, as shown in Table 2–4. Compared to the
adult population, university graduates are statistically overrepresented in these
elites roughly ten or twenty to one. Education is particularly crucial for entrance
into the administrative elite; only in Great Britain does the figure fall below 98
percent. University education is generally somewhat less common among British
elites (including business elites) than in other industrialized democracies. This
fact may imply greater opportunity for the less well educated, or it may simply
mask more subtle social discrimination, based, for example, on differing types of
secondary education. Still, in Great Britain, as elsewhere in the West, university
education is the royal road to the top.

For the political elites of developing countries the importance of university

---

[12] Brzezinski and Huntington, 1964, p. 138; Barton, Denitch, and Kadushin, 1973, p. 25. The
relatively large number of Yugoslav managers from humble origins may be related to the
recency of industrialization there.

[13] Wildenmann, 1968, p. 10; Barton, Denitch, and Kadushin, 1973, p. 125; Abegglen and
Mannari, 1960; Parsons and Barton, 1974, p. 6; Keller, 1963, pp. 292–317; Kourvetaris and
Dobratz, 1973.

Table 2–4   Rates of University Education
among Western Elites

Group	United States	Great Britain	Italy	West Germany
National legislators	88%	65%	76%	59%
Senior civil servants	98	83	100	99
Adult population (1970 est.)	11	2	3	3

education is greater still. For example, three-quarters of India's parliament and more than nine-tenths of the Council of Ministers are college educated, two-thirds of the ministers holding postgraduate degrees. In Mexico, four-fifths of the "Top 88" political leaders in a 1969 study had completed university. Fully 183 of 186 Egyptian cabinet ministers between 1952 and 1973 had college degrees, and 46 percent had doctorates.[14] Because less than 1 percent of all adults in these countries have a university education, graduates are statistically overrepresented in the political elite by a factor of 100 or more. (Elites in some earlier underdeveloped countries, too, were "overeducated": two-thirds of the American presidents, vice-presidents, and cabinet members from 1789 to 1824 had attended college, while 99 percent of their fellow citizens had no more than a grade-school education.)[15] In discussing political stratification in developing countries, Suzanne Keller concludes: "Formal education is the single most important entrance requirement into the higher circles."[16]

The importance of educational credentials persists through many changes of regime. Between 1920 and 1969, for example, Turkey was ruled by four successive elites: the traditional Ottoman rulers, Atatürk's revolutionary modernizers, the parochial conservatives of the Democratic party, who were ousted by a military coup, and the civil-military coalitions that followed. Yet throughout this kaleidoscopic half century the proportion of university graduates in the National Assembly never fell below 70 percent.[17] An even more remarkable illustration comes from Albania, where reactionary royalists of the 1930s were succeeded in 1945 by Communist revolutionaries. Although the ideologies and social origins of the two elites were very different, a majority of each was university educated, this in a country where roughly one citizen in 500 has attended a university.[18]

[14] Arora, 1972; Gruber, 1971; Dekmejian, 1974.

[15] Anderson, 1935, p. 512.

[16] Keller, 1963, p. 121.

[17] Frey, 1965, p. 176; Tachau and Good, 1973, p. 557.

[18] Moskos, 1965, p. 212.

Higher education is becoming an essential credential for leadership in Communist countries. For example, three-quarters of the Yugoslav elite and nineteen out of twenty members of the 1972 Polish Central Committee were college trained. The Chinese case is still more striking: roughly two-thirds of the members of the Eighth Central Committee had received higher education, as contrasted with less than one-thousandth of the population. A graduate of higher education in China is more than two thousand times more likely than his less-educated compatriot to enter the national political elite.[19]

CLASS, EDUCATION, AND POWER: FOUR MODELS

Elite recruitment based on educational credentials is often seen as a means of breaking the patterns of political inheritance by which elites have traditionally bequeathed power to their children. When success rests on learned and testable skills rather than on inherited prerogatives, access to elite positions is presumably meritocratic.

Yet this argument is problematic, for where educational credentials are essential for elite membership, the schools in effect screen elite aspirants. If access to education depends on social status, then selecting a well-educated elite may be tantamount to selecting an elite from the upper social strata. Mosca argued precisely this:

> *Even when academic degrees, scientific training, special aptitudes as tested by examinations and competitions, open the way to public office, there is no eliminating that special advantage in favor of certain individuals which the French call the advantage of* positions déja prises *[positions already captured]. In actual fact, though examinations and competitions may theoretically be open to all, the majority never have the resources for meeting the expense of long preparation, and many others are without the connections and kinships that set an individual promptly on the right road.*[20]

To interpret the correlation between education and political status, we must take into account the ubiquitous link between social status and access to education. After reviewing studies of university entrants in eighteen different countries during the years when today's elites were educated, C. A. Anderson concluded that "in all countries the majority of students come from non-manual

---

[19] Barton, Denitch, and Kadushin, 1973, p. 135; Waller, 1973a, p. 173. Some of the higher education of Communist elites occurs in party schools and is thus in part a consequence of, rather than a precondition for, political involvement. As the regimes become increasingly established, however, university education tends to supplant special party training in the curriculum vitae of younger elite members. Changing educational patterns in Communist elites are discussed in detail in Chapter 7.

[20] Mosca, 1939, p. 50.

(non-farm, non-labor) families, who of course [were] a distinct minority of the population." Children of professional families were between 5 times and 500 times more likely to attend university than were children of manual workers.[21]

In both East and West the educational bias in favor of middle-class children declined after World War II as a result of enlarged enrollments and (in Eastern Europe) quota systems. Nevertheless, in proportion to their numbers in the total population, working-class children remain statistically underrepresented in universities by roughly 1.5 to 1 in Eastern Europe, and by between 2.5 to 1 and 10 to 1 throughout Western Europe. Similar findings are reported even for such countries as the United States, Australia, and Canada, where the norm of equal educational opportunity has deeper historical roots.[22]

The causes of this link between social status and educational opportunity are complex. In both capitalist and communist societies, middle-class parents and middle-class children have higher educational aspirations, and once in school, middle-class children outperform their working-class compatriots.[23] In addition, as Mosca pointed out, economic circumstance and social connections encourage middle-class children to continue their education long after most working-class children have been forced into the labor market.

The complex interconnections among social origin, education, and political status can be clarified with the help of Figure 2–1. Our initial discussion implied that education and social background are each linked independently to elite membership, as indicated in Model I. The discovery of a direct link between social origins and education means, however, that this simple conception may be misleading. At least three alternatives deserve attention.

In Model II the impact of social origins on political status is only indirect and is mediated by education. Higher-status groups gain a disproportionate share of elite positions only insofar as they have an advantage in acquiring education. Once past the educational hurdles, well-educated children of the lower classes are just as likely to enter the political elite as are well-educated middle-class children. Social bias in the educational system simply means that fewer lower-class children will gain the educational credentials necessary for elite status.

Elite recruitment in traditional China usefully illustrates Model II. For nearly a millennium China's Mandarin rulers were selected in competitive examinations for which candidates often spent decades preparing. Confucian laws required that these exams be open to virtually all men, and among successful candidates career advancement was relatively independent of family background. For these reasons, many scholars have termed traditional China a meritocracy.

---

[21] Anderson, 1956, pp. 255, 259.

[22] Parkin, 1971, pp. 109–111; Lane, 1971, pp. 110–116; Blau and Duncan, 1967, pp. 165–170, 430; Encel, 1970, pp. 148–151; Porter, 1965, pp. 180–191.

[23] Lane, 1971, pp. 110–116.

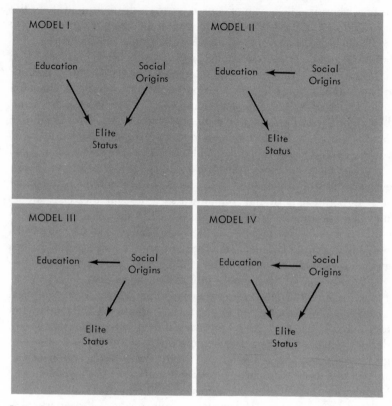

Figure 2–1   Class, Education, and Power

In the terms we have been using, the link between educational achievement and elite membership was very strong, and the direct link between social background and elite membership was relatively weak. However, historians have shown that sons of upper-class families were much more likely than sons of lower-class families to prepare successfully for the state examinations; that is, the link between social background and educational achievement was powerful. Hence, recruitment patterns closely followed Model II: a strong impact of social background mediated by education.[24]

Model III is more subtle. Here higher social status brings with it higher education, but it is social origin and not education that is crucial for entry into the elite. Because most scions of the upper classes happen to be well educated, the political elite is incidentally overeducated by comparison with the nonelite. But

---

[24] Marsh, 1961, and Ho, 1962. Ping-ti Ho finds that the direct impact of wealth and social standing on elite recruitment increased toward the end of the imperial era.

the link between education and political status is fundamentally spurious. Any lower-class child who manages to slip through the educational system discovers that without the approved social background his educational certificate is worthless as a credential for elite recruitment.

Examples fitting Model III are rare in the modern world, but probably more common in traditional societies. Admission to the Moroccan political elite is said to depend on traditional family status rather than on education per se, although most upper-class children acquire much formal education. Many members of the nineteenth-century British elite were well educated, but not all were. Social eminence, not education, was their common denominator.[25]

Model IV combines elements of Models II and III. Education itself counts as a credential for elite membership and mediates some of the impact of social origin, but social origin is also directly linked to political status. Unlike Model III, Model IV implies that among both lower-class and upper-class children, education itself increases the odds of making it into the elite. But unlike Model II, Model IV implies that among the well-educated, upper-class children are more likely to enter the elite than those from more modest backgrounds.

Consider, for example, the French administrative elite. The correlation between social background and access to education is unusually high in France, and in turn virtually all senior officials must have a university education. Hence, there is a strong indirect link between social background and elite status. But, in addition, there is a direct link, for among university graduates, those from upper-class backgrounds have a better chance for admission to the elite than those from working-class backgrounds. Hence, in the case of the French administrative elite, all three links in Model IV are relatively strong.[26]

The differences among Models II, III, and IV are matters of degree. Imagine differing weights attached to each of the links in Model IV representing the strengths of the direct association between each of the variables. As the direct link between social origin and elite membership weakens, we approach Model II, and as the direct link between education and elite membership weakens, we approach Model III. The strength of the link between education and social origin is also variable, though the link itself exists in every society yet studied.[27]

In principle, the link between social and political status, controlling for education, might actually be negative, so that among equally well-educated persons, upper-class origins would be a disadvantage for political advancement. This pattern apparently occurs in some working-class movements and may

[25] Waterbury, 1970, p. 85; Guttsman, 1963.

[26] Ehrmann, 1971, pp. 153–154; Suleiman, 1974, pp. 41–99.

[27] When the link between social status and education becomes very strong, it becomes difficult to tell which is really most important for elite recruitment. In Iran, for example, where most elite members are the educated children of educated, well-to-do, former elite members, it is virtually impossible to determine the critical variable. See Zonis, 1971, pp. 155–175.

account, for example, for the combination of high education and modest social origins characteristic of the Yugoslav political elite.[28]

Thus, if access to education is socially biased, reliance on educational credentials for political recruitment by no means assures a socially representative elite. In Communist Eastern Europe the direct impact of social background on elite membership is relatively slight, but the link between education and political status is growing ever stronger. Because the link between social background and education persists (and is perhaps also growing), the indirect effect of social background on political status may increase, even though the direct link is broken. The net result may well be, as some have argued, a "new class" of rulers in these societies.[29] Because education is also increasingly significant for elite recruitment in the West, the emergence of a socially exclusive meritocracy is possible in these countries, too.

Many contemporary developing societies face the same dilemma. Reformist regimes in such countries as Egypt and India have tried to break the direct link between social and political status, but as we have seen, the link between education and political status is extremely strong in these countries. Moreover, the link between social class and education is also very strong; it has been estimated, for example, that the chances of a middle-class Indian getting a university education are one hundred times greater than the chances of his lower-class compatriots.[30] Hence, the indirect impact of social standing on political stratification will probably continue to be very strong.

ETHNICITY, GEOGRAPHY, GENDER, AND POLITICAL STRATIFICATION

The impact of social structure on elite composition extends far beyond social class and education. For example, lower status ethnic and religious minorities usually are underrepresented in the higher political strata. Blacks and Catholics in America illustrate this phenomenon, as do non-Slavic minorities in the Soviet Union, French Canadians in Canada, Croats and Slovenes in pre-Titoist Yugoslavia, and assorted ethnic minorities in various developing countries. Geographically, many elites are drawn disproportionately from cities, especially metropolitan areas. The underrepresentation of farm, village, and small town characterizes both developed and underdeveloped countries, both capitalist and communist systems. As with social class, geography and ethnicity affect political status sometimes directly and sometimes indirectly via access to education.

In statistical terms, women are the most underrepresented group in the political elites of the world. The world of high politics is almost universally a

---

[28] Barton, Denitch, and Kadushin, 1973, pp. 125, 136.

[29] Lane, 1971, p. 119; Djilas, 1957.

[30] Subramaniam, 1967, p. 1018.

man's world. The extent of this underrepresentation of women within the elite varies surprisingly little from country to country. In most parliamentary democracies, women constitute about 5 percent of the national legislature, and a virtually identical ceiling seems to apply to membership in the Central Committees of the Communist party in such countries as China and Russia.[31]

Scandinavia provides the only significant exception to the general exclusion of women from positions of political leadership. Women's movements have been strong historically in these countries, and in each of the Scandinavian legislatures women hold 10 to 20 percent of the seats. This relatively prominent role of women in Nordic politics dates from the earliest years of this century. Indeed, in 1905 Finland became the first country in the world to have a woman in the national legislature.

Because women's suffrage is only half a century old, one might expect their share of the top political strata to have grown steadily. But with the marked exception of Scandinavia, the role of women in national political elites has remained stable or declined over the last quarter century, as Figure 2–2 illustrates. Even in India and Israel, where Indira Gandhi and Golda Meir have reached the top of the political hierarchy, the proportion of women in the national legislatures tended to drift inexorably downward from postwar peaks toward the 4-to-8-percent level typical of most countries. There is, it seems, an "iron law of andrarchy."

The Women's Liberation Movement may have a significant impact on these patterns in coming years, but the obstacles to be overcome are substantial. Moreover, because female aspirants to elite status often come from somewhat higher social backgrounds than male aspirants, the immediate impact of a growth in female elite representation may be to increase the statistical overrepresentation of higher socioeconomic strata; this has been the pattern, for example, in the British administrative elite over the last two decades.[32]

THE	The disproportionate advantage of male, educated, high-status elite recruits increases as we move up the
LAW	political stratification system. This "law of increasing
OF	disproportion" seems to apply to nearly every political
INCREASING	system; no matter how we measure political and social
DISPROPORTION	status, the higher the level of political authority, the greater the representation for high-status social groups.

[31] Blondel, 1973, pp. 78–79; Donaldson and Waller, 1970, p. 629; Lapidus, 1975. Women constitute a somewhat higher proportion of the legislatures of Eastern Europe, but these institutions are not really equivalent to Western parliaments in terms of political significance. See also Means, 1972; Costantini and Craik, 1972; Kirkpatrick, 1974; Brichta, 1974–1975. For a stimulating early, yet still fresh, discussion of women in political elites, see Comstock, 1926.

[32] Kelsall, 1974, p. 182.

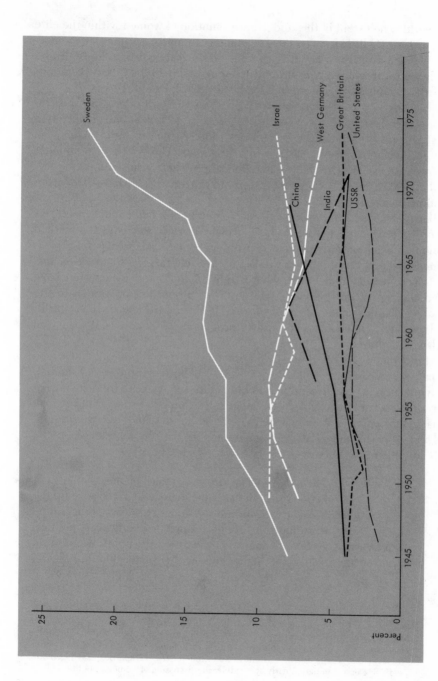

Figure 2-2 Women as Percent of National Elites: 1945–1973

Sources: Dahlström, 1971, p. 300; Waller, 1973b; Zidon, 1967, p. 341; Butler and Pinto-Duschinsky, 1971, and other volumes in that series;
Congressional Record index volumes; national consulates. Data are for lower house of parliament or (in the case of China and the USSR) party
central committee.

This phenomenon can be easily observed in Western parliamentary democracies. In America governors tend to come from higher social origins than do state legislators, congressmen from higher origins than governors, senators from higher origins than congressmen, and presidents from the highest average social origins of all.[33] In Britain, a degree from Oxford or Cambridge is an excellent mark of social status, and as Table 2–5 shows, the disproportionate advantage for "Oxbridge" graduates increases at each rung of the political hierarchy.

Table 2–5   Oxbridge Education in the British Political Elite, 1955–1974

	Percent Educated at Oxford or Cambridge
Prime ministers	100
Cabinet ministers*	72
Ministers not in cabinet*	67
Parliamentary secretaries*	48
Members of Parliament	37
Defeated candidates for Parliament	23
Total British population	<1

Sources: Butler and Pinto-Duschinsky, 1971, and other volumes in that series; Dod's Parliamentary Companion, 1955–1971; Johnson, 1973.
* Immediate postelection governments only.

The law of increasing disproportion also applies to elites in the Second and Third Worlds. For example, Figure 2–3 shows that from 1947 to 1967, while the rate of university education in the Soviet population as a whole was increasing from 1 percent to 3 percent, the educational level of Communist party members was growing even faster, and the educational level of the full-time party elite reached such a high plateau that further growth was virtually impossible. Table 2–6 draws illustrative evidence from the case of Tunisia. Beginning with a population two-thirds of whom are still illiterate, the importance of secondary or university education increases at each step up on the political ladder.

Analogous patterns apply in the case of ethnicity. For example, the modern state of Israel was founded by European Jews as an avowedly egalitarian society, but in the years following independence large numbers of poor, uneducated Sephardic Jews immigrated from North Africa and Asia. In accord with the law of

[33] Matthews, 1954, p. 30.

Table 2-6   Advanced Education in the Tunisian Elite

	Percent with University Education or Modern Secondary Degree
Cabinet	100
Assembly	70
Governors	50
Secretaries general	55
Regional committees of coordination	27
Local branch presidents	30
Local branch members	7

Source: Quandt, 1970, p. 186.

increasing disproportion, these "Oriental" Jews are found in ever fewer numbers as we move up the Israeli political hierarchy. In 1972 they constituted three-fifths of the Israeli population, but provided only two-fifths of all local councillors, less than one-fifth of the national legislature, less than one-twentieth of the senior civil service, and none of the members of the "inner cabinet."[34]

Even working-class political parties fit the same pattern. One study of the Italian Socialist party, for example, found that the working class constituted 83 percent of the mass membership, but only 64 percent of the local leaders and 53 percent of the provincial elite. Further up the hierarchy, other studies show, less than 10 percent of the delegates to the national party congress held working-class jobs, and only 4 percent of the Socialists in parliament were in the working class when they became deputies.[35]

The law of increasing disproportion also applies in many other contexts. Within each strategic elite the proportion of women declines as we move from lower to higher strata. Generals and admirals are drawn from more exclusive social backgrounds than are lower-ranking officers, and bishops have higher social origins than local clergy. Directors of large firms come from more privileged backgrounds than do those in smaller firms, and within any given firm, the higher a post, the less likely it is to be filled by a Horatio Alger from humble origins.[36]

[34] Shimshoni, 1975.

[35] Barnes, 1967, pp. 95–96; Stern, Tarrow, and Williams, 1971, p. 539; Sartori, 1963, pp. 123–124.

[36] Kourvetaris and Dobratz, 1973; Stanworth and Giddens, 1974, p. 82; Thompson, 1974, p. 202.

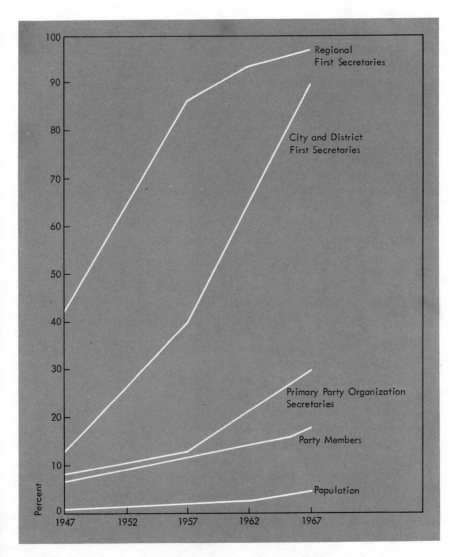

Figure 2–3   Graduates of Higher Education as Percent of the Soviet Elite
Sources: Mickiewicz, 1973; Hodnett, 1965; Frank, 1971.

**IDEOLOGY
AND
AGGLUTINATION**

The degree to which an elite diverges from the independence model of statistically perfect representation is closely related to its ideological orientation. The more conservative a party or regime, the greater the overrepresentation of upper-status social groups within its leadership. Throughout Western Europe, as well as in such countries as Australia, Japan, and Israel, the more conservative a party, the greater the disparity between the social background of its voters and the social composition of its parliamentary delegation. Even though the leaders of left-wing parties come from less modest origins than do the electorates that support them, it remains considerably easier for someone raised in the working class or the lower middle class to rise within one of these parties than within one of the conservative parties.[37] Similarly, the exclusion of women is more pronounced in parties of the Right than in Socialist and Communist parties.

Nor is this pattern confined to parliamentary democracies. In the chaotic politics of interwar China, leaders of the conservative Kuomintang came from higher class origins than did the leaders of their main competitors, the Communists, and this divergence increased over time, as the peasantry rallied to the Communists. The relatively modest social origins of political leaders in Eastern Europe, particularly as contrasted with Western elites, also illustrate the link between ideology and elite composition.[38]

The main exception to the generalization that leaders of left-wing parties come from lower-status backgrounds than leaders of right-wing parties is the United States. Democratic elites come from no less privileged origins than Republican elites. This anomaly helps to explain why the American political elite as a whole deviates from the independence model even more than most other political elites. The absence of a genuine working-class party in America has meant the absence of the main channel through which men and women from modest social backgrounds have risen to top political positions in other countries.[39]

AGGLUTINATION: WHY?

The available evidence strongly supports the agglutination theory of elite composition, for political elites everywhere are drawn disproportionately from groups toward the top of the social hierarchy.[40] To be sure, upper-status groups rarely monopolize elite posts completely, and only a fraction of those who are socially "eligible" actually enter the elite. One ingenious American study, for example, found little overlap

---

[37] Encel, 1961; Langdon, 1967, pp. 227–229; Akzin, 1967, pp. 144–146; Valen, 1966; Holmberg, 1974.

[38] North and Pool, 1965, pp. 376–402; Baylis, 1973, p. 13.

[39] Working-class persons are also more underrepresented among ordinary political activists in America than in other countries because of the lack of a strongly organized working-class movement. See Nie, Powell, and Prewitt, 1969, pp. 823–824. Canada is another partial exception to the link between ideology and elite composition, and for similar reasons. See Kornberg and Winsborough, 1968.

[40] Apparently agglutination applies even to physical well-being. Quint and Cody (1970) report that elites, defined operationally as persons listed in *Who's Who*, live longer than nonelite members of the same occupations.

between entries in the *Social Register* and in *Who's Who*, particularly for political and governmental posts.[41] In the case of Britain, W. L. Guttsman reports that "of a sample of 100 peerage families in which the title had descended uninterruptedly between 1800 and 1900 the title holders in 31 families had never been politically active while in the case of 34 families *two-thirds* or more of the peers had been politically active."[42] In most countries at most times, most people of great wealth and status do *not* enter the highest political stratum. Yet the correlation between social and political status, if not perfect, is still very strong. Why should this be so?

The most obvious explanation for statistical bias at the top of the political hierarchy would be social and political bias. The pathway into the political elite is blocked by a series of gates, and the gatekeepers may consider the candidates' social backgrounds. For example, many observers attribute the underrepresentation of certain groups in the elite to *voter preference*. "Voters seem to prefer candidates who are not like themselves but are what they would like to be."[43] Perhaps, as Frederick Frey argues, "it is less ego-humbling and restrictive to be influenced by a socially established, clear status-superior than by a peer."[44]

The difficulty with this explanation is that agglutination is often even more marked in contexts where voting plays no role at all. In fact, elected elites are typically more representative demographically than are other strategic elites, and there is some evidence that universal suffrage and high voter turnout actually weaken the link between social and political status.[45] Voter bias can hardly explain most agglutination.

A more plausible version of the gatekeeper hypothesis might apply to both elected and nonelected elites. As I shall discuss in Chapter 3, in every political system it is possible to find *selectorates* who screen elite aspirants. Examples include local party nominating committees in Britain, the party secretariat in Russia, and corporate personnel committees. Selectorates occasionally strive for demographic "ticket balancing," but more frequently the criteria that they use are socially discriminatory. If the selectorate is itself controlled by the social establishment, the result may be nepotism. However, discrimination may also be unintentional. The use of educational criteria, for example, normally introduces an upper-class bias to the outcome. In other cases, selectors may innocently assume that high social status itself is a good indicator of ability.

Agglutination also stems from the *conversion of social or economic resources* into political resources. Money or social status can sometimes buy politi-

[41] Baltzell, 1966. See also Prewitt and Eulau, 1971, p. 304.

[42] Guttsman, 1974, n. 43.

[43] Matthews, 1960, p. 45.

[44] Frey, 1965, p. 404.

[45] Wences, 1969; Dahl, 1961, pp. 85–86. See also Chapter 7 below.

cal power. For example, traditional American campaign practices involving personal organizations and private financing help explain the striking lack of elected officials from working-class backgrounds. Public campaign financing and strong working-class movements have minimized this effect in other countries. Nearly everywhere, however, aspiring politicians from the upper classes find it easier to skip the first few rungs of the political ladder and are therefore more likely to make it to the top. But one should not exaggerate the importance of private economic wealth as an explanation for agglutination, for the law of increasing disproportion applies in socialist as well as capitalist societies.

Most discussions of sociological bias in elite composition focus on the external handicaps imposed on lower-class candidates. But the distribution of political motivation and aptitudes is also relevant, because the supply of candidates flowing from different social groups may be quite unequal. As Amitai Etzioni has pointed out, we should not conclude from the sociological characteristics of the membership of the NAACP that its admissions criteria exclude white southerners.[46]

Education and high social status increase participation rates both by stimulating political interest and ambition and by fostering political skills and self-confidence. To some extent, therefore, the law of increasing disproportion results from *self-selection.* Even among party activists, for example, ambition for higher office is correlated with socioeconomic status.[47]

One important proposition relevant here is Kenneth Prewitt's *overexposure hypothesis:*

> As a result of political socialization experiences, a small segment of the population are "overexposed" to public affairs; this group of persons are exposed more frequently and intimately to politics than is the case for the average member of society. . . . The correlation between status and political leadership holds only because moving up the status hierarchy increases the proportion of the class belonging to the segment of society frequently exposed to the political world. Increasing the political sensitivity of the worker and middle classes, via the union movement, neighborhood organizations, and the like, should increase their contribution to political leadership circles.[48]

Thus, levels of political interest and aspiration help explain the link between social structure and elite membership.

[46] Etzioni, 1961, p. 153.

[47] Schwartz, 1969, p. 567.

[48] Prewitt, 1965, pp. 105, 110; see also Lasswell, 1948, pp. 47–50.

	The most important question to ask about any finding
AGGLUTINATION:	of social science is "So what?" But this question has too
SO	seldom been asked about the findings reported in this
WHAT?	chapter. Hence, we know much more about the social
	backgrounds of political elites than we do about what
	difference it all makes for politics.

SELF-INTEREST

The most obvious hypothesis—so obvious that it has rarely been scrutinized carefully—is that decision makers will favor the interests of the social groups from which they come. "The power elite is rooted in the upper class," it is argued, "and serves the interests of the members of the upper class."[49] Some evidence supports this proposition. For example, one study has shown that upper-class members of the Indian Parliament are more likely than MPs from "have-not" backgrounds to oppose land reform and the redistribution of income.[50] And we have already seen that politicians from lower-status backgrounds are more frequently found in parties that pursue policies favorable to the lower classes.

A related argument is that ordinary citizens from the same social groups as political leaders will have easier access to the decision-making process, because "they 'speak the same language,' share much the same style of life, have had many of the same experiences and training."[51] For example, Israelis from European backgrounds may find it easier to gain a fair hearing from the political elite than their compatriots from Asia and North Africa. Perhaps an elite that is demographically more representative is also more broadly responsive.

That political elites look after their own is a plausible thesis that deserves more systematic testing than it has yet received. Do elites of differing sociological composition, but facing similar decisions, actually produce different policies? Individual cases illustrating this kind of sociological determinism are common, but so are exceptions: revolutionaries from upper-class backgrounds and self-made persons from humble origins who become energetic defenders of the status quo. C. Wright Mills, an ardent critic of social bias in American elite recruitment, nevertheless argued that

the fact that members of the power elite come from near the top of the nation's class and status levels does not mean that they are necessarily "representative" of the top

[49] Domhoff, 1968, p. 144.

[50] Kochanek, 1968.

[51] Matthews, 1967, p. 209.

levels only. And if they were, as social types, representative of a cross-section of the population, that would not mean that a balanced democracy of interest and power would automatically be the going political fact. We cannot infer the direction of policy merely from the social origins and careers of the policy makers. [52]

SOCIALIZATION

In recent years a more subtle defense of social background studies has emphasized political socialization. It is well established that among ordinary citizens social background is associated with political outlook, and it is reasonable to suppose that among elite members, too, behavior is a function of past experience. Leaders who grow up in middle- and upper-class homes are, according to this theory, likely to develop political perspectives that are different from those held by leaders who are raised in lower-class homes.

The main difficulty with this hypothesis is that—as we shall see in more detail in Chapter 4—most research to date has tended to disconfirm it. At the elite level the correlations between social background and policy preferences are remarkably weak and unpredictable. And precisely those features of childhood experience highlighted by socialization theory seem to be the most weakly related to current views.

There are several reasons why members of the political elite might be less bound to their social origins than are ordinary citizens. The filters of elite recruitment may favor "class traitors" whose views deviate from the climate of opinion in the groups from which they come. Moreover, learning does not end in childhood, and adult political experience often tends to dilute the impact of social origins on political behavior. The impact of early experience is probably particularly weak when a highly mobile elite member has moved away from his origins early in life, when he has served a lengthy apprenticeship in an ongoing organization, and when the role requirements of his institutional position are clear-cut.

If these speculations are correct, social background studies may be much more useful in some circumstances than others. For example, because postrecruitment socialization in such institutions as parties and legislatures weakens the link between background and behavior, the inference from origins to outlook is weakest where political institutions are strongest. In fact, some evidence suggests that the significance of social background for elite behavior is greater in developing societies than in societies with more stable political institutions. As William Quandt has argued:

In more highly developed societies, the role of politician is probably clearer than in the developing nations, the rules of the game of politics are more nearly codified and expectations of other members of the political system may act to define the appro-

[52] Mills, 1956, pp. 279–280.

priate forms of behavior. Whatever predispositions are brought by the individual to the job of politician may count for little in comparison with institutional or legal constraints. [53]

We shall see in Chapter 4 that it is sometimes possible to detect the impact of social origins on a leader's outlook, but the link between background and behavior is neither simple nor direct.

SEISMOLOGY

A rather different answer to the "So what" question has been offered by some scholars: The social background of elite members is relevant less as a predictor of individual behavior than as an indicator of the structure of social power. Background studies may tell us more about the selecting than about the selected. For example, even though working-class members of the political elite may be no more progressive than their middle-class colleagues, the fact that they have achieved elite status may reflect the importance of the working class in a given society. Instead of holding that social structure influences policy outcomes indirectly by affecting elite composition, this theory argues that both elite composition and policy are directly influenced by social structure. Because elite composition is more easily observable than are the underlying patterns of social power, it can serve as a kind of seismometer for detecting shifts in the foundations of politics and policy. This theory will be examined in Chapter 7, when we discuss change in elite composition over time.

ELITE INTEGRATION

Some scholars have offered a fourth justification for studying the social composition of political elites. The greater the homogeneity of backgrounds within an elite, it is argued, the greater the integration of the elite. Some observers fear that elite integration enables the elite to act in concert contrary to the interests of ordinary citizens. Ralph Miliband believes that the socioeconomic homogeneity of British and American elites is so great that they constitute veritable ruling classes, insulated from and exploiting the rest of society. On the other hand, students of some developing societies fear the incapacitating effects of excessive elite diversity. José Luis de Imaz, a student of the Argentine elite, has argued that the root of Argentina's political difficulties is the extreme heterogeneity of the elite's social backgrounds. [54] We shall examine the dimensions and consequences of elite integration in Chapter 5.

---

[53] Quandt, 1970, p. 198. See also Searing, 1969.

[54] Miliband, 1969; Imaz, 1970, p. 246.

It is sometimes argued that the stability of a political system depends on the degree to which elite composition approaches the independence model of proportionate representation for all social groups. Even the classical elite theorists believe that a modest degree of circulation from the lower classes into the elite was socially stabilizing, and one contemporary political scientist has argued that "the stability of an elite rests in great measure on the degree of its representativeness. An elite must be both symbolically and functionally representative."[55] Agglutination implies a marked gap in experience and outlook between those at the top of the political system and those at the bottom, a gap most vivid where leaders with Ph.D.'s govern societies that are still largely illiterate. As Mosca put it, "A ruling class is the more prone to fall into errors . . . the more closed it is, actually if not legally, to elements rising from the lower classes."[56]

In many societies political legitimacy rests in part on some notion of equality of opportunity. America's "log cabin" legend and Russia's myth of proletarians in power echo the traditional Chinese proverb that "Ministers and generals are not born in office." Practical politicians apparently believe that a sociologically unrepresentative elite may impair the legitimacy of their rule. Hence, "token" elites—representatives of underprivileged groups given posts with formal authority, but little real power—are ubiquitous. Many ethnically fragmented societies, from Yugoslavia and India to New York City, have formal or informal rules requiring proportionate elite representation for ethnic minorities. Yet no rigorous evidence is yet available to test the underlying assumption that greater social mobility into elite roles actually generates legitimacy and stability.

In summary, the impact of elite social background on politics and policy remains plausible, but ambiguous and unsubstantiated. We cannot be certain that an elite that represents all social groups proportionally would actually foster stability or effectiveness or responsiveness. Yet it is scarcely debatable that agglutination is a prima facie violation of justice and equality of opportunity. This moral answer to the "So what?" question remains the bedrock on which interest in the social composition of elites is founded.

---

[55] Seligman, 1964, p. 16. Ironically, other social scientists have argued that violations of the law of increasing disproportion are actually destabilizing, because groups with high social status will resent being ruled by their social inferiors. See Lasswell, Lerner, and Rothwell, 1952, pp. 35–36, and Quandt, 1969, p. 133.

[56] Mosca, 1939, p. 119.

ELITE
RECRUITMENT
3

After each recent American presidential election, president-watchers have eagerly greeted the quadrennial installment of Theodore White's series on "the making of the president," for most people reasonably assume that how one of us gets to be president helps determine what kind of president the rest of us get. Presidential aspirants are sifted and screened by a long and complex process—a process climaxed and symbolized by the primaries, the conventions, and the electoral campaign. However, this process was actually begun years earlier, as a group of young people reached for the first rung of the political ladder. Similarly, observers of British politics ask about the making of the prime minister, Kremlinologists about the making of the general secretary, and Brazilians about the making of the chief of staff. This process of elite recruitment is the subject of this chapter.

As conceived here, political recruitment refers to the processes that select from among the several million socially favored and politically motivated citizens comprising the political stratum those several thousand who reach positions of significant national influence.[1] Recruitment in this sense is affected by many factors studied by political scientists—party organization and party competition, electoral laws and electoral behavior, pressure groups and personnel administration, and many more. It is impossible here to detail all these factors, and I shall focus instead on five critical issues:

1. *Channels.* Through what routes do aspirants for political leadership most commonly reach the top?
2. *Gates and gatekeepers.* How and by whom are the chosen few actually chosen?
3. *Credentials.* What criteria must successful aspirants meet?

[1] In the case of national elites, it is safe to assume that aspirants outnumber posts, so that the task of recruitment is to winnow the few from the many. In other contexts, however, recruiters must actively draft candidates. See Schwartz, 1969.

4. *Turnover and succession.* How (and how often) do incumbents leave office?
5. *So what?* How do recruitment patterns ultimately affect the character of the elite and its politics?

CHANNELS	For aspirants seeking the path to the political summit, distinguishing thoroughfares from dead ends is a practical concern.

Should a politically ambitious youth in America aim first for a job in the state legislature, or the federal bureaucracy, or a prestigious law firm? Should a would-be Soviet leader set his sights on the state administration, or the party's "agit-prop" apparatus, or the secret police? Should an ambitious Latin American enter local politics, or the army, or some multinational corporation?

PERMEABILITY

Institutionally speaking, the preferred paths of recruitment constitute channels for finding, sifting, and training leaders. From this perspective, recruitment channels vary, first of all, in their permeability. At one extreme, hereditary systems prescribe a single path to the top, from which all but the fortunate few are barred at birth. Less restrictive, but more common, are what we might call "guild" systems, which require long apprenticeship within a single institution as a prerequisite for admission to the elite.

Bureaucratic regimes often employ guild systems of recruitment. The vast Ottoman Empire was ruled for many centuries by a cadre of eunuch officials, enslaved as youths, excluded from the rest of society, and trained in the arts of war and government. Entrance into the administrative elites of Western Europe, though less traumatic, is almost equally restrictive; in recent years, for example, virtually all the highest British civil servants have entered government immediately after leaving university and have followed a single *cursus honorum* to the top.[2]

Recruitment practices that discourage lateral entry into top posts without prior service in lower grades are also characteristic of some nonadministrative elites. Very few British, German, Japanese, Italian, or Norwegian politicians reach the cabinet without first serving an apprenticeship of a decade or more in parliament. In the economic sphere, too, there is some evidence that the paths to the top are becoming more specialized and bureaucratic, and movements between firms less common. In the case of British elite recruitment, Richard Rose concludes that "intensive apprenticeship is a prerequisite for success in many aspects of English life today."[3]

---

[2] V. Parry, 1969; Harris and Garcia, 1966.

[3] Rose, 1974, p. 214; Schlesinger, 1967, pp. 286–287; von Beyme, 1971, p. 122; Cheng, 1974; Putnam, 1973a, pp. 13–14; Martin, 1972, p. 6; Granick, 1962; Dahrendorf, 1959, p. 46.

Some scholars have argued that permeable recruitment channels are more characteristic of emergent countries, whereas apprenticeship systems inevitably accompany industrialization and political modernization.[4] However, recruitment channels in some highly developed countries are quite permeable. In the parliamentary systems of Canada, the Netherlands, France, and Australia, most cabinet members reach that rank after serving fewer than 5 years in the national legislature.[5] Moreover, students of Communist elites in Eastern Europe have often noted the frequency of lateral transfers from jobs in the party apparatus to managerial posts in the state-run economy and back again. In fact, the Communist party in East Germany has formally endorsed "an astutely planned exchange and rotation of leaderships cadres from socialist enterprises and the state apparatus into the party apparatus and vice versa."[6] More important, as we shall see in Chapter 7, these "dual executives" seem to have become increasingly important over the last several decades, thus casting doubt on any simple proposition linking modernity and impermeable recruitment channels.

Perhaps the most striking case of permeability and lateral entry is found in the United States. Cabinet and subcabinet positions are typically filled by men and women from industry, commerce, education, and the professions. As one administration succeeds another, many officials return to their private jobs, only to reappear in Washington when their party regains power. One study found that two-fifths of the American business elite have served in high government jobs at one time or another, and that five out of every six government leaders based their careers primarily in the private sector. Such "in-and-outers" illustrate the relative openness of recruitment channels for political executives in America.[7]

The career patterns of American politicians illustrate that elective recruitment channels are not completely permeable. Nearly nine-tenths of all congressmen have previously held public office, mainly in state or local government, half of all senators have served in Congress or statewide office just prior to their election to the Senate, and every Republican and Democratic presidential nominee since 1960 has previously served in the Congress. Moreover, the seniority system has meant that the most powerful congressional posts require an apprenticeship of several decades. But in general, guildlike recruitment is less marked in America than in many other countries. Based on his study of elective careers in the United States, Joseph A. Schlesinger concludes: "There is no clearly marked *cursus honorum* or set stages of office advancement. Nor are

---

[4] Marvick, 1968, p. 279.

[5] Schlesinger, 1967, pp. 286–287; Dogan and Scheffer-van der Veen, 1957–1958, p. 100.

[6] Cited in Baylis, 1974, p. 170. See also Barghoorn, 1972, p. 187 and the studies cited there.

[7] Neustadt, 1966; Dye and Pickering, 1974, p. 912.

there any offices, including the very highest, which have not gone to men from outside the ranks of officeholders or active party workers."[8]

<hr>

Recruitment channels also differ from country to country in institutional locus. Political parties, bureaucracies, and local governments are the most common institutional channels into the political elite, although, as we shall see, other social institutions can also be important in political recruitment.

Concern with recruitment is often made a defining characteristic of the *political party*. However, the specific role of parties in recruitment varies considerably from one system to another. In the Communist countries of Eastern Europe, the party apparatus has consistently been the best springboard to national leadership. More than 80 percent of the members of the Soviet Politburo have served previously as party functionaries, and in each of the three succession crises of Soviet history the first secretary of the Central Committee—Stalin, Khrushchev, and Brezhnev—has successfully outmaneuvered powerful rivals holding important posts in other institutions.[9] In some parliamentary democracies, such as Austria, Italy, and India, the party organization itself is an important source of elite recruits, while in others, most notably Britain, the party's parliamentary delegation supplies virtually all national political leaders.[10] Parties in the Third World are frequently evanescent, but many political leaders in Asia, Africa, and Latin America have achieved power by virtue of their role in party activities or nationalist movements. The path to power in Mexico, for example, lies through the *Partido Revolucionario Institucional* (PRI), the dominant party that has held power for nearly four decades.[11]

In the United States, too, for most aspiring politicians affiliation with one of the two major parties is a prerequisite for advancement to national elective office. However, U.S. parties are only loosely organized, and thus they are less able than their foreign counterparts to control recruitment. The role of parties in the United States is, as Joseph Schlesinger puts it, "less a case of an organization's

<hr>

[8] Schlesinger, 1965, p. 781; Schlesinger, 1966, p. 103; Schlesinger, 1967, p. 279; Davidson, 1969, pp. 49–54; Matthews, 1960, p. 55. Note that impermeability of recruitment channels is not necessarily related to specialization in a professional sense. American in-and-outers may be quite specialized professionally, whereas British civil servants, though recruited through a highly impermeable channel, tend to be generalists, not specialists.

[9] Hough, 1972, p. 44; Ciboski, 1974, p. 180; Barghoorn, 1972, pp. 190–191; Rush, 1974.

[10] Steiner, 1972, p. 218; Sartori, 1967, p. 172; Nicholson, 1975, pp. 536–544; Schlesinger, 1967, pp. 286–287.

[11] Von der Mehden, 1969, p. 85; Johnson, 1971, pp. 60–80.

selecting candidates according to qualifications than it is of providing the framework within which they contest for the nomination."[12]

In many countries the *bureaucracy*, in addition to its administrative role, serves as a primary channel of recruitment into the top political elite. For example, of the 186 cabinet members who governed Egypt between 1952 and 1973, more than half had served in the civil bureaucracy before entering the cabinet, and more than a third had begun their careers as military officers. In Greece, from 1843 to 1965, under monarchy, dictatorship, and republic alike, between one-third and one-half of the cabinet were military officers or civil servants by profession. On average, William Quandt has found, a quarter of the seats in the legislatures of developing countries are held by government bureaucrats.[13]

Nor is the presence of public administrators in the political elite peculiar to less developed countries, for civil servants have traditionally constituted roughly a quarter of the national legislatures of such countries as Sweden, Germany, and Japan; in recent years France too has moved toward this pattern of bureaucratic recruitment. In Eastern Europe, bureaucratic and party careers are more difficult to disentangle, as we have seen, but Brzezinski and Huntington accurately conclude that "the top leader in the Soviet Union is a politician *and* a bureaucrat."[14] In fact, in comparative perspective the Anglo-American democracies are quite unusual in the relative insignificance of the bureaucratic channel for recruitment to elective office, probably in part because in these countries political parties antedated the emergence of a strong, centralized civil service.

A third institutional locus of elite recruitment, overlapping the political party to some extent, is *local government*. In many countries local elective office is typically the first rung of the political ladder. In centralized systems, such as France, Italy, Sweden and Ireland, as in the federal systems of West Germany, Austria, and the United States, more than two-thirds of all national legislators have served previously in local or regional government. Indeed, in Sweden and France more than half the members of the national parliament are simultaneously local officeholders. And in the Soviet Union the key step up the political hierarchy seems to be the post of *obkom* (district) party secretary.[15]

[12] Schlesinger, 1965, p. 781. The classic urban machines, of course, have played a more direct role in elite recruitment; see Snowiss, 1966.

[13] Quandt, 1970, pp. 192–193; Dekmejian, 1975; Legg, 1969, p. 305. On the state bureaucracy as a channel for recruitment into the economic elite, see Harbison, 1959, pp. 154–168, and Granick, 1962, pp. 75–76.

[14] Brzezinski and Huntington, 1965, p. 170 (italics added); Hancock, 1972, p. 182; Loewenberg, 1967, pp. 116–117; Ike, 1972, p. 86; Ehrmann, 1971, p. 149; Quandt, 1970, pp. 192–193.

[15] Pierce, 1973, pp. 256–260; Galli and Prandi, 1970, p. 158; Hancock, 1972, p. 95; Cohan, 1973, pp. 221–222; von Beyme, 1971, pp. 74–75; Steiner, 1972, p. 217; Schlesinger, 1967, p. 279; Hough, 1969, especially pp. 272–288.

Local government is often an especially important channel for political recruitment among parties of the Left. That is the case, for example, in such diverse countries as Norway, Britain, Chile, Italy, West Germany, and Australia.[16] Left-wing parties must develop leadership from the grassroots, for in comparison to parties of the Right, they are less able to draw on established sources of recruitment, such as privileged socioeconomic classes, elite educational institutions, and the civil service.

Local government is not universally an important channel for recruitment to the national elite; Britain is a good counterexample. Moreover, "both in America and Europe, evidence suggests that about half the incumbents in public power at the lower and middle reaches of power and governance are serving for the first—and last—time."[17] Nevertheless, prior experience in lower elective office is among the most widely shared characteristics of national legislators.

In many countries *educational institutions* play key roles in sifting and channeling aspirants. For example, the ancient Oxbridge colleges of England, the elite *grandes écoles* of France, the Law School of Tokyo University, Makerere University College in East Africa, Tunisia's Sadiki College, the National University of Mexico City, and the Political Science Faculty of Ankara University in Turkey have traditionally furnished a very disproportionate share of the recruits to their respective national elites.[18] Graduation from one of these schools increases so substantially a youth's chances of "making it" politically that the educational and political recruitment systems are virtually merged.

Other social institutions may also be significant channels of political recruitment. Most leftist parties in the industrialized world have traditionally relied heavily on labor unions to supply potential leaders. Religious organizations, such as *Azione Cattolica* in Italy and *Opus Dei* in Spain, sometimes provide a substantial share of the elite. In the United States, civic associations often assume the recruitment function performed elsewhere by political parties. And, as we shall see later, within many parties and bureaucracies, informal groups—patron-client networks, factions, and cliques—provide the effective channels of recruitment.[19]

Recruitment channels do not finally determine who will occupy elite positions, for in the end most party members, most bureaucrats, most local government officials, and most alumni of prestigious schools do not become

---

[16] Valen, 1966, p. 152; Schlesinger, 1967, p. 279; Valenzuela, 1976; Barnes and Farah, 1972, p. 14.

[17] Marvick, 1968, p. 280.

[18] Vaughan, 1969; Langdon, 1967, p. 227; Kubota, 1969, pp. 69–71; McGowan and Bolland, 1971, pp. 71–72; Smith, 1974; Szyliowicz, 1971. On the Ivy League and American elites, see Dye and Pickering, 1974.

[19] Steiner, 1972, p. 218; Langdon, 1967, p. 229; Galli and Prandi, 1970, p. 159; Lewis, 1972, p. 100; Prewitt, 1970, pp. 84–86, 143. Dogan (1961, p. 83) argues that the role of unions as recruitment channels declines as the leftist parties' share of the parliamentary elite grows.

national political leaders. Recruitment channels provide the pool of eligibles. Choosing among them is a further task.

GATES

AND

GATEKEEPERS

AUTOMATIC AND QUASI-AUTOMATIC SELECTION

Political systems have evolved a variety of automatic, quasi-automatic, and discretionary techniques for deciding who among the eligible aspirants for leadership will actually rule. The simplest of these are the automatic mechanisms that require no real exercise of judgment about the candidates' qualifications. Hereditary succession is virtually ubiquitous as a recruitment device in traditional political systems, as well as in a substantial but declining proportion of contemporary capitalist economic elites. Random selection by lot or rotation is equally simple, but it provides for little continuity and socialization and has been used only along small groups of peers, as in the Athenian forum. The market is another automatic social process, and elite positions have been filled by direct purchase during some periods in France and China. Wealth is a powerful resource under almost any system, of course, for it can often be used to buy credentials required for recruitment—education, prestige, contacts, and so on. However, pure market mechanisms of selection are relatively rare.[20]

A pair of quasi-automatic selection mechanisms—examinations and seniority systems—are more common. Both involve relatively little discretion, yet unlike the fully automatic devices, each discriminates among aspirants in terms of skills and experience. Examination-based selection has always been attractive to political reformers, because it has seemed to promise meritocracy—rule by the brightest and the best. In practice, however, examination systems have been largely confined to bureaucratic elites, probably because examinations cannot effectively measure political skills and values. Tests of various sorts are used to winnow civil service candidates in most modern countries, but the most important example of a political elite selected essentially on the basis of examinations was Mandarin China, as discussed in Chapter 2.

Seniority-based mechanisms for designating top leaders are found very frequently in both bureaucratic and political contexts, usually in combination with other mechanisms and criteria for selection. As we have seen, seniority is particularly important in guild systems of recruitment, although rarely is a seniority system as unadulterated as it is in the U.S. Congress. Selection by

---

[20] Keller, 1963, p. 180. On the decline of inheritance within the U.S. business elite, see Newcomer, 1955, 1965.

seniority has several advantages. First, its quasi-automatic nature minimizes conflict about promotion; as Samuel Huntington points out, "Selection by seniority is, in effect, selection by heredity: power goes not to the oldest son of the king but the oldest child of the institution." Moreover, seniority requirements allow intensive socialization of leaders into the "rules of the game" and permit candidates' qualifications to be assessed over a long period in a variety of contexts.

Even the revolutionary regimes of China and Eastern Europe have recognized the stabilizing virtues of the seniority principle. On the other hand, selection by seniority may limit a political system's adaptability, for seniority systems imply impermeable recruitment channels and generally produce an elite that is both old-aged and old-fashioned. The seniority system, concludes Huntington, "purchases institutional integrity at a high price in terms of institutional isolation."[21]

In practice quasi-automatic selection devices require some discretion, because someone must set and grade the examinations, and typically someone must decide who among the candidates "tried" by seniority is really "true." A third set of selection mechanisms, including appointment, cooptation, and election, are more fully discretionary. Someone must appoint, coopt, and elect. Thus, we must pay special attention to the characteristics of those who do the selecting.

SELECTORATES: SOME EXAMPLES

Monocratic regimes are usually characterized by a selectorate of one. In the difficult years after the Turkish revolution of 1919, Atatürk, undisputed leader of the new regime, took personal charge of nominations to the Grand National Assembly, and, more recently, Richard Daley is reported to have taken a similar interest in congressional nominations in Chicago.[22] In complex political systems, however, it is difficult for one person to review all nominations, and selectorates must be correspondingly larger.

One particularly interesting example is the *nomenklatura* system used in the Soviet Union to screen recruits for all influential positions, whether in the party, the government, the military, education, agriculture, industry, trade unions, the press, and other sectors of society. The term *nomenklatura* refers to a list of key positions, appointment to which is under the supervision of a specific party secretariat. These officials serve as the ultimate selectors in Soviet political recruitment.[23]

Analogous selectorates are found within some Western political parties.

---

[21] Huntington, 1973, p. 35.

[22] Frey, 1965, p. 430; Royko, 1971.

[23] Harasymiw, 1969.

Electoral systems of proportional representation, such as those in Norway, Italy, Israel, and Austria, require each party to compile an ordered list of candidates. The higher the ranking of a given candidate, the greater the likelihood of his election. Final decisions about candidate placement usually rest with a selectorate composed of the party's most senior leaders.

Cooptation by incumbent elites characterizes recruitment to senior positions in many organizations. For example, our best evidence is that new members of the Soviet or Chinese Politburo are effectively chosen by the incumbent members, who then submit the names to the Central Committee for formal ratification. Similar patterns have appeared in such diverse contexts as Meiji Japan and Western corporate management.[24]

A variant of this system is illustrated by recruitment to the British cabinet. Formally, cabinet members are appointed by the prime minister. Many of his choices, however, are predetermined, because some members of his party have gained such a solid reputation with their parliamentary colleagues that as a practical matter the prime minister would find it difficult to exclude them. Thus, one can reasonably describe the members of each parliamentary party as the selectorate for cabinet recruitment, though obviously the views of the senior members of this selectorate are weighted more heavily than those of ordinary back-benchers.

Thus far I have ignored elections, presumably a form of recruitment in which elite members are directly chosen by the citizenry. Mosca had little patience with this view:

> When we say that the voters "choose" their representative, we are using a language that is very inexact. The truth is that the representative has himself elected by the voters, and, if that phrase should seem too inflexible and too harsh to fit some cases, we might qualify it by saying that his friends have him elected.[25]

Without denying that (as we shall discuss in chapter 6) elections can have political and occasionally even historic significance, we can nonetheless agree with Mosca that as selection mechanisms, elections are easily overrated.

For example, more than two-thirds of all seats in Congress and in the House of Commons are "safe": nominees of the majority party are virtually assured of election, regardless of personal character or the gales of national politics. In these constituencies (and often even in competitive districts), control over the nominating process is tantamount to control over elite recruitment. In the United States, the direct primary has to some extent diffused this power, but

---

[24] Cheng, 1974.

[25] Mosca, 1939, p. 154.

in Britain the selectorate for parliamentary recruitment consists of the small group of activists who run the local party organizations.[26]

As our discussion of the British case suggests, selectorates at different levels in a given political system may vary considerably in composition and operation. In Britain and throughout most of Western Europe, for example, selectorates for parliamentary seats are typically composed of local activists, whereas the selectorate for cabinet posts is restricted to national party leaders. These primary and secondary selectorates may well apply quite different criteria.

The size, homogeneity, and centralization of selectorates also differ cross-nationally. The selectorate for the British prime minister is composed of senior members of the parliamentary party, sharing many common values and experiences, whereas the selectorate for the U.S. presidency (including convention delegates, campaign contributors, congressmen, influential journalists, and even primary voters) is much larger and more diverse in political, social, and geographic background. Moreover, the rate of turnover among members of the selectorate is much higher in the United States than in Britain.[27]

The difference between American and British elite recruitment is illuminated by Ralph H. Turner's distinction between "contest" and "sponsored" mobility:

> Contest *mobility [which he ascribes to American recruitment patterns] is a system in which elite status is the prize in an open contest and is taken by the aspirants' own efforts. . . . Under* sponsored *mobility [as in Great Britain] elite recruits are chosen by the established elite or their agents. . . . Upward mobility is like entry into a private club where each candidate must be "sponsored" by one or more of the members.*[28]

In each system diverse criteria for recruitment may be applied—intelligence, popularity, tactical ability, vision, and so on. But in a contest system the criteria are established and interpreted by a selectorate that, though still relatively small, is far wider and more heterogeneous than in a system of sponsored mobility. As Heclo notes:

> *The British apprentice moves upward by ingratiating himself with his guild masters; the American entrepreneur moves through a wide-ranging series of contests against*

---

[26] Ranney, 1965, pp. 4–7.

[27] Heclo, 1973.

[28] Turner, 1960, p. 855.

other largely isolated contenders attempting to arrange their own combinations of political resources. For purposes of his own advancement, the apprentice's constituency is largely internal; the scrutineers in his selectorate are his own political superiors [and, I would add, peers] in Parliament, while the American entrepreneur looks far more to an outside constituency of disparate party leaders whose self-interest must be mobilized on his behalf.[29]

We may distinguish between *intramural* and *extramural* selectorates, depending on both their breadth and their responsiveness to the opinions of outside groups and individuals. No doubt all selectorates are concerned about the candidates' acceptability to certain key reference groups, but these reference groups are more diverse and more influential in extramural than in intramural selection. The American selectorate would probably fall toward the extramural end of this dimension, the Soviet selectorate toward the intramural end, and the British selectorate somewhere between the two.

SELECTORATES: SO WHAT?

The character and composition of selectorates are fundamentally important for two reasons. First, the selectorate constitutes the effective constituency to which the elite member will respond, for the behavior of leaders is guided by their "perception of the interests, wishes, and demands of those who control their tenure in office."[30] The primary constituency of a Soviet politician, for example, is composed of his superiors in the party apparatus. Frederick Barghoorn concludes that "the nomenclature system is a powerful factor in the maintenance of party dictatorship in the USSR."[31] A purely coopted elite is by definition a self-perpetuating oligarchy. Critics of Mexico's dominant party, for example, argue that "The Revolutionary Family"—a self-recruited cabal composed of past and current Presidents, the principal Cabinet members, and the heads of certain public and semipublic corporations—controls the recruitment and promotion of all other elite members.[32] Similarly, much contemporary criticism of business elites in America is based on the intramural character of the corporate selectorate.

The influence of selectorates is also illustrated where control over the nomination of cabinet members has been ceded to a dominant interest group —where the minister of agriculture is effectively named by farm organizations, the minister of labor by trade unions, and so on. In such cases the nominee will

---

[29] Heclo, 1973, p. 33.

[30] Prewitt and Nowlin, 1969, p. 301.

[31] Barghoorn, 1972, p. 182.

[32] Brandenburg, 1964; Gruber, 1971.

naturally be more responsive to the interest group than to the party that formally appointed him, for the group and not the party is the real selectorate.

The second reason why selectorates are important is that they define and apply the standards that successful aspirants must meet. A selectorate that values technical skills will generate a different type of elite from a selectorate more concerned with "character." Or to take another example, Kenneth Prewitt and Alan Stone theorize that "persons who have some control over the pathways to membership in the political elite tend naturally to favor persons of similar ideology, status, and background."[33] All the evidence for and against this hypothesis is not yet in, but like the previous example, it underlines the importance of examining the credentials that are required of aspirants in different recruitment systems.

CREDENTIALS

What makes a person fit to lead? A society's answers to this question tell us much about its structure and culture. Qualifications for elite membership are sometimes specified in law. The U.S. Constitution, for example, limits eligibility for the presidency to native-born Americans at least 35 years old, and in some societies posts in the elite are legally reserved to members of specific ethnic groups. But nowhere do juridical provisions fully define the credentials required of leaders.

Scholars often distinguish between *ascriptive* and *achievement* criteria. In traditional societies leaders are thought to be chosen primarily because of who they are—their lineage, ethnicity, religion, sex, and so on—whereas in modern societies an individual's own talents and achievements are supposed to be more important. In practice, however, achievement and ascription are blended in almost every recruitment system, from Confucian China to contemporary America, and some credentials, such as formal education, seem in themselves to link inheritance and performance inextricably. Broadly speaking, we can classify the criteria applied in different nations and eras into three broad categories: skills, perspectives, and affiliations.

SKILLS

Anthropologists have found that in all societies the most highly valued skills tend to become the basis for elite recruitment.[34] In hunting societies leaders are drawn from the best hunters, in pastoral societies, from the best herdsmen, and so on. In contemporary societies, on the other hand, *technical expertise* is universally important as a credential for leadership. We noted in Chapter 2 that

---

[33] Prewitt and Stone, 1973, p. 142.

[34] Broussard, 1956. See also Lasswell, Lerner, and Rothwell, 1952, pp. 10–11.

education, especially university education, distinguishes elites from nonelites throughout the world. In both Communist and capitalist countries, training in management and technology is of growing importance, as we shall discuss in Chapter 7. No longer can the untutored peasant revolutionary or the uneducated "self-made man" rise to the top, either in the Kremlin or in American corporate boardrooms. In the Third World, too, the demands of economic planning and technological change have given a decisive advantage to the expert—the agronomist, the engineer, the economist.

Technical expertise is not equally valued by all selectorates, however. For example, specialized training and professional skills seem to be less important for advancement into British elites—administrative, political, and even economic—than is true of other industrial countries.[35] And in most political systems, selectorates for party and legislative elites give less weight to technical skills than do their counterparts in business and public administration.

A second skill universally demanded of aspiring leaders is the *ability to persuade and organize*. Studies of leadership in Mexico, the United States, the Philippines, Britain, Algeria, Japan, and the USSR all stress the importance of interpersonal skills—the ability to charm, cajole, conciliate, and coordinate people and groups with different backgrounds and goals.[36] Politics invariably involves conflict, and those most adept at building coalitions have a decisive advantage in the recruitment process, whether the coalitions link competing families (as in Renaissance Italy), or competing parties and factions (as in Fourth Republic France), or competing government agencies (as in contemporary Washington and Moscow).

It is important, however, to distinguish two types of interpersonal skill: the ability to mobilize masses of ordinary citizens, and the ability to maneuver effectively in small groups of colleagues. In extramural recruitment systems, and especially in revolutionary movements, oratorical and agitational skills—sometimes loosely termed "charisma"—are highly valued. Trotsky, Gandhi, Nasser, and the Kennedy brothers rose to power in part because of their ability to capture the emotions of large numbers of people, although each also had great tactical proficiency in smaller groups. In intramural recruitment systems such as Britain, Japan, and today's Soviet Union the quieter skills of bargaining and negotiation are more important. Churchill, Tanaka, and Khrushchev stood out precisely because most of their colleagues lacked public flamboyance.[37]

The disproportionate representation of certain *occupations* in political

[35] Rose, 1974, pp. 199–203; Granick, 1962, pp. 242–247.

[36] Johnson, 1971, pp. 78–80; Prewitt, 1970, p. 117; Grossholtz, 1964, pp. 221–222; Kavanagh, 1974, pp. 28–31; Quandt, 1969, p. 156; Ike, 1972, p. 84; Brzezinski and Huntington, 1964, p. 150.

[37] British selectorates prize rhetorical skill, but mainly before small, politically sophisticated audiences. See Rush, 1969, pp. 281–283.

elites is one reflection of the importance of specific skills as credentials for leadership.[38] For example, intellectuals, journalists, and teachers are found in large numbers in many political elites. Intellectuals' traditional prestige, together with their ability to manipulate the symbols of sacral and secular ideologies, accounts for their political prominence in such countries as Italy, France, Poland, Yugoslavia, and many non-Western nations.[39]

Almost everywhere lawyers are politically prominent. They comprise roughly 15 to 25 percent of most national legislatures and in many countries their share rises to one-third or more. Lawyers have also traditionally supplied the lion's share of the bureaucratic elite in many countries; more than half the senior civil servants of West Germany, Italy, and Japan, and approximately a quarter of their Swedish and American counterparts have legal training.[40]

Max Weber offered the classic explanation for the high number of lawyers in political elites. Of primary importance are the lawyer's twin skills—familiarity with the law, that traditional tool of statecraft, and the ability "to plead effectively the cause of interested clients." Moreover, the hazards of politics can best be assumed by one whose private occupation can be performed intermittently. Businessmen, scientists, farmers, and manual workers generally must sacrifice occupational security in order to enter politics. But lawyers find it relatively easy to return to their private profession.[41] (The same is true for journalists, party and trade union officials, and, in some countries, civil servants, which doubtless helps to account for their growing prominence in many national elites.)

PERSPECTIVES

Loyalty and *political reliability* are crucial credentials in all political systems, but they are particularly critical in revolutionary and authoritarian contexts. Membership in the official party—and the ideological orthodoxy that it usually signifies—has been the most fundamental credential of all in such regimes as Communist China, the Soviet Union, Fascist Italy, and Nazi Germany. In more

---

[38] The role of military and quasi-military specialists in violence is a topic too vast to summarize here. See Lasswell, 1941; and Nordlinger, 1976.

[39] Sartori, 1967, p. 165; Dogan, 1961, pp. 63–72; Cohen, 1973, p. 45; Benda, 1960, pp. 205–218.

[40] Blondel 1973, pp. 160–161; Quandt, 1970, p. 192; Putnam, 1973*b*, p. 267; Kubota, 1969, p. 79. Lawyers are much less prominent in Communist elites and in the Scandinavian legislatures; and in some countries, such as France and Italy, the lawyers' traditional dominance in parliament has been significantly reduced in the postwar period. See Pedersen, 1972, Ehrmann, 1971, p. 148, and Sartori, 1967, p. 166.

[41] Weber, 1958, pp. 85, 93–94. No other developed nation has so high a proportion of lawyers in national politics as the United States; the extraordinary role of lawyers in this country is enhanced by the unusual importance of law enforcement posts on the American electoral ladder. See Schlesinger, 1966, pp. 72–73, 90–93, and Eulau and Sprague, 1964.

personalistic regimes, such as Atatürk's Turkey or Nasser's Egypt, personal loyalty to the ruler becomes an important criterion for advancement.

In revolutionary regimes, one good index of political reliability is participation in the prerevolutionary conspiracy. "Early membership [in the Party] was one of the most important distinctions a Nazi could claim."[42] Veterans of Mao's arduous "Long March" into the hills of Yenan in 1934–1935 still constituted the core of the Chinese Communist elite three decades later. Tito's guerrilla partisans provided the bulk of the Yugoslav political elite for more than a quarter century after the Communists took power. Fascists *della prima ora* ("from the first hour")—those who joined the party before the march on Rome in 1922—held most key posts throughout Mussolini's rule.[43]

The preeminence of such "charter groups" in newly established regimes is not limited to authoritarian settings. From the establishment of the Fourth French Republic in 1945 until its demise in 1958, veterans of the anti-Nazi Resistance constituted more than two-thirds of the National Assembly, although less than 2 percent of the population had been active in the Resistance. For the first quarter century of Israel's independence, political power was virtually monopolized by settlers who had arrived in Palestine from Eastern Europe in the early years of this century. And fully half of the Sixth U.S. Congress, elected in 1799, had served two decades earlier in General Washington's Continental Army.[44] Members of such charter groups typically have great postrevolutionary prestige and close personal ties to other leaders. More important, each can claim to have proved his fidelity to the fledgling regime in the fires of battle.

As new regimes turn to the practical tasks of governing, political reliability can no longer be the prime criterion for elite recruitment. A recurrent pattern in the postrevolutionary years is the emergence of a conflict between elite members recruited because of their ideological loyalty and those recruited because of their technical expertise—the so-called "Red-expert" cleavage. One of the first objectives of the Soviet regime was the training of a new generation of technically competent and ideologically reliable "Red directors." Nevertheless, the latent tension between technical and ideological criteria for advancement has persisted for more than half a century. In the case of China the turmoil of the Cultural Revolution and its aftermath involved in part a conflict between ideological purists and pragmatic technicians.[45]

Ideological orthodoxy is also a criterion for recruitment in Western democracies. Except in the United States, acceptance of the basic strategy and philoso-

---

[42] Lerner, Pool, and Schueller, 1965, p. 236.

[43] Klein, 1966, p. 83; Barton, Denitch, and Kadushin, 1973, pp. 49, 108; Lasswell and Sereno, 1965, pp. 190–192.

[44] Dogan, 1961, pp. 85–87; Fein, 1967, pp. 151–153; Biographical Directory of the American Congress, 1961. See also Dekmejian, 1975.

[45] James, 1959, especially p. 329; Schram, 1973. See also Schurman, 1965, pp. 50–53.

phy of one's party is a prerequisite for admission to the political elite. And even in America, as Prewitt and Stone point out, "the recruitment process filters out . . . those whose views are 'bizarre': the rabid racist, the nineteenth-century laissez-faire capitalist, the serious socialist."[46] Each administration tries, not always successfully, to replace high-ranking executives from the previous administration with men and women presumably more loyal to the political philosophy of the new president.[47] Starkly or subtly, political perspectives are a credential of importance in all recruitment systems.

This third category of credentials includes both ascribed and achieved traits. *Family ties*, for example, play a significant role in political recruitment even in nonhereditary systems. It is not surprising, perhaps, that lineage affects recruitment in semitraditional societies, such as Morocco, Sri Lanka, Lebanon, Ireland, Greece, and Republican China. But it is striking that 43 percent of the cabinet ministers who ruled Holland between 1848 and 1958 were bound by kinship to other ministers, that approximately one-seventh of the deputies of the Third French Republic (1870–1940) were related to one another, and that about one-tenth of all U.S. congressmen from 1790 to 1960 had relatives who also served in Congress. On the other hand, in these last three cases the importance of family ties for recruitment has steadily declined, and though statistically significant, political lineage is now rarely politically significant, the Kennedy dynasty to the contrary notwithstanding.[48]

Patron-client affiliations and personal recommendations are virtually universal credentials for recruitment. In its classic settings, such as in southern Italy, the Philippines, Bolivia, and traditional Japan, clientelism takes the form of networks of political loyalty and obligation between members of different social strata, especially peasants and landlords. The political power of high-status patrons is reinforced by highly personalistic support from their clients, who in turn gain favors and protection. Analogous patron-client patterns have been found to be important for promotion in such modern, achievement-oriented settings as the Communist party of the Soviet Union, American big business, the Chinese People's Liberation Army, the Japanese Diet, and parties and bureaucracies in many industrialized nations. Even in that very model of modern government, the British Civil Service, the school tie and the "Old Boy Net-

---

[46] Prewitt and Stone, 1973, pp. 150–151.

[47] Aberbach and Rockman, 1974.

[48] Waterbury, 1970, pp. 94–110; Singer, 1964, pp. 101–102; Dekmejian, 1975; Cohan, 1972, pp. 41–42; Legg, 1969, pp. 265–267, 307–309; North and Pool, 1965, pp. 415–416; Dogan and Scheffer-van der Veen, 1957–1958, p. 117; Clubok, Berghorn, and Wilensky, 1969, pp. 1043–1044.

work," reflecting personal relationships dating back to prep-school days, seem to have an impact on the recruitment process.[49]

Factional ties are frequently important in partisan recruitment, particularly when a single party dominates politics, restricting alternative routes into the elite. Hence, for example, in the Italian Christian Democratic party, the Indian Congress party, the Japanese Liberal Democratic party, and the Mexican PRI—each of which has been in power for two decades or more—political advancement is dependent on the candidate's factional affiliation, and the leaders of the factions or cliques constitute a kind of primary selectorate. Less reliable evidence suggests, too, that faction-based "crypto-politics" affects elite recruitment in single-party Communist regimes.[50]

The relative importance of *cosmopolitan* and *localist affiliations* varies considerably from selectorate to selectorate. In most electoral democracies, parliamentary candidates with personal ties to their constituency are strongly favored, constituting three-quarters or more of the national legislative elite. In Britain, on the other hand, members of Parliament are drawn from a national pool, and most have no local connections at all. Revolutionary regimes, from Kemalist Turkey to Communist China and the Soviet Union, have made strenuous efforts to root out localism in elite recruitment, but not always with success. In a broader sense cosmopolitan affiliations are often a badge of distinction in colonial and postcolonial regimes. For example, education in England and the ability to speak fluent English were important credentials for aspiring leaders in the former British colonies of India and East Africa in the period just after independence, although as we shall see in Chapter 7, parochial backgrounds have become more advantageous recently.[51]

In almost all political systems, certain socioeconomic, ethnic, geographic, and political groups can successfully demand that the elite include individuals from those groups. Such *corporate representation* assumes three distinct forms, depending in part on who controls the selectorate and in part on the durability of group loyalties. The first form, *ceremonial representation*, involves merely symbolical representatives, whose selection and loyalties are owed to a national and not a corporate selectorate. For example, most federal systems, including Austria, Germany, India, Australia, and the United States, have a convention that cabinet posts will be divided among candidates from several states or

---

[49] J. D. Powell, 1970; Legg, 1972; Stewart et al., 1972; Newcomer, 1955, pp. 9–10; Whitson, 1972; Nakane, 1970, especially pp. 78–79; Sampson, 1965, pp. 259–261.

[50] Zuckerman, 1975; Robins, 1975; Totten and Kawakami, 1965; Johnson, 1971, pp. 67–76; Rigby and Churchward, 1962, p. 5; Nathan, 1973.

[51] Legg, 1969, pp. 285–288, and sources cited there; Oksenberg, 1969, pp. 177–179, 207; Kau, 1969, pp. 229–230; Hough, 1972, p. 33. The East African example and the concept of "credentials" itself are borrowed from my colleague Ali A. Mazrui.

provinces.[52] Although an aspirant's geographic origin is one relevant credential in such a system, there is little reason to believe that he is particularly responsive to the region from which he comes.

Cooptive representation, the second form of corporate representation, occurs when a central selectorate attempts to ensure the loyalty of some group by including representatives of that group in the elite. This sort of ticket balancing is common in political parties wishing to appeal to ethnically or politically diverse constituencies. It has been noted in such contrasting contexts as the Israeli Knesset, the Egyptian cabinet, the Indian Congress party, the Yugoslav Communist elite, and American local government.[53] Cooptive representatives may be genuinely responsive to the group from which they are drawn, but as with ceremonial representation, final discretion in the recruitment process rests with a central selectorate.

In the third form of corporate representation, *sponsored representation,* the corporate group itself serves as the selectorate and hence controls the nominating process. One example has been mentioned already—the nomination of a cabinet minister by the interest group representing the clientele of his ministry. Another example is provided by cases—including Israel, Britain, West Germany, and Mexico—in which parties allow affiliated interest groups to name candidates for certain safe seats. Perhaps the most striking case of full-blown corporatism in the modern world is the Swedish system of royal commissions, which are charged with formulating most national policy initiatives and are composed for the most part of nominees from the major socioeconomic interest groups.[54]

In some cases it is not clear whether corporate representation is sponsored, cooptive, or merely ceremonial. There has been much speculation, for example, about the appearance in the Soviet Central Committee of representatives of each of the main centers of bureaucratic power—the party apparatus, the state administration, the military, and (frequently) the secret police. But there is little firm evidence about the selectorate (and the consequent loyalties) of these representatives. If they are coopted by the central elite primarily to symbolize and preserve the unity of the regime, as representatives to the Supreme Soviet clearly are, then their affiliations are of little political significance. If, on the other hand, they are admitted as sponsored delegates, their appearance may signify genuine, if limited, pluralism in the higher circles of the Soviet Union.[55]

---

[52] Steiner, 1972, p. 249; Nicholson, 1975; p. 55; Encel, 1970, p. 234; Fenno, 1959, pp. 78–79.

[53] Medding, 1972, pp. 188–189; Dekmejian, 1971, pp. 209–210; Robins, 1975; Cohen, 1973, p. 60.

[54] Czudnowski, 1972, p. 575; Ranney, 1965, pp. 222–235; Loewenberg, 1967, pp. 75–77; Scott, 1964, pp. 162–176; Ruin, 1974.

[55] Barghoorn, 1972, pp. 187–188.

The credentials demanded of aspirants for leadership can be indirectly inferred by examining the distinctive traits of successful candidates. Unfortunately, more direct (and hence more convincing) evidence, drawn, for example, from interviews with selectors themselves, is rare. One Norwegian study reports that provincial politicians in all parties value the same qualities in prospective candidates: political and professional knowledge; experience in public office; voter appeal and eloquence; moral qualities, such as honesty and reliability; party loyalty; and representative links to interest groups.[56] The responses of

Table 3–1   Credentials for Leadership in Britain and Italy: Answers Given to the Question "What Are the Most Important Characteristics of a Good Party Leader?" by British and Italian Politicians

	British Members of Parliament		Italian Deputies		
	Labour (N = 44)	Conservative (N = 34)	Communist (N = 12)	Non-Communist Left (N = 21)	Center and Right (N = 31)
Policy-making and problem-solving skills	39%	29%	33%	33%	32%
Ideological and intellectual skills	11	3	58	52	52
Public stature and inspirational ability	30	76	17	38	32
Personal character and morality	36	26	8	29	42
Organizational and administrative skills	7	15	58	29	39
Conciliatory and persuasive skills	70	18	17	33	16
Party loyalty	9	6	25	10	13

Source: Unpublished data from the study reported in Putnam, 1973a.

[56] Valen, 1966, p. 124.

members of the British and Italian parliaments to a question about the characteristics of "a good party leader," given in Table 3–1, reveal both cross-national and cross-party differences in the credentials emphasized by parliamentary selectorates. For example, British Labourites stress the ability to conciliate, while Conservatives emphasize the ability to inspire. By contrast, Italians give greater weight to ideological and organizational credentials. These studies illustrate the need for more rigorous and more comparative analysis of selectorates and the credentials they require of applicants.

**TURNOVER
AND
SUCCESSION**

How leaders leave the top—and how often—is nearly as important as how they arrive. In some times and places individuals move into and out of the elite with stroboscopic speed, while elsewhere incumbents remain in office for many decades. Little is known systematically about how turnover rates vary from country to country, but within a single system turnover seems to vary in accord with two general rules.[57]

1. *High turnover is associated with periods of crisis,* while low turnover is associated with institutional stability and political tranquillity. In Germany, for example, turnover has peaked around each of this century's historical turning points—from the Kaiser's Empire to the Weimar Republic to the Third Reich to the Bonn Republic. In each case the increase in numbers of new elite members preceded the collapse of the old regime; "the dam leaked before it completely burst."[58] In the aftermath of World War II, new regimes were established in France and Italy as well as in Germany, and the prewar political elites were almost completely replaced by men and women with little previous political experience. The newly installed elites showed considerable staying power, and turnover rates declined significantly. At the birth of de Gaulle's Republic in 1958, however, French turnover rates rose sharply once again, symptomatic as well as symbolic of the change in regimes. Similarly, longitudinal studies of the Greek, Lebanese, Mexican, Syrian, and Soviet political elites confirm that spurts of higher turnover are associated with political crises.[59]

2. *Turnover within an elite institution tends to decline as the institution*

---

[57] For a preliminary cross-national comparison of elite turnover, see Nagle, 1973*b*. Strictly speaking, the average tenure of incumbents must be distinguished from the regularity with which turnover occurs, for holding average tenure constant, the renewal of the elite could occur gradually or in concentrated spurts. See Smith, 1973. Nor is personnel turnover equivalent to elite circulation, as that concept was understood by the classical elite theorists; in Chapter 7 we shall discuss long-term, macroscopic changes in elite composition.

[58] Knight, 1953, pp. 11–14; Zapf, 1965, especially p. 136.

[59] Pierce, 1973, p. 262; Sartori, 1967, pp. 158–159; Legg, 1969, pp. 299–301; Dekmejian, 1975; Smith, 1973; Winder, 1962, p. 422; Brzezinski and Huntington, 1965, p. 177; Rigby, 1970.

ages. Jean Blondel has found this negative correlation between institutional longevity and turnover rates in such diverse systems as Canada, Switzerland, Chile, Colombia, and the United States. For example, the proportion of freshman representatives in the U.S. Congress has been falling for more than a century, from 50 percent in the 1850s to roughly 15 percent at present. Consistent with this link between turnover and institutional age is the fact that legislative turnover is highest in the newer regimes of the Third World, and lowest in the older parliamentary democracies. Analogously, after successful revolutions turnover rates tend to decline as the new regime matures; there is evidence of this pattern in China, Japan, and post-Stalinist Russia.[60]

What difference do turnover rates make for politics and policy? This question has evoked much speculation, but little hard research. Interest has centered on three broad hypotheses.

1. *The higher the degree of elite turnover, the greater a system's innovativeness and flexibility in terms of policy.* More new leaders means more new ideas. Of course, if the new elite resembles its predecessors in background and outlook—if Tweedledee follows Tweedledum—high turnover may not lead to new policies. But in both electoral and nonelectoral systems, spurts of turnover are often associated with bursts of innovation and even shifts in budgetary allocations.[61] One study of the effects of turnover on the Swedish Riksdag found that within each party "attitudes of new members differed most drastically from the attitudes of former members on 'new' [that is, recently politicized] issues."[62] It seems reasonable to conclude, as Brzezinski and Huntington do for the United States and the Soviet Union, that elite turnover "does not guarantee new policies, but it makes them possible."[63]

If turnover declines as institutions age, it would seem to follow that older institutions should be less innovative. The "petrification" theory of Soviet politics, for example, holds that as the regime has matured, it has become more rigid and less adaptable to social change. The evidence for this thesis is far from convincing, however, and despite declining congressional turnover, it would be difficult to show that U.S. policy making is markedly less innovative now than a century ago. The relationship between elite turnover and policy innovation is not a simple one.[64]

2. *The higher the degree of elite turnover, the lower the average level of elite experience, expertise, and effectiveness.* Older leaders, though perhaps less imaginative, may be wiser in the ways of government. Getting new ideas is quite different from getting new ideas implemented. For this reason "the capacity of a

---

[60] Blondel, 1973, pp. 85–87; Kau, 1969, pp. 256–257; Kuroda, 1974, p. 4; Hough, 1972, p. 32.

[61] Bunce, 1975. See also Chapter 6, for a discussion of the consequences of electoral turnover.

[62] Holmberg, 1974, p. 382.

[63] Brzezinski and Huntington, 1963, p. 181.

[64] Hough, 1972.

political system and its ability to make *effective* policy changes . . . might be associated with stability of executive tenure."[65] Because of Mexico's very high turnover rates, for example, it has been suggested that her leaders have little opportunity or incentive to develop skills in policy analysis or to undertake long-range projects, for they are not around long enough. The operative rule becomes instead, "grab the money and run."[66]

Where turnover rates among different institutions or subelites within the same political system diverge, the balance of power among those institutions or subelites may be affected, for those with low turnover rates are likely to accumulate greater expertise and hence more power than their competitors. Where turnover is lower among senior civil servants than among ministers or members of parliament, for example, political control over the bureaucracy may be severely limited; evidence of this pattern has been found in such countries as France, Britain, and Japan. Conversely, low turnover in the U.S. Congress, combined with relatively high turnover in the top layers of the executive branch, increases the ability of congressional leaders (in concert with permanent civil servants) to resist administration initiatives.[67]

3. *The higher the degree of elite turnover, the greater the number of persons who will have a chance to attain elite status.* From this mathematical certainty it is sometimes inferred that high turnover is a prerequisite for democracy. Both Karl Marx and Andrew Jackson believed that the progressive simplification of the tasks of government made it possible to approach the democratic ideal of permanent, rapid circulation of individuals through leadership posts. Roughly the same logic lies behind legal limitations on elite tenure in such countries as the United States, Yugoslavia, and Mexico.

For similar reasons, high turnover is sometimes thought to be politically stabilizing. As Dwaine Marvick has said, "One of the basic questions about any system of public order is how smoothly it provides career opportunities to each successive generation."[68] Pareto and Mosca believed that, within limits, high turnover prevents the build-up of frustration among potential challengers of the regime, by allowing them to be coopted, however briefly, into positions of leadership. Conversely, as we shall discuss in Chapter 7, in successful revolutionary movements the durability of the revolutionary generation often creates a destabilizing blockage to the advancement of younger leaders.

The manner of elite turnover is as significant as its frequency. There is no necessary link between the two; across a large number of countries there is virtually no correlation between the frequency and the constitutionality of

---

[65] Hopkins, 1969, p. 84 (italics added).

[66] Smith, 1974, pp. 28–31.

[67] Rose, 1969; Cheng, 1974; Brzezinski and Huntington, 1964, pp. 175–182; MacGregor, 1974, p. 24.

[68] Marvick, 1968, p. 279.

leadership changes.[69] How people leave power is an important basis for classifying political systems, and the diversity is very great—coups, electoral defeats, assassination, loss of key factional support, foreign intervention, occasionally even retirement in old age. Regularized and peaceful succession is historically rare, and practices involving any sort of representation are rarer still. Robert Daniels has pointed out that Nikita Khrushchev's ouster in 1964 by a vote of the Politburo was an intriguing milestone: "This was the first time in the entire history of Russia . . . that the established leader of the country was removed by the rules of representative procedure."[70]

From *Oedipus Rex* to *Hamlet*, the poet and the playwright have been fascinated by the drama of political succession, for the inevitable crisis exposes the strengths and weaknesses of human character. Succession exposes, too, the strengths and weaknesses of political systems, and therein lies its fascination for the more prosaic political scientist. Succession politics differs markedly from "normal" politics, whether we consider the deposing of a Soviet general secretary, the election (or the impeachment) of a U.S. president, the formation of a new Italian cabinet, or the latest military coup in Latin America. In a typical succession crisis, the number of participants increases, major policy issues get caught up in the struggle, and latent personal, social, and political conflicts become more visible and more acrimonious. All political systems are most vulnerable to attack from within or without at the time of succession, but the stress is greatest for immature systems. It is the mark of a strongly institutionalized system that it is able to weather the seasonal storms of succession.

POLITICAL RECRUITMENT: SO WHAT?	The consequences of recruitment patterns are both direct and subtle. Reformers have often learned to their dismay that changes in recruitment practices (such as the direct primary or the Twenty-second and Twenty-fifth Amendments to the U.S. Constitution) can have quite unintended effects. Broadly speaking, recruitment influences elites in three ways: the selection effect, the incentive effect, and the socialization effect.

tion effect, the incentive effect, and the socialization effect.

SELECTION

Most clearly, the recruitment system determines who gets through and who is screened out. As we have seen, different selectorates demand different credentials, and an elite screened primarily for rhetorical skills, for example, will differ markedly from one selected on the basis of political outlook. Another illustration:

[69] Hopkins, 1969, p. 84n.

[70] Daniels, 1971, pp. 22–25. See also Rush, 1974.

intramural selectorates, as in Britain, tend to produce an elite that is cautious and orthodox, whereas extramural selectorates, as in America, favor innovative and frenetic self-starters.[71]

But selection is not the only way that recruitment influences the character of the elite. In Prewitt's words, "irrespective of who [the leaders] are, the pathways taken to office by political leaders certainly affect the way in which they will govern."[72] For ambitious politicians, the paths leading to the top constitute a structure of opportunities and incentives. Recruitment patterns, therefore, encourage leaders to behave in certain ways and not in others. Any theory of recruitment must include a theory of careers and ambition.[73]

Aspirants must satisfy present and (especially) prospective selectorates. This is precisely the rationale for elections: If leaders must win votes to gain office, they have an incentive to attend to the wishes of the voters. Moreover, as a number of American studies have found, politicians eager to grasp the next rung of the electoral ladder tend to adopt a political posture appropriate to the office they desire. State and local politicians who dream of higher office take a broader view of public problems than do their less ambitious colleagues and are more sympathetic to the expansion of the role of higher levels of government.[74]

A similar logic applies to nonelectoral settings. Where advancement depends on seniority and the good will of party superiors, party loyalty and discipline will be stronger than where recruitment is decentralized to local selectorates. And the incentives provided by monocratic recruitment systems are equally compelling. Under the Stalinist regime, for example, ambitious leaders "learned that success was to be had by winning the favor not of those below them but of those above them, which was exactly what Stalin wanted them to learn."[75]

Patterns of departure from the elite also create powerful incentives. Politics is everywhere a "greasy pole," but in what Seligman terms "high-risk" political systems, the costs of a fall from power are very great, ranging from ignominious oblivion to execution. In low-risk systems, on the other hand, a variety of "cushions"—company directorships, a seat in the House of Lords, a university presidency—are available to limit the discomfiture associated with leaving the elite. High-risk systems are likely to be more authoritarian and to

---

[71] Waltz, 1967, pp. 46–55.

[72] Prewitt, 1970, p. 22.

[73] Schlesinger, 1966, especially pp. 3–6.

[74] Prewitt, 1970, pp. 190–192; Prewitt and Nowlin, 1969; Soule, 1969; Fiellin, 1967.

[75] Feldmesser, 1966, p. 532.

suffer more severe succession crises, for incumbents will hardly leave without a struggle. Michels traced the roots of oligarchy in working-class movements in part to the very sharp drop in status and income that awaited ex-leaders, and a similar theory may fit some developing countries today. Khrushchev's relatively gentle treatment at the hands of his successors may have reflected a decision on their part to reduce the risks (and hence the severity) of future succession crises.[76]

SOCIALIZATION

Recruitment patterns also affect elites by the lessons they impart. David Easton has suggested that "the process of competing for positions of authority in itself trains the leadership in many of the competences required by the system."[77] American politicians learn to make and break alliances of convenience with a minimum of fuss, whereas recruitment in Britain teaches the importance of teamwork. Everywhere political recruits are trained in, and tested on, the informal rules of the game, but in seniority-based guild systems, apprentices can be taught a particularly intricate code to guide their use of power. Career socialization is less effective (or at least less uniform) for the in-and-outers of high-turnover, high-permeability systems. Donald Matthews found, for example, that ex-congressmen learn the norms of the Senate more quickly than do ex-governors.[78]

Certain features of recruitment systems may have special importance for elite socialization. Elites recruited from local government, for example, are probably more sympathetic to demands for decentralization than are elites recruited entirely through national channels. Where a few schools supply most recruits, the curricular and extracurricular training they provide and the friendships they foster will be an important influence on elite behavior. British administrators differ from French administrators in part because the humanist colleges of Oxbridge differ from the technocratic *grandes écoles*, and both groups are more integrated than their American counterparts in part because the education of American elites is more pluralistic. Soviet leaders whose path to the top has included lengthy service in nonparty posts (such as factory management) differ from lifelong party *apparatchiki* partly because their career experiences have imparted different lessons.[79] We shall return to these issues of elite socialization in the next chapter.

---

[76] Seligman, 1971, pp. 9–12; Michels, 1959.

[77] Easton, 1965, p. 451

[78] Matthews, 1960, pp. 103–108.

[79] Fleron, 1973; Lodge, 1973; Barton, 1973, pp. 254–259. It would be wrong, however, to assume full uniformity of socialization and outlook among officials from a given career path; see Hough, 1971.

MOTIVES, BELIEFS, AND THEIR SOURCES

4

Thus far we have considered where members of the political elite come from and how they reach positions of power. This chapter discusses the motivations that lead them to seek power and the perspectives they bring to bear on their exercise of that power.

THE MOTIVATIONS OF POLITICAL ELITES

Throughout the world men and women seek public power. Why? One broad answer was offered decades ago by Harold D. Lasswell, who argued that political leaders in their public behavior merely act out private drives and conflicts, cloaking this fact in publicly acceptable rhetoric. In Lasswell's concise formula, "We sum up the political type in terms of the development of motive as follows:

Private Motives

Displaced on Public Objects

Rationalized in Terms of Public Interest."[1]

According to this approach, a leader's public behavior derives from his unconscious emotional needs, not his conscious political values. To understand his behavior we should look, not to the "logic of the situation," but to his own private "psycho-logic."

But most of us suffer inner conflicts. Why do only a few of us choose to fight our private battles in the public arena? Why are the private motives of some people displaced onto public objects? How and why do political leaders differ psychologically from ordinary citizens?

[1] Lasswell, 1948, p. 38.

By definition, elites are distinguished by their greater power. Hence, it is natural to assume that motivationally they are distinguished by an unusual need for power. Michels, for example, wrote of "a natural greed for power" in leaders, and in contemporary formal models of political systems the power-maximizing political man is often postulated by analogy with profit-maximizing economic man.[2]

Lasswell has formulated the most influential account of the power-seeking political personality: "He pursues power as a means of compensation against deprivation. *Power is expected to overcome low estimates of the self,* by changing either the traits of the self or the environment in which it functions."[3] Damaged self-esteem may stem from a physical handicap, or from social deprivation, or from exaggerated parental expectations. Or power may be sought to compensate for childhood bereavement and the absence of parental affection; an astonishing two-thirds of British prime ministers over the last two centuries have lost one or both parents in childhood.[4] But whatever the genesis of damaged self-esteem, it is hypothesized, "in order to overcome or compensate for low self-estimates, the power-seeking personality attempts to carve out a sphere of activity in which he can demonstrate his competence and worth."[5]

Many children, perhaps even most, are deprived in some way, of course, and not all deprived children become political leaders. Activity in other spheres, withdrawal, isolated aggression, and even suicide are alternatives. For political involvement to be the result, Lasswell argues, the damage to the child's self-esteem must not be so great as to incapacitate the potential politician from effective action in the public arena, and the objective situation must invite (or at least allow) both displacement and rationalization. In a general sense, Lasswell concludes, "All men are born politicians, and some never outgrow it."[6]

But if a wounded sense of self is not a sufficient condition for seeking power, many political psychologists believe it may be a predisposing one. And if this account of political motivation is substantially correct, it may mean that political leaders are all potentially psychopaths. The archetype for this theory is Shakespeare's lamed and murderously ambitious Richard III:

> I, that am rudely stamp'd, and want love's majesty . . .
> Cheated of feature by dissembling nature,
> Deform'd, unfinish'd . . .
> I am determined to prove a villain.

[2] Michels, 1959, p. 205; Downs, 1957.

[3] Lasswell, 1948, p. 39.

[4] Iremonger, 1970; Berrington, 1974.

[5] George, 1968, p. 38.

[6] Lasswell, 1954, p. 210.

What evidence is there for this hypothesis tracing political leadership to damaged egos, compensatory power seeking, and psychopathology? Members of the top political elite rarely accommodate the curiosity of social scientists by undergoing psychological testing, and hence the best available evidence comes from studies of activists in intermediate political strata.

Some of this evidence tends to confirm Lasswell's hypothesis. A study of the Connecticut state legislature found that although the most effective (and presumably the most influential) members are characterized by *above*-average ego strength, the majority of the sample "appear in the interviews as people with rather severe deficiencies in self-esteem."[7] An ingenious survey of patients in an Illinois mental hospital found that their reported level of political involvement prior to admission was at least as high as that of "normal" citizens. More intriguingly, those patients who had been most active politically (and who continued to be most active in the patients' self-governing councils) showed a peculiarly high rate of paranoid schizophrenia, a mental illness that involves projection and aggression, combined with relatively high self-confidence, intelligence, and sensitivity to social norms.[8]

That paranoids are unusually active politically, however, does not establish that most political leaders are paranoids. The more typical finding is that political participation is positively, not negatively, associated with ego strength, self-esteem, and a sense of personal efficacy. Among American college students, for example, it is apparently the political apathetics, not the political activists, who harbor deep-seated feelings of insecurity and aggression. One study of the Yugoslav League of Communists found activists to be more optimistic and less anxiety-ridden than ordinary Yugoslav citizens. Several studies of somewhat higher levels of the American political stratification system confirm that political involvement is positively correlated with ego strength, self-esteem, and a minimum of neurosis. This is true, for example, of South Carolina legislators, regional administrators, California party officials, national-security policymakers, Washington lobbyists, and delegates to the national political conventions. On balance, the available evidence speaks against Lasswell's theory, at least at the higher levels of the political elite.[9] Damaged egos and psychopathic symptoms seem to be rarer among political leaders than in the mass public.

MOTIVATION AND POLITICAL RECRUITMENT

One important intervening variable that may account for these mixed findings about psychopathology and leadership is the political recruitment process. For

[7] Barber, 1965, p. 217. See also Di Renzo, 1967.

[8] Rutherford, 1966.

[9] See Milbrath, 1965, pp. 76–86, and sources cited there; Mussen and Warren, 1952, pp. 65–82; Zaninovich, 1970, p. 314; McConaughy, 1950, pp. 897–903; McConaughy and Palmer, 1971; Costantini and Craik, 1972, p. 226; Etheredge, 1974; Mennis, 1971; Sniderman, 1975, pp. 254–304; Milbrath, 1963, pp. 99–107.

even if persons with damaged egos and neurotic tendencies are drawn toward the political arena to vent their emotions, institutional mechanisms may in some circumstances tend to exclude them from positions of real influence. Indeed, Lasswell has conceded that "It is probable that a basically healthy personality is essential to survive the perpetual uncertainties of political life."[10] Based on his study of prominent politicians, Victor Wolfenstein concludes: "Great leaders are not permanently incapacitated by blows, public or private, which would destroy lesser men."[11]

If established political institutions do tend to screen out psychological deviants, then leaders who rise through unstructured or unconventional political movements should be more likely to display psychopathological tendencies. In fact, one study found that officials in a traditional urban political machine displayed fewer psychoneurotic abnormalities than did a sample of unconventional community activists. More dramatically, according to a clinical study of defendants at Nuremberg, the Nazi elite was composed disproportionately of paranoid schizophrenics.[12] Based on a study of Hitler and Stalin, Robert Tucker concludes: "An individual who might be psychologically disqualified for successful leadership in very many large-scale organizations need not be so in the very special context of a fighting organization [such as a totalitarian political party], in which his very psychopathology may be 'functional' for leadership purposes."[13]

Similarly, the success of aspiring leaders may depend on the "fit" between their psychic needs and the requirements of the political situation. For example, intense, ego-defensive power seekers, rejected by political institutions in normal times, may be especially favored during political crises. Winston Churchill's career—remarkably successful during World War II, but relatively unsuccessful during the calmer prewar and postwar periods—may illustrate this phenomenon.[14]

Other findings, too, suggest that recruitment and personality are jointly important. In one study, local politicians and businessmen were asked to make up fantasy stories about six ambiguous pictures, stories that could be used to measure latent needs for power, achievement, and friendship. In the aggregate, politicians showed no striking motivational differences from nonpoliticians. However, politicians holding positions of more power and opportunity for advancement displayed greater need for power and achievement and lower need for friendship than either dead-end politicians or politically inactive businessmen. Politically active businessmen, on the other hand, showed the same syndrome of high need for power and achievement and low need for affiliation,

[10] Lasswell, 1954, p. 223. For supportive empirical evidence, see Sniderman, 1975, pp. 254–304.

[11] Wolfenstein, 1969, p. 16.

[12] Marcus, 1969, pp. 913–931; Gilbert, 1950; Di Renzo, 1967, pp. 108–110.

[13] Tucker, 1965, p. 582.

[14] Wolfenstein, 1967a; Kavanaugh, 1974. See also Edinger, 1964, p. 672.

but unlike the professional politicians, they came from apolitical families, so that partisan politics did not seem so natural an outlet for their personal drives. Personal motivation and early exposure to politics seem independently necessary and jointly sufficient to explain political leadership.[15]

Exposure and motivation are themselves related, of course, as Prewitt's "overexposure" hypothesis implies. Robert Salisbury writes that political activity "is an aspect of a life-style that has been accepted uncritically since childhood by a relatively small number of people in the society. . . . Such people, though a very small part of the total population, make up a very large portion of the political participants."[16] Psychologically speaking, political involvement is for many men and women a family legacy. Nearly half of the members of the British, German, and Italian parliaments report that some older relative of theirs had been active in politics, half recall that politics was a prime topic of conversation in their childhood, and three-quarters say that they became actively interested in politics before the age of 25.

The proportion of these early starters seems to vary from political stratum to stratum in accord with a law of increasing disproportion: At each step up the political hierarchy—from voters to activists to local leaders to national leaders—persons whose interest in politics was precocious become more common. Moreover, several studies suggest that at each level these "home-grown" politicians have a more realistic, "political" conception of their role than do late starters, are more professional in their approach to politics, have stronger programmatic interests, and harbor stronger ambitions for political advancement. These distinctive traits no doubt help explain why early starters make it to the top of the political hierarchy in disproportionate numbers.[17]

The research reviewed so far has focused on politicians as single-minded power seekers, but the need for power is actually multifaceted. On the basis of studies in France, Colombia, Brazil, the Dominican Republic, and the United States, James L. Payne and Oliver Woshinsky describe six different political incentives, six emotional needs that drive political leaders to make the sacrifices required by political involvement.[18] (See Table 4–1.)

Woshinsky has argued that differences in incentives are associated with differences in behavior. French deputies who seek status through politics, for example, devote most of their effort to activities that bring personal publicity, whereas those whose emotional satisfactions come from programmatic accomplishments spend more time in areas requiring legislative expertise and less time

---

[15] Browning and Jacob, 1964, pp. 75–90; Browning, 1968, pp. 93–109.

[16] Salisbury, 1965–1966, p. 564.

[17] Kornberg and Thomas, 1965; Kesselman, 1973, pp. 27–31; Prewitt, 1970, p. 103; Soule and Clarke, 1970, pp. 891–892; Soule, 1969; Black, 1970; Kornberg, 1967, pp. 50–51, and sources cited there. However, see also Prewitt, Eulau, and Zisk, 1966–1967.

[18] Payne and Woshinsky, 1972.

Table 4–1   Incentives for Political Participation: A Typology

A leader driven by this incentive	seeks this satisfaction through political participation	and is typified by these traits
I. Adulation	Personal affection and praise	Enjoys campaigning; gregarious; preoccupied with own reputation.
II. Status	Socially defined "success"	Preoccupied with climbing career ladder; cynical about others' motives and about politics in general.
III. Program	Solution of policy problems	Interested in substance of public policy and policy-making process; concerned for stability; favorable to compromise and incrementalism.
IV. Mission	Identification with a "cause"	Focused on ideology; consumed by missionary zeal; committed to complete social transformation.
V. Obligation	Sense of civic duty	Preoccupied with normative principles rather than with concrete outcomes; averse to politics in general and compromise in particular.
VI. Game	Exercise of skill in political competition	Preoccupied with strategy and tactics; enjoys political haggling and manipulation; has detached view of political game, though a supporter of its rules.

Source: Payne and Woshinsky, 1972.

on personal exhibitionism. Deputies driven primarily by a sense of duty rather than by any positive incentive withdraw from most legislative activity and leave politics sooner. Participants who gain satisfaction from serving a mission or cause enter politics early in life and devote more energy to party activities than to legislative duties.[19]

Viewed from afar, all politicians may seem to be purely power seekers, but viewed close up, the diversity of motivation is more impressive. Distinctive national motivational patterns may help explain distinctive behavioral patterns. An elite of status seekers is prone to public posturing and probably less effective at solving policy problems than is an elite whose personal satisfactions are programmatic in nature. More research is needed to explore this and similar hypotheses.

[19] Woshinsky, 1973; see also Payne, 1972. Such studies must take care to measure motivation and behavior independently, in order to avoid methodological circularity.

Even within a single office the personality and motivations of successive incumbents may differ markedly. For example, James David Barber has used a simple fourfold typology to array the diverse personalities of American presidents and to show how presidential performance varies as a function of presidential character. "Active-positive" presidents are marked by high self-esteem and relish manipulating their environment; Harry Truman and John Kennedy are among Barber's examples of this type. "Active-negative" presidents are equally intense in their efforts to control people and events, but they are suspicious, aggressive, and compulsive. Such men—Lyndon Johnson and Richard Nixon illustrate this type—fit Lasswell's model of the compensatory power seeker. "Passive-positive" presidents derive pleasure less from self-initiated activity than from compliance with external pressures; life for a passive-positive politician, such as William Howard Taft, is "a search for affection as a reward for being agreeable and cooperative rather than personally assertive." "Passive-negative" types, by temperament withdrawn and self-deprecating, reach high office only rarely. Like Woshinsky's "obligation" participants, they are driven less by a zest for politics than by a sense of duty; Dwight Eisenhower is said to exemplify this pattern.[20]

The personality and motivation of political leaders may also vary as a function of their social backgrounds. For example, two contrasting personality types have been detected among the classic American urban bosses—"game" politicians and "gain" politicians. The game politician normally came from a stiff, upper-class home and was molded psychologically by a lack of love and approval in his childhood. He sought in public life—"the great game of politics"—the satisfactions of power, prestige, and adulation. The gain politician, on the other hand, was typically raised in a working-class immigrant home and was deprived, not of affection, but of physical comforts. Politics for him was a source of wealth and the venal rewards of office. In sum, both types sought power, but for quite different reasons, and both used power, but in quite different ways.[21]

High-quality research on the personalities and motivations of political leaders is still rare. We know virtually nothing in a rigorous way about the psychic origins of political involvement, except among American local leaders and activists. Studies comparing matched samples of national politicians and ordinary citizens, or of conventional and unconventional politicians, or of political and bureaucratic or economic elites, or of American and foreign leaders are very rare. Moreover, the link between personality and political behavior is rarely demonstrated. It is, for example, plausible to suppose that paranoid politicians resist compromise, but this hypothesis is more often illustrated than tested.[22]

---

[20] Barber, 1972; see also Barber, 1965, and George, 1974. For some interesting comparable findings from a sample of California city councilmen, see Black, 1970, p. 865.

[21] Rogow and Lasswell, 1963, pp. 45–54.

[22] However, see Mennis, 1971, and Etheredge, 1974, for evidence that among national-security officials, personal dogmatism, rigidity, dominance, hostility, competitiveness, and paranoia are associated with support for hard-line foreign policies.

The relative importance of role, situation, and psyche in determining behavior remains unclarified in empirical terms.[23]

Finally, studies of personality and politics have often undervalued cognitive or ideological impulses. Lasswell himself has argued that while many ordinary citizens displace private drives onto public objects, "the distinctive mark of the *homo politicus* is the rationalization of the displacement in terms of public interests."[24] But this "rationalization" may itself affect the behavior of the politician. It made a great difference for German history that Hitler's "rationalization" was fascist, rather than, say, social democratic.[25] The study of the psychology of political elites must pay special heed to their beliefs and values.

ELEMENTS OF ELITE BELIEF SYSTEMS

Political observers often attribute considerable importance to the beliefs and values of political leaders. Each day's newspapers report the shifting tides of elite opinion. Historians stress the significance of sweeping ideological and intellectual movements—liberalism, Marxism, nationalism, Confucianism, Maoism. And an American president explains his economic policies by saying, "We're all Keynesians now," a comment that would have amused John Maynard Keynes himself, who once wrote of policy makers that "madmen in authority, who hear voices in the air, are distilling their frenzy from some academic scribbler of a few years back."[26]

Yet only recently have elite attitudes been studied systematically. Most commonly, these studies have focused on leaders' *opinions* on topical issues. One study of British elites, for example, inquired, "How valuable would you say membership of the Common Market [would be] for Britain—very valuable, fairly valuable, no real value or actually harmful?"[27] Drawing on the familiar techniques of polling and making the plausible assumption that elite preferences count for more than mass preferences, the logic of this approach is quite simple—if you want to discover whether Britain is likely to join the Common Market, find out the views of British leaders.

However useful this approach may be in some contexts, as a basis for

---

[23] Space does not permit a full review of the literature on personality and politics. Among the most useful introductions to this approach to the study of political elites are Greenstein, 1969, Greenstein and Lerner, 1971, Edinger, 1964, 1965, George and George, 1964; George, 1968; Wolfenstein, 1967*b*.

[24] Lasswell, 1960, p. 262.

[25] Edinger, 1965, p. 294n.

[26] Keynes, 1936, p. 383.

[27] Abrams, 1965, p. 242. See also Free, 1959; Deutsch et al., 1967; Lerner and Gorden, 1969; Bell, 1964. Occasionally such surveys ask respondents to *predict* future developments; for example, Deutsch asked, "What do you think the map of Europe will look like in 1975?" (p. 308). This approach entails two difficulties: (1) leaders are not necessarily very good at this sort of prediction, and (2) their predictions are at best an ambiguous guide to their underlying orientations or their behavior.

understanding elite behavior it has several serious flaws. First, elite preferences often do not accurately predict outcomes. One study, for example, found that French elite preferences measured in this way during the 1960s coincided with French government policy only about half the time.[28] Part of the difficulty here is that even among elites not everyone's "vote" has equal weight. A second flaw is that, as we shall see later in this chapter, a leader's behavior is a function, not just of his personal opinions, but also of the objective situation in which he finds himself. The link between opinion and behavior is never simple.[29] A third, fundamental flaw is that most interesting problems of political analysis involve issues not yet faced by policy makers, and unless we understand how specific opinions fit into a broader pattern of beliefs, we can neither predict nor understand elite behavior.

Prediction and understanding can be enhanced by considering the fundamental orientations that underlie leaders' day-to-day opinions and actions. I shall discuss here four basic classes of elite attitudes: (1) *cognitive orientations* —assumptions about how society works; (2) *normative orientations*—views about how society ought to work; (3) *interpersonal orientations*—attitudes about other players in the political game; and (4) *stylistic orientations*—structural characteristics of elite belief systems.

COGNITIVE ORIENTATIONS

Social facts rarely speak for themselves. "Students of human behavior have long agreed that any individual must necessarily simplify and structure the complexity of his world in order to cope with it."[30] A policy maker's attention must be focused on certain "facts" and not on others that are, for him, less significant. The conceptual lenses that accomplish this focusing are his cognitive orientations —predispositions that lead him to see and interpret reality in a particular way. As one illustration of a key cognitive orientation, consider leaders' perspectives on social conflict.

Some policy makers assume that conflict is the essence of politics and that public affairs is inevitably a "zero-sum" game in which the gains of one person or group are the losses of another. On this assumption, the size of the social pie is fixed, and bitter conflict about the slices is inevitable. Others believe instead in a natural harmony of interests. In this view, policy making is a technical matter of solving common problems. The pie can always be made larger, and there need be no losers.

These almost philosophical assumptions about social conflict and consensus

---

[28] Lerner and Gorden, 1969, pp. 381–382; see also Cavala and Wildavsky, 1970.

[29] Greenstein, 1969.

[30] George, 1969, p. 200.

seem to guide the everyday perceptions and behavior of practical politicians. Those whose cognitive orientations highlight conflicting interests believe that economic policy, for example, must inevitably favor some groups at the expense of others, while the consensualists believe that skillful policy makers can satisfy everyone. Conflict-oriented politicians typically act as partisan advocates for some group they view as exploited, whereas those who believe society to be essentially harmonious discount particularistic demands as selfish and shortsighted.[31]

The orientations to conflict generally characteristic of a national elite condition its political behavior, to some extent independently of social reality as might be perceived by an external observer. An elite for whom conflict is highly salient is likely to be fragmented and paralyzed, for their cognitive lenses magnify conflicting interests and minimize mutual interests. If the size of the pie seems fixed, one must be hard-nosed; as a member of the Malaysian elite told James C. Scott, "The big fish eat the small fish and the small fish eat worms." In such a society, government is apt to be unstable and policy incoherent. Recent evidence suggests that orientations of this sort characterize elites in Italy, Morocco, and Malaysia. On the other hand, an elite that is insensitive to social conflict has an equally constricted view of reality, for their cognitive orientations tend to screen out instances of genuine conflict. Such an elite is prone to reject awkward demands from dissident and dispossessed groups as being inconsistent with the national interest. Government in such a system may be stable, but it is likely to be unresponsive to public demands. Elites in India, Japan, traditional China, and imperial Germany seem to have had orientations of this sort. Stable and responsive government seems to be most likely where leaders have a balanced perspective on conflict and consensus. Scattered evidence suggests that most leaders in Britain and the United States are sensitive in this way to both interests that divide and interests that unite.[32]

NORMATIVE ORIENTATIONS

The reasoning that leads leaders to act as they do implicitly involves both "is" premises and "ought" premises. The former are shaped by cognitive orientations, while the latter are undergirded by normative orientations. Everyday judgments about specific political objects—for example, social welfare programs or membership in the European Economic Community—rest on commitments

[31] Putnam, 1973a, especially pp. 118–128; see also George, 1969, especially pp. 201–202.

[32] Putnam, 1973a, pp. 137–156; Waterbury, 1970, pp. 5–6; Scott, 1968, pp. 99–149; International Studies of Values in Politics, 1971, pp. 70–80, 129; Dahl, 1971, pp. 152–162; Austin, 1975; Solomon, 1971; Dahrendorf, 1969, pp. 129–203. On the complex interaction between perception and reality that lies behind the concept of cognitive orientations, see Putnam (1973a) and the sources cited there.

to more fundamental values—individual self-reliance, social justice, national independence, material progress, and so on. Although specific evaluations are often of interest to students of elites, I want here to stress the importance of the underlying criteria in terms of which these evaluations are made.

The range of human values is as wide as the world and as long as human history, and this diversity is recorded in the great controversies of religious, social, and political philosophy. The mighty ideological currents that have swept across the last several centuries—liberalism, nationalism, socialism, fascism, and so on—have each embodied more or less consistent systems of values, and each has found adherents among the political elites of the world. In some countries a single such ideology has been embraced by nearly all members of the elite, while in other countries elite value systems are more variegated.

The texture of politics in any age is provided by the interplay among conflicting visions of the good society. For example, Table 4–2 shows the responses of British and Italian members of parliament to a question about "the kind of society [they] would like to see for [their] children and grandchildren." Certain desires are widely shared, but both national and ideological divergences are apparent. For example, politicians of the Left are more concerned for social and political equality, while representatives of the Center and Right give priority instead to liberty. These diverse definitions of social progress inevitably condition leaders' day-to-day policy preferences.

Political controversy in the twentieth century has revolved around the issue of equality, more than any other single value.[33] For radicals almost everywhere, social and economic equality is a moral imperative, whereas conservatives fear leveling and laud diversity. As an English Tory once complained to me:

> *The trouble with democracy as it's working out at the moment is it tends to assume, in a horseracing analogy, that every horse has got to be fit to run in the Derby, when in fact a draft horse may pull the brewer's dray better than a thoroughbred would. Similarly, a cart horse cannot win the Derby.*

A leader who sorts his fellow citizens into thoroughbreds and cart horses is hardly likely to favor broad welfare programs, progressive income taxes, workers' participation in management, and other policies dear to egalitarians.

Evidence on the commitment of national elites to socioeconomic equality comes from a study of the values of community leaders in India, Poland, Yugoslavia, and the United States. Figure 4–1 summarizes their views about the proper distribution of income. The results disconfirm any simple link between formal regime ideology and elite values, for leaders in the two Communist nations are less extreme egalitarians than are the Indians. On the other hand,

---

[33] For evidence illustrating this contention in the case of British elites, see Searing, 1974.

Table 4–2   Visions of the Future in Britain and Italy: Answers Given to the Question "How Would the Society You'd Like to See for Your Children and Grandchildren Differ from Today's Britain [or Italy]?" by British and Italian Politicians

	British Members of Parliament		Italian Deputies		
	Labour (N = 49)	Conservative (N =30)	Communist (N = 20)	Non-Communist Left (N = 26)	Center and Right (N = 36)
Political reform	16%	3%	70%	58%	61%
More social justice	76	37	100	88	56
Greater freedom	6	80	35	46	53
Higher moral standards	47	33	10	35	50
Improved Standard of living	65	73	70	73	58
More education and culture	67	37	35	50	44
Security and sense of community	39	23	10	38	28

Source: Unpublished data from the study reported in Putnam, 1973a.

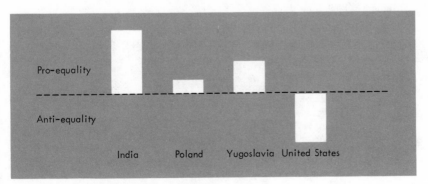

Figure 4–1   Economic Egalitarianism in Four Elites
Source: International Studies of Values in Politics, 1971, p. 79.

these data (together with other evidence) suggest that American leaders are very dubious about socioeconomic equality and are committed to socioeconomic *laissez-faire.* This pattern of elite values helps explain the striking reluctance of American governments (in comparison with governments in other industrialized countries) to intervene in socioeconomic affairs.[34]

Leaders also differ in their openness to social and technological innovation. Some are eager to adopt the most "modern" policies, while others, hostile to the mercurial, secular religions of science and technology, favor a cautious approach that respects national traditions. Aversion to innovation and skepticism about equality are two quite different brands of conservatism. For example, American elites, though more conservative than British elites with regard to socioeconomic equality, are less conservative about social and technological change.[35]

Another important set of normative orientations concerns not the substance, but the process, of government, for elites have diverse notions about what political procedures are fair and proper. For example, in contemporary pluralist democracies elite norms legitimize criticism of, and even organized opposition to, incumbent rulers. But the pages of world history record how remarkably rare is elite commitment to such values. Even today most leaders in most countries doubt the capacity of their subjects to participate fully in the governing process and reject the right of discontented groups to contest the status quo. Moreover, the tensile strength of elite support for political liberty and popular participation varies within the pluralist democracies. Table 4–3 shows how national leaders in four countries of Western Europe respond to a series of questions about political rights and wrongs. These data suggest that British elites are the most firmly committed to political democracy, Italian elites the most dubious, with the Dutch and the Germans in between.

Elite attitudes toward political equality and socioeconomic equality are not perfectly correlated. This distinction is highlighted by evidence (presented in

---

[34] International Studies of Values in Politics, 1971, pp. 78–79, 92, 390; McClosky, 1964, p. 367; King, 1973.

[35] Hargrove, 1969; King, 1973.

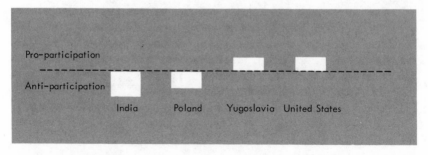

Figure 4–2   Political Egalitarianism in Four Elites
Source: International Studies of Values in Politics, 1971, p. 79.

Table 4–3   Democratic Norms Among Five
Western Legislative and
Administrative Elites*

	Great Britain	West Germany	Netherlands	Italy
1. The freedom of political propaganda is not an absolute freedom, and the state should carefully regulate its use.	21%	33%	†	43%
2. Citizens have a perfect right to exert pressure for legislation that would benefit them personally.	99	83	84%	58
3. Few people know what is in their real interest in the long run.	48	60	70	84
4. Certain people are better qualified to lead this country because of their traditions and family backgrounds.	20	23	20	37
5. In a world as complicated as the modern one, it doesn't make sense to speak of increased control by ordinary citizens over governmental affairs.	36	27	36	53

* Civil servants' and politicians' responses weighted equally.
Entry is percent "agreeing" or "agreeing with reservations" with
each statement.
† Question not asked in Netherlands.

Figure 4–2) on the political egalitarianism of leaders in India, Poland, Yugoslavia, and the United States. American elites, so conservative in economic
terms, are fully as supportive of popular participation as the Yugoslavs, while the
Indian leaders, whose commitment to social justice was noted in Figure 4–1,
here show considerable skepticism about citizen involvement in public affairs.
(This pattern of Indian elite values, as revealed in a 1966 survey, is strikingly
consistent with the posture of the Indian government in the aftermath of the 1975
coup.)

Attitudes toward socioeconomic equality, innovation, and political democracy do not exhaust the panoply of normative orientations important for understanding elite behavior. For example, the International Studies of Values in Politics explored leaders' orientations to economic development, conflict avoidance, national commitment, selflessness, and honesty; and Donald Searing has measured the commitment of British elites to a list of thirty-six values including such things as free enterprise, fellowship, privacy, compassion, and security.[36] Our brief discussion here can merely illustrate the diversity of leaders' views about the good society and the good polity.

INTERPERSONAL ORIENTATIONS

Some elites are riven by personal and partisan antagonisms, while others bridge practical differences by mutual tolerance. Three broad patterns can be distinguished here. Studies of elites in such countries as Morocco, Algeria, and Iran describe a culture of conspiracy, mutual suspicion, and cynicism. Mistrust of all competitors in this Hobbesian war of all against all forces leaders to engage in a "defensive use of power." The result: "A high degree of political tension . . . goes hand in hand with stalemate, and the recognized need for action [on concrete public problems] is paired with a pervasive lack of initiative."[37]

In a second group of countries, including Italy and Austria, political enmity is more narrowly focused, but no less virulent. Characteristically, leaders in these countries have dogmatic, dichotomous political maps—all actors are sharply classified into "us good guys" and "them bad guys." For such people, politics is essentially a morality play, a continual struggle between good and evil, and compromising with one's opponents is deemed dangerous because it inevitably risks the betrayal of one's own side. Trust and tolerance are extended only to one's party (or factional) colleagues, and the atmosphere of partisan hostility smothers cooperative initiatives on common problems. The operative question remains, as Lenin once said, "*Kto . . . kovo?*" ("who [does in] whom?").[38]

In a third group of countries, including Sweden, Britain, and the United States, elite interpersonal orientations generally follow the "norm of restrained partisanship."[39] Tolerance and trust cross party boundaries, and leaders see one another as legitimate contestants in a mutually beneficial game, rather than as belligerents in a ruleless war. Cooperation and reciprocal concession allow public problems to be confronted and social conflicts to be accommodated. On

---

[36] International Studies of Values in Politics, 1971, pp. 73–79; Searing, 1974.

[37] Waterbury, 1970, p. 5; Quandt, 1969, pp. 266–271; Zonis, 1968.

[38] Putnam, 1973*a*, pp. 56–59, 82–87; G. B. Powell, 1970, pp. 69–95; Powell, 1975; see also George, 1969, pp. 202, 217–221.

[39] Manley, 1965, as cited in Di Palma, 1973, pp. 10–13; Putnam, 1973*a*, pp. 56–59, 82–87; Hancock, 1972, pp. 62–64, 68–70.

the other hand, politics in such a system is not cuddly and conflictless, for most politicians believe their own programs correspond best to the needs of the country and the demands of social justice. As a British member of Parliament once described his opponents to me, "Well, they're different men with different policies, and some of them I quite like. They seem decent chaps, but . . . I don't agree with their policies."

Mutual intolerance limits the ability of an elite to grapple with public problems and undermines its willingness to abide by the self-restraining rules of democratic politics. It is no accident that those American leaders who proved most eager in the early 1970s to violate the rules of the game were distinguished by an intense partisanship and cynicism quite unusual among American politicians. It is also no accident that most of them were newcomers to the game of politics, for they took the outcome too seriously and the rules of play not seriously enough. The reaction of more experienced politicians revealed in the end a willingness to depose a powerful incumbent in order to vindicate the "norm of restrained partisanship." Historically, this may be the most important "lesson of Watergate."

It would be wrong to assume that some countries are naturally and permanently blessed with low political temperatures or that intense political hostility betokens immaturity or ignorance. Trust and cynicism, tolerance and dogmatism, amity and enmity have deep roots in a nation's past and its social structure. Against a background of class and ethnic cleavages, unresolved dilemmas of development, and historical experiences of mutual betrayal and exploitation, it is hardly surprising that in many countries even intelligent, well-intentioned leaders find it difficult to trust their opponents.

STYLISTIC ORIENTATIONS

It is important to consider, finally, the structure of a leader's belief system and his style of policy analysis. Much evidence from a number of countries suggests that elite belief systems are in several ways richer and more structured than the views that most of us have about politics. Political leaders and activists have more information about politics and society, and they have more sophisticated concepts for interpreting, storing, and using this information.[40] Leaders are more likely than most of us to grasp the significance of reports that the "forces of imperialism" are becoming more threatening, or that the cabinet is "drifting to the Left," because such "facts" are meaningful only in terms of conceptual frameworks that elites are more likely to have mastered. (In a precisely analogous way, my mother-in-law does not know what to make of a report that the Jets have strengthened their secondary, and I am mystified by the news that Shostakovich's latest symphony combines lyricism and modernism.)

---

[40] Converse, 1964; Cobb, 1973; Budge et al., 1972, p. 262.

The political views of elites are also more intensely held and more stable over time than are the views of most of us. Like participants in any sport, political activists care more about the state of play, and their loyalties and preferences are more durable (though not always more emotionally intense). Even on such perennial issues of public debate as government intervention in the economy, relatively few ordinary citizens appear to have any fixed view at all, whereas members of the political elite are likely to hold firm and broadly constant positions for decades.[41]

The belief systems of political elites are also more coherent, in the sense that knowing their views on one issue will allow us to predict their views on many other topics. Sometimes this sort of constraint among the elements of a leader's belief system is based in logic. For example, among U.S. congressmen, support for spending on social services is inversely related to concern about high taxes and balanced budgets, whereas "among adult American citizens, those who favor the expansion of government welfare services tend to be those who are more insistent upon reducing taxes 'even if it means putting off some important things that need to be done.' "[42] On the other hand, the linkage among elements in elite belief systems is often less logical than ideological. There is no unassailable logical link between foreign economic aid and federal support for school construction, and in fact support for the former among American voters is virtually unrelated to support for the latter. Among congressmen, however, those who favor foreign assistance are likely to favor aid to education as well.[43]

Elite beliefs are usually structured by partisan ideological commitments, often along the familiar Left-Right continuum. In such diverse countries as France, Britain, Israel, Sweden, India, Germany, Canada, and Italy, a leader's party affiliation is the best predictor of his position on a wide range of issues.[44] As Allan Kornberg has said, "For a political elite . . . party affiliation constitutes a kind of 'conceptual net' for capturing, organizing, and evaluating incoming information which may be politically relevant."[45] Nearly everywhere the opinions of conservatives and progressives differ sharply and consistently, whether the issue is religious laws (in Israel), decentralization of government (in Sweden), extension of the welfare state (in Canada), colonialism (in France), land reform (in India), negotiations with Eastern Europe (in West Germany), or race relations (in Britain). In fact, it is precisely because of this stable underlying structure that

---

[41] Butler and Stokes, 1969, pp. 195–199.

[42] Converse, 1964, p. 209.

[43] Converse, 1964, p. 228.

[44] Hunt, 1969; Kornberg and Frasure, 1971; Arian, 1968, pp. 37–40; Holmberg, 1974; Nanda, 1973, p. 745; Fishel, 1972; Kornberg, 1967, pp. 100, 117, 136; Clarke, Price, and Krause, 1975; Putnam, 1973a, especially p. 239. For evidence that internal party factionalism, too, can be based on coherent ideological differences, see Stern, Tarrow, and Williams, 1971, and Leonardi, 1974.

[45] Kornberg, 1967, p. 137, n. 5.

the studies of elite opinion mentioned earlier in this chapter are useful in interpreting elite behavior: Knowing where a leader stands on one issue is likely to help us understand and predict his stance even on tangential or as yet undiscussed matters.

It is perhaps not surprising that where politics are overtly ideological and parties cohesive, a leader's party affiliation provides a remarkably economical index of his political outlook. But even in the case of the motley and undisciplined American parties, studies of the attitudes and values of state politicians, national convention delegates, congressmen, senators, senior civil servants, judges, labor leaders, business elites, and journalists have consistently found sharp and comprehensive differences between Republicans and Democrats.[46]

Nor are the effects of the Left-Right ideological structuring limited to opinions on issues. In Canada, Italy, Britain, France, and the United States, politicians of the Left and the Right conceive their roles differently, interpret the world on the basis of different cognitive orientations, are committed to different normative orientations, and even define "democracy" differently.[47] To be sure, there are mavericks in all but the most totalitarian political parties, but for most politicians on most topics most of the time, partisan ideology provides a strong and enduring framework for organizing information, opinions, norms, and commitments.

Studies of mass political behavior have taught us how alien to most people are the complex systems of ideas traditionally used to interpret politics and history. The debate continues about just how conceptually impoverished ordinary voters are, but there is general agreement that elite beliefs about politics are characteristically richer and more structured.[48] As Alan Arian has said:

> Members of an elite not only produce ideology, they are also its largest distributors and consumers. They distribute it to their constituents in their programs and statements; they consume ideological output because, trained in the language of ideological discourse, they tend to communicate with their peers in that idiom and they are the most alert and sensitive to messages which have an ideological cast.[49]

If this is so, it is important to ask about causes and consequences. Why are elites more sophisticated ideologically, and what difference does it make?

---

[46] Searing, 1969, p. 478; McClosky, Hoffmann, and O'Hara, 1960; Fishel, 1973, pp. 64–94;Matthews, 1960, pp. 119–123; Aberbach and Rockman, 1974; Grossman, 1967, p. 346; Parsons and Barton, 1974; Russett and Hanson, 1975.

[47] See footnote 44.

[48] Cobb, 1973, especially p. 126; Bennett, 1973. For evidence on the relative degree of Left-Right structuring in elite and mass attitudes, see Converse, 1964, Barnes, 1971, and Kornberg, Mishler, and Smith, 1975, but also Nie and Anderson, 1974, pp. 565–566.

[49] Arian, 1968, p. 15.

That elites are characteristically well-educated is part of the explanation, for education strengthens cognitive skills, furnishes concepts essential for organizing political information, and fosters a firmer sense of what goes with what, politically speaking. But even among equally educated citizens, the more active politically are more sophisticated ideologically. In part, their sophistication reflects greater exposure to political information and comment. Political activists at all levels are more avid consumers of the mass media and more frequent participants and kibitzers in informal political discussions.

Involvement in a party organization can itself provide a surrogate education, particularly for leaders from less privileged backgrounds, who are concentrated, as we have seen, in the parties of the Left. Indeed, the success of the Socialist and Communist parties of Europe in providing political education (and the failure of left-wing parties in America to do so) helps explain the greater incidence of working-class backgrounds among European political leaders.[50]

A final part of the explanation for the greater ideological sophistication of the elite is, of course, that practice makes perfect. Leaders learn the lingo and lore of politics for the same reason that golf buffs learn "linksmanship." Citizens whose only contact with public affairs is a periodic trip to the polling booth have little need and less occasion to develop coherent, stable positions on the myriad of topics that daily confront a political leader, just as my mother-in-law cannot remember from one Superbowl to the next whether wet weather is good or bad for the Jets.

If, as Clifford Geertz has suggested, political ideologies are "maps of problematic social reality," then the fact that members of the political elite are distinctively better cartographers and map readers than the rest of us has important political consequences.[51] In the first place, because (as we have already seen) rich and differentiated belief systems allow more information to be received and stored, and because (as psychologists have shown) beliefs that are stable and consistent are more likely to be acted on, elites are better equipped than most of us to respond appropriately to political cues and trends. Greater political sophistication means greater knowledge of which strings to pull and when and why.

Second, the broader range and articulation of the belief systems of elites greatly increases leaders' capacity to discern and interpret novel social problems. An unemployed worker knows very well that he has lost his job, but the correct attribution of unemployment to the secular decline of a dying industry, or to the changing terms of international trade, or to reduced defense spending requires a conceptual framework that most of us have not acquired. Hence, the formulation of society's agenda of unresolved problems is usually a virtual monopoly of the

---

[50] Barnes, 1967, pp. 119–125; Budge et al., 1972, pp. 124–164. The link between political participation and ideological sophistication is probably reciprocal; that is, participation is probably both a cause and an effect of sophistication.

[51] Geertz, 1964.

political elite, at least in the first instance. To be sure, many leaders—whether out of a desire to serve the people or a hope of reelection—strive to articulate the concerns of ordinary citizens, and problems that are common to many citizens typically force themselves onto the agenda over the long run. But the long run may be fairly long—health insurance has taken decades longer to reach the national agenda in America than in Europe—and in any event, by virtue of their greater ideological sophistication, elites typically control the terms of the debate. As we will see in Chapter 6, only in special circumstances does the agenda of the political elite mirror the private concerns of ordinary citizens.[52]

Finally, there is the nagging possibility that because leaders know more (and know they know more), they will think they know better. For democrats, the gravest risk implicit in the empirical generalizations we have been exploring is the fact that in politics—here, *un*like sports or music—knowledge is power. Inequalities in political sophistication and information help perpetuate inequalities in political power and influence.

Although elites' beliefs are more structured—and in this sense, more ideological—than those of nonelites, all elites are not equally ideological in the way they analyze public problems. Some focus on the particular details of each issue: the regulations governing the school lunch program, for example, or the administrative organization of police departments. They "morselize" the problem and reason inductively from personal experience. Others, however, analyze public issues synoptically, casting specific problems in terms of broad abstractions, like "capitalism" or "African socialism" or "our Judeo-Christian heritage," and deducing solutions from general social or political or economic theories. These characteristics of what we can term a leader's *political style* are closely related to the structural features of his beliefs. Leaders who analyze policy ideologically tend to have more complex conceptual schemes for interpreting political affairs than do their empiricist colleagues, though, contrary to Anglo-American mythology, politicians whose style of policy analysis is ideological are *not* characteristically more ruthless, dogmatic, intolerant, and uncompromising than nonideologues.[53]

The structure and style of elite belief systems vary cross-nationally, as well. Table 4–4, for example, shows that Italian politicians are markedly more ideological than British politicians on several measures of conceptual complexity, cognitive structure, and political style. These differences derive both from recruitment patterns and from contrasting national histories. As we saw in Table 3–1, ideological skills rank high among the credentials required of aspiring Italian political leaders. More fundamentally, an ideological political style is the product of the rapid and violent social change that has wracked Italy in the last century.

---

[52] Converse, 1964, pp. 249–254; Barnes and Farah, 1972, p. 19; Wildenmann, 1971, p. 58.

[53] Putnam, 1973a, pp. 34–63. For useful discussions of the tactical rules of thumb or "political axioms" that decision makers follow, see George, 1969, pp. 205–216, and Dahl, 1961, pp. 94–95.

Table 4–4   The Intensity of Ideology among Italian and British Politicians

	Italy (N = 82)	Britain (N = 93)
Abstractness of interpretation of party politics		
High	84%	25%
Medium	13	46
Low	3	29
	100%	100%
Constraint: Correlation (gamma) between Left-Right ideological position and:		
Support for political equality	.65	.39
Sensitivity to social conflict	.60	.29
Opposition to European unity	.71	−.11
Ideological Style Index		
High	65%	25%
Low	35	75
	100%	100%

Source: Putnam, 1973a.

As Geertz has pointed out, "It is in country unfamiliar emotionally or topographically that one needs poems and road maps."[54] In few countries has the pace of political change been as measured and the social continuities as great as in Britain. In world perspective, the ideological style of Italian politics is probably more common than the muddling pragmatism of the British.

ORIGINS OF ELITE BELIEF SYSTEMS

A full explanation of how elites come to hold the views they do about politics and society would touch on many factors discussed elsewhere in this book: social structure, recruitment processes, communication patterns within the elite and between elites and nonelites. Here I shall discuss the socialization of individual members of the elite. There is no reason to suppose that this process is identical in all countries, nor for all

[54] Geertz, 1964, p. 63. For a fuller discussion of the causes and consequences of an ideological political style, see Putnam, 1973a, pp. 75–82.

elites, nor for all the elements that comprise a belief system; indeed, there is considerable evidence to the contrary.[55] Nevertheless, certain patterns recur in studies of how leaders acquire their beliefs.

CHILDHOOD EXPERIENCES

Studies of the socialization of ordinary citizens stress the importance of childhood experiences, for beliefs acquired early in life are thought to be especially powerful and enduring. Moreover, because political leaders tend to come from politically conscious families, it is likely that many of their basic beliefs were learned in the home. The most extreme example of family-centered elite socialization was the traditional practice in upper-caste Indian homes of having a bard recite family sagas to the children, in order to inculcate loyalties and lessons from the history of the lineage.[56] Anecdotal evidence of the impact of his family occurs in the autobiographical musings of nearly every public leader. In fact, however, we know very little in a rigorous way about this process.

Broadening our focus to include other aspects of a leader's childhood, it is natural to assume that his adult political outlook would enduringly bear the marks of his social origins. Indeed, the assumption of a correlation between attitude and social origin lies behind most studies of the social backgrounds of elites. But as foreshadowed in Chapter 2, most of the available evidence tends to disconfirm this assumption. Studies of elites in Germany, France, Venezuela, Israel, Yugoslavia, Canada, Korea, Argentina, and the Soviet Union, as well as in the United States, uniformly conclude that such characteristics as region of birth, size of home town, ethnicity, and parent's occupation or education have little consistent relationship to current political opinions or behavior.[57] The implication would seem to be that a leader's views are influenced less by the social circumstances of his youth than by his adult roles and affiliations.

These studies have effectively challenged blanket assumptions about the impact of social background on elite attitudes. However, these studies have concerned primarily opinions on contemporary issues rather than fundamental cognitive and normative orientations, and, on reflection, we should probably expect such opinions to be more responsive to contemporary experiences and constraints. In fact, it would be surprising if a leader's position on economic

[55] Searing, 1969, especially pp. 484–485; International Studies of Values in Politics, 1971, pp. 111–112.

[56] Rudolph and Rudolph, 1974, pp. 20–21.

[57] Edinger and Searing, 1967; Searing, 1969; Schleth, 1971; Barton, 1973; Zaninovich, 1973; Clarke, Price, and Krause, 1975; Woo and Kim, 1971; Wellhofer, 1974; Lodge, 1973; Prewitt, Eulau, and Zisk, 1966–1967; Parsons and Barton, 1974; Suleiman, 1974, pp. 100–108; Meier and Nigro, 1975.

planning or his interpretation of his role as a legislator revealed any lingering effects of the size of his home town or his father's occupation.[58]

These studies have cast a wide net in seeking significant correlations between heterogeneous sets of background characteristics and attitudes. More narrowly defined inquiries into the effects of specific background characteristics on more basic orientations have discovered some intriguing patterns. For example, some evidence suggests that leaders from upper- and middle-class backgrounds are cognitively less sensitive to social conflict and normatively more hostile to redistributing wealth and authority than leaders whose social origins are more humble.[59] Another example: research in such diverse settings as Venezuela, Yugoslavia, Germany, Canada and North Africa has found that a leader's orientations on some matters are closely associated with his religious affiliation, which is, of course, normally acquired in childhood.[60] Fundamental cognitive and normative orientations are probably initially acquired by adolescence, and, unlike opinions on transient issues, these basic orientations are probably relatively stable and perhaps even self-confirming. Although unfortunately we have no good evidence on the long-term stability of elite beliefs, these scattered findings invite continued investigation of the early origins of elite beliefs.[61]

EDUCATION

From Plato's *Republic* to contemporary American graduate schools of public affairs, it has been recognized that how a nation is ruled depends on how its rulers are trained. Education is universally a key credential for elite recruitment, as we have repeatedly seen. Although studies of elite socialization have found little or no consistent impact of the quantity of education a leader has received. different types of education do have discernibly different effects on elite attitudes. For example, Donald Emmerson has reported that "evidence from nineteen countries shows that, on the whole, students in the social sciences, law, and the humanities are more likely to be politicized and leftist than their

---

[58] One methodological difficulty is introduced by the fact that social background strongly and directly affects elite recruitment, for that linkage makes it difficult to detect the independent impact of background on attitude. If virtually no one in the elite is from the working class and virtually no one in the elite supports nationalization of basic industries, it is difficult to tell whether the support for free enterprise is related to the middle-class character of the elite. For further discussion of the attenuated links between background and attitude, see pages 42–43 above.

[59] Putnam, 1973a, pp. 129–134, 218–220. Jerzy Wiatr reports a similar finding in the Polish data from the International Studies of Values in Politics, 1971.

[60] Searing, 1969, p. 475; Zaninovich, 1973, pp. 285–286; Schleth, 1971, pp. 111–113; Clarke, Price, and Krause, 1975; Suleiman, 1973.

[61] However, see Johnson, 1976, especially Table 1.

colleagues in the natural and applied sciences."[62] Similarly, the norms and behavior of Europe's senior civil servants reflect the type of education to which they have been exposed—the proud technocrats from the French *grandes écoles*, the relaxed humanists from Oxbridge, the formalistic, cautious lawyers of the traditional German *Juristenmonopol*. Some researchers have suggested, too, that the mentality of the Soviet elite betrays the effects both of training in engineering and of indoctrination in Party schools.[63]

Another example of the impact of education on elite values is provided by the Western-educated nationalist revolutionaries of Asia and Africa. Even when their political activities led them into conflict with the imperial authorities, leaders like Nehru of India, Mboya of Kenya, Nyerere of Tanzania, Bourguiba of Tunisia, and Senghor of Senegal often revealed an abiding commitment to political beliefs and a political style learned in Oxbridge, Edinburgh, or the Sorbonne. Some of these imported cultural traits were jarringly out of tune with the character and traditions of the Third World countries, and many have been discarded in the ensuing decades. For example, elite politics in India in the quarter century after independence demonstrated both the surprising persistence of political values inculcated by English education, and the unfortunate but probably inevitable erosion of those values, as newer cohorts of leaders rose to positions of power.[64]

Sometimes an elite is educated in specially segregated institutions. This pattern is almost universal among military and religious elites, but probably the clearest political example is the English system of "public" schools. Although these select private boarding schools educate only about 5 percent of the population, they provide 20 percent of the Labour members of Parliament, more than 40 percent of Labour cabinet members, roughly 65 percent of the top ranks of the civil service, about 75 percent of the Conservative members of Parliament, more than 90 percent of Conservative Cabinet Members, and roughly 80 percent of the top men in the army, the judiciary, the foreign service, the church, and the leading financial, industrial, and commercial institutions. Nor is there any evidence that the rate of public school education within the elite is declining.[65]

Like all schools, the English public schools influence their students both by what is taught and by what is inadvertently learned. Their curriculum has traditionally stressed moral character, expository rigor, and intellectual flexibil-

---

[62] Emmerson, 1968, p. 403; see also Ladd and Lipset, 1972.

[63] Price, 1957; Brzezinski and Huntington, 1964, pp. 143–146.

[64] On Western education among Third World elites, see also Chapter 7, pp. 193–194.

[65] On segregated elite education, see Wilkinson, 1969, and Prewitt, 1970, pp. 77–81. On the English public schools, see Wilkinson, 1964, Weinberg, 1967, McQuail et al., 1968, R. W. Johnson, 1973, pp. 40, 46, Sampson, 1971, p. 131, and Boyd, 1973. By way of comparison, only 11 percent of the American business elite and 6 percent of the American governmental elite have attended one of the nation's prestigious prep schools; see Dye and Pickering, 1974, p. 914.

ity. Science, technology, and imagination have been less emphasized. School customs and extracurricular activities have been even more important in inculcating the peculiar blend of initiative, strong leadership, self-restraint, loyalty, conformity, and team play that characterizes products of the public schools. (It is no doubt this that Wellington had in mind when he opined that the Battle of Waterloo had been won on the playing fields of Eton.) Many of the distinctive features of British elite culture can be detected *in vitro* in the public school experience: a reliance on internalized norms rather than on codified rules to govern the exercise of power, a preference for amateur generalists rather than technically trained specialists, a finely tuned sensitivity to emergent consensus, a gradualist approach to problems of social change.

A segregated system of elite education like the English public schools (or similarly, the French *grandes écoles*) concentrates the educational resources of a society on those destined to lead and is thus in one sense highly efficient. Part of the explanation for the ability of the tiny Victorian ruling class to control a vast empire lies in the social and intellectual skills provided by the public school system, and from time to time critics of American government have urged that "a truly common elite program of recruitment and training" be provided for American leaders. [66] On the other hand, the very centralization of such a system means that important reservoirs of talent may be excluded from positions of leadership.

Another consequence of the public school system is to increase the homogeneity and integration of the British elite, for common educational experiences and long-standing ties of friendship and trust increase the ability of an elite to cooperate effectively. By the same token, however, the elite produced by such a segregated system necessarily lacks ties to the masses of ordinary citizens. The mutual incomprehension between leaders and followers that some have seen at the root of Britain's recent political and economic difficulties may stem in part from the divergent educational experiences of the two groups.

A third important source of elite beliefs and values is the training and experiences acquired by the aspirant after entering an elite institution. Study after study has found that much of the variation in outlook within the elite is related to role differences. In the pluralistic elites of Germany, France, and the United States and in the more homogeneous elites of Yugoslavia and the Soviet Union, members of each subelite—economic managers, civil servants, the military, journalists, intellectuals, legislators, party and union officials—have more in common with one another than with their counterparts in other subelites. Allen Barton concludes: "Value-socialization is not parental, or even based on early

[66] Mills, 1956, p. 295.

political experience, but apparently takes place from working in a given field or institutional setting."[67]

What accounts for this relationship between role and outlook? The most obvious explanation is situational. Role constraints may demand certain beliefs and behavior. East or West, any industrial manager is likely to want autonomy to make economically sound investment decisions, any intellectual is likely to favor the free expression of ideas, and any legislator will be wary of the unfettered power of bureaucrats. As Arthur Clun has put it, where you stand depends on where you sit.

An alternative explanation for the role-outlook link is that where you get to sit depends on where you stand. Selectorates or self-selective processes may tend to exclude those whose views are institutionally heterodox. Conversely, candidates may acquire the appropriate attitudes prior to assuming a particular role. It has been suggested, for example, that working-class recruits into the British administrative elite learn to behave as "proper" senior officials long before they reach the top. Both selective recruitment and anticipatory socialization reduce the organizational imperative for on-the-job training. The more an institution can rely on preformed incumbents for crucial roles, the less the need for smoothing off rough edges.[68]

Where rough edges remain, genuine postrecruitment socialization is very common. An acute dilemma for revolutionaries who attempt to subvert established institutions from within is the risk that they will find themselves captured by the ethos of those institutions. A Chilean Socialist senator has described the classic process:

> *Unfortunately, as a result of the tasks a legislator must perform and the spirit of life Congress imposes, a professional congressman is created who is the antithesis and negation of what an authentic revolutionary agitator should be. This system of gradual and subtle assimilation unconsciously transforms one into support of the status quo versus being against it.*[69]

If where a leader stands depends (at least in part) on where he has sat in the past, postrecruitment socialization may also undermine institutional solidarity.[70] The quandary for Soviet leaders striving to maintain party control over economic management is that, on the one hand, party *apparatchiki* placed in managerial posts may come to assume the outlook of those they were sent to control, while, on the other hand, economic managers imported into the party organization may

---

[67] Barton, 1973, p. 242. See also Edinger and Searing, 1967; Lodge, 1973; Schleth, 1971; Parsons and Barton, 1974.

[68] Rex, 1972, p. 25; Prewitt, 1970, pp. 155–156; Marvick, 1968a, pp. 275–276.

[69] Senator Carlos Altamirano, quoted in Agor, 1971, p. 153.

[70] Kaufman, 1960.

continue to sympathize with their former colleagues in industry and agriculture. The key issue here is the relative influence of early and late postrecruitment socialization.

Under what conditions is involvement in a given organization most likely to affect a leader's outlook? First of all, the organization is likely to have less impact on preexisting attitudes than on issues that arise in the course of the job. Policy opinions and role conceptions are probably more subject to postrecruitment socialization than are fundamental values. Moreover, indoctrination is likely to be less effective on matters not directly related to the functioning of the organization. A corporate executive's views on free speech are probably less influenced by his role than are his views on free enterprise.

Postrecruitment socialization is likely to be more important in strongly institutionalized settings, because new or unstable institutions are less able to inculcate distinctive norms in their members. Hence, in developing societies such as Algeria or Venezuela the effects of social background are less masked by institutional socialization than in more stable settings.[71]

At the other extreme are the highly institutionalized legislatures of the Anglo-American world. Many observers have commented on the speed with which the British House of Commons absorbed and "reeducated" the fire-breathing Labourites who entered Parliament in large numbers after 1918. But probably the clearest example of postrecruitment socialization is provided by the committee system in the U.S. Congress. Richard Fenno has shown how the House Appropriations Committee inculcates a firm set of norms in new members—"guard the Federal Treasury," "cut whatever budget estimates are submitted," and so on. Fenno lists five factors that explain the effectiveness with which new members are inducted: (1) the deep, clear consensus within the committee on its goals; (2) its ability to coopt task-oriented members; (3) the extraordinary attractiveness that service on the committee holds for its members; (4) the unusual stability of its membership; and (5) the repetitive and incremental nature of its decisions. With the possible exception of the last, these traits probably characterize all elite institutions that succeed in socializing their members.[72]

CROSS-NATIONAL DIFFERENCES

Childhood experiences, social origins, education, and postrecruitment socialization help explain why members of an elite hold varying views about society and

---

[71] Quandt, 1969, p. 182n; Searing, 1969, p. 486.

[72] Guttsman, 1963, p. 247; Fenno, 1962. See also Brand, 1973, p. 486, and Kornberg, 1967, pp. 148–149. Political parties are an important agency of postrecruitment socialization, which helps explain the correlation noted earlier between party and ideology.

politics. But systematic comparative surveys of elites have consistently found that differences across these categories are less marked than are cross-national differences.[73] Members of an elite typically share many beliefs and values that distinguish them from their counterparts in other countries.

Regime characteristics provide only marginal help in explaining cross-national contrasts in elite perspectives. For example, elite value profiles in India, Yugoslavia, Poland, and the United States seem not to parallel the Communist versus non-Communist distinction. On some dimensions, such as economic egalitarianism, U.S. leaders are closer to Polish leaders and Indians to Yugoslavs, whereas other values, such as support for decentralization, pair the Americans and the Yugoslavs against the Poles and the Indians.[74]

A more promising explanation involves differing levels of economic development. This factor could account, for example, for the fact that on most value dimensions Indian and American elites are found at opposite poles. Similarly, my own comparison of elite political culture in Britain and Italy revealed many traces of Britain's historically higher level of development. However, not all differences between British and Italian elite beliefs followed developmental lines. Similarly, a recent study of younger and older elites in Japan and the United States found sharp and often increasing cross-national disparities in fundamental orientations. Such findings cast doubt on any simple theory that economic development means convergence toward a single pattern of elite beliefs.[75]

These important and continuing cross-national differences invite us to examine the impact of a nation's history on contemporary elite beliefs, for "symbolic universes are social products with a history. If one is to understand their meaning, one has to understand the history of their production."[76] The unique cultural traditions of each nation—its "national character"—must not be treated as a question stopper, but rather as a question poser. Of course history matters, but *how* does it matter?

Consider, first, the continuities of history. Each nation's past sets for its current leaders a series of problems and conflicts—race in the United States, social class in Britain, ethnicity in India, religion in Northern Ireland, and so on. Each of these major issues (along with many minor ones, of course) has accumulated encrustations of loyalties, antipathies, values, and cognitive assumptions, and this pattern of beliefs serves as the template for the socialization of each new generation.

[73] Edinger and Searing, 1967; Searing, 1969; International Studies of Values in Politics, 1971; Putnam, 1973a, Austin, 1975.

[74] International Studies of Values in Politics, 1971, pp. 97–100.

[75] International Studies of Values in Politics, 1971, pp: 79, 99–100; Putnam, 1973a; Austin, 1975.

[76] Berger and Luckmann, 1969, p. 115.

On the other hand, each nation's past also provides its leaders with a repertoire of familiar responses to political problems. For more than a century, for example, Austrian leaders have dealt with deeply divisive religious and class conflicts by the technique of *Proporz*—an agreement to guarantee each side an irreducible minimum share of political posts and power. Recourse to *Proporz* is part of the cultural inheritance of all Austrian leaders.[77]

But history also has discontinuities, which are reflected in elite perspectives. Dramatic events in the adult lives of leaders can occasionally shatter their opinions and even, very occasionally, their fundamental cognitive and normative orientations. A leading American isolationist like Senator Arthur Vandenberg was moved by the events of World War II to support internationalism in the postwar world, and a generation later an internationalist like Senator Frank Church was so shaken by the Vietnam tragedy as to become more suspicious of foreign involvement.

But normally our basic beliefs, once formed, are self-sustaining and resistant to the pressure of passing events. As Robert Dahl has pointed out:

> *Most people acquire their beliefs during a period when they are particularly receptive. Typically, a person is highly receptive during, and only during, the first two decades of his life. At the end of this period, one's outlook becomes fixed or crystallized.*[78]

Thus, social conditions and upheavals during a youth's years of greatest receptivity are likely to leave a permanent imprint on his political perspectives, whereas these events may have only a transient effect on the views of those outside the critical age bracket. When society is changing, the result of this process will be a succession of distinct *political generations*. In Karl Mannheim's words:

> *The fact of belonging to the same class, and that of belonging to the same generation or age group, have this in common, that both endow the individuals sharing in them with a common location in the social and historical process, and thereby limit them to a specific range of potential experience, predisposing them for a certain characteristic mode of thought and experience, and a characteristic type of historically relevant action.*[79]

Generational contrasts are likely to be sharpest during periods of great upheaval and rapid change. Protracted revolutions produce the greatest discon-

---

[77] Steiner, 1972, especially p. 27.

[78] Dahl, 1971, p. 167.

[79] Mannheim, 1952, p. 291.

tinuities in socialization. For example, five distinct and mutually antagonistic generations have been detected within the elite that led the multifaceted struggle for Algerian independence from 1930 to 1962. Or again, a 1968 study of the Yugoslav elite found that views about "the most important achievements of Yugoslav socialism" depended on when the respondents had entered politics. Those who joined the clandestine prewar party stressed workers' self-management; wartime partisan recruits, the attainment of national independence; those from the bleak years of the immediate postwar period, economic development; and the youngest generation, freedom and democracy. One permanent legacy of the dramatic events of the 1960s in American politics is likely to be enduring generational differences among the cohorts who came of age politically before, during, and after this decade.[80]

Political generations also emerge from periods of more gradual historical change. For example, a substantial minority of contemporary Italian politicians have only a tenuous understanding of, and commitment to, liberal democracy. Figure 4–3 shows how this group of "antidemocrats" is heavily concentrated among those whose formative years were spent under Fascism. Even though all Italian leaders have now experienced more than a quarter century of democratic government, only those who have come of age in the postwar period seem wholly at home in the institutions of democracy. Interestingly, the generational impact

[80] Quandt, 1969, especially pp. 14, 22–24; Pantic, 1971, p. 6; Allison, 1970–1971

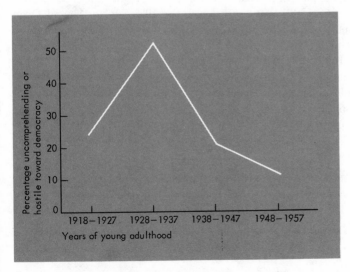

Figure 4–3   The Fascist Generation in the Contemporary Italian Elite
Source: Putnam, 1973a, p. 223.

of Fascism on the political outlooks of ordinary citizens seems to have been much less marked, which conforms to our earlier discussion of the degree to which political perspectives are crystallized among elites and masses.[81] At the elite level, the effects of the long waves of social and political history have been discerned also in the distinctive outlooks of the Great Depression generation of British politicians, the prewar and wartime generations of Soviet leaders, and the postwar generation of European administrative elites.[82]

Epochs are never homogeneous in their impact on elite beliefs, for contemporaries may not share identical places in the flow of history. What is important for the socialization process is how history is personally experienced. For example, Mao Tse-tung and Liu Shao-Ch'i were both deeply affected by their experiences in the Chinese guerrilla campaigns of the 1930s, Mao as an inspirational national leader, Liu as a grassroots organizer. But their respective roles in the Communist movement gave them different perspectives on the events of the period, and their disagreements during the Cultural Revolution have been traced at least in part to their divergent experiences 30 years earlier.[83] On the other hand, the great tides of history usually affect large numbers of people similarly, and hence "they help to produce those broad and decisive changes in outlook that historians describe when they write about the Renaissance, the Enlightenment, or the growth of democratic ideas."[84]

Thus, elite values do respond to social change, but only after a considerable lag, for most societies most of the time are led by men and women socialized decades earlier. To many of their younger compatriots, these leaders often seem to be—and in some sense are—living in a different era. History seems out of joint, particularly if the pace of social and political change is rapid and the pace of elite turnover slow. Both Sir Anthony Eden in the 1956 Suez crisis and Dean Rusk in the Vietnam affair interpreted events in terms of maxims they had learned as young men, observing the disastrous capitulation of the Allies to Hitler at Munich. But their youthful critics, formed in a different era, found the analogies unintelligible.

Even in revolutionary times this dynamic gives history a subsurface inertia. But the study of political generations also sensitizes us to the ways in which the lessons of history are eventually—if often inappropriately—learned by leaders. As Keynes wrote:

I am sure that the power of vested interests is vastly exaggerated compared with the gradual encroachment of ideas. Not, indeed, immediately, but after a certain

[81] Putnam, 1973a, pp. 222–224; Barnes, 1972.

[82] Putnam, 1973a, pp. 139–149; Hough, 1967b, p. 25; Nagel, 1975; Putnam, 1973b.

[83] Lewis, 1968.

[84] Dahl, 1971, p. 181.

interval; for in the field of economic and political philosophy there are not many who are influenced by new theories after they are twenty-five or thirty years of age, so that the ideas which civil servants and politicians and even agitators apply to current events are not likely to be the newest. But, soon or late, it is ideas, not vested interests, which are dangerous for good or evil.[85]

CONSEQUENCES OF ELITE BELIEF SYSTEMS

Several important traditions of political inquiry challenge this chapter's assumption that leaders' beliefs count in politics. The psychoanalytic school argues that conscious beliefs are mere rationalizations for emotional compulsions, while Machiavellians and Marxists claim that ideologies simply cloak self-interest or class interest. Values and beliefs are discarded from political analysis as froth on the mouths of madmen or froth on the waves of history.

These critiques are forceful, for elite behavior clearly is influenced both by emotional needs and by material and structural incentives. But, as I argued earlier, psychodynamic explanations can only supplement and not supplant explanations that refer to public purpose and conscious intention. And, on the other flank, although it is true that leaders are not selfless saints, it is not true that their calculations of self-interest are unaffected by beliefs and ideologies. Studies of the attitudes of American business leaders to foreign policy, for example, have shown that their ideological commitments tend to govern their estimates of economic self-interest rather than the reverse.[86] "The main defects of the interest theory," Clifford Geertz has concluded, "are that its psychology is too anemic and its sociology too muscular."[87]

A leader's role carries with it structural and situational constraints that often counterbalance the impact of his beliefs. In many European parliaments, for example, the pressure of party discipline overwhelms the effects of individual preferences on legislative voting. But the impact of leaders' beliefs and values can occasionally be detected even in such contexts. When in 1971 the British House of Commons faced the issue of joining the Common Market, Labour party leaders announced strong opposition and the pro-market Conservative cabinet demanded support from its own back-benchers. But the issue sharply divided the parliamentary parties internally, and (as Table 4–5 shows) the votes of individual members of Parliament were determined jointly by the obligations of party discipline and the imperatives of personal conscience. This example illus-

---

[85] Keynes, 1936, pp. 383–384.

[86] Bauer, Pool, and Dexter, 1963, pp. 224–225; Russett and Hanson, 1975. See also Powell, 1975.

[87] Geertz, 1964, p. 53.

Table 4–5   Role and Beliefs as Determinants of Elite Behavior: British Members of Parliament Vote on the Common Market

		Party			
			Personal Attitude to European Unity*		
		Conservative			Labour
		Pro (N = 24)	Con (N = 22)	Pro (N = 22)†	Con (N = 9)
Vote on Common Market Entry	Yes	100%	59%	55%	11%
	No	0	41	45	89
		100%	100%	100%	100%

* Attitude measured by agreement or disagreement with the statements that "It is desirable that the Common Market evolve toward the political formation of the United States of Europe" and "It is acceptable to me that there be, over the British government, a European government responsible for foreign affairs, defence, and the economy."

† Two pro-European Labourites who abstained on the vote are excluded from this table.

trates both the power of beliefs to affect elite behavior and the limits of that power.[88]

Political scientists, however, can rarely compete with well-informed journalists in predicting the behavior of individual leaders in specific situations. Underlying cognitive and normative orientations are instead important in accounting for broader patterns of system performance. Let me illustrate.

Leaders have considerable freedom in deciding what to decide and, conversely, what issues need not be raised, and here elite political culture is of fundamental importance. "Issues come into existence and remain alive as long as they conform to a minimum set of shared criteria which opinion-makers use to estimate whether a situation . . . is sufficiently urgent or controversial to be publicly discussed."[89] Prevailing outlooks among American elites have traditionally excluded from the sphere of public responsibility such topics as economic equality or the role of women. Orthodox Marxism denies that class conflicts can exist in socialist societies, and hence exploitation of the working class is barred by definition from the agenda of Communist countries. Nationalist

[88] The attitude data were gathered in January–March 1971; the vote was on October 28, 1971; see also Stassen, 1972. The discrepancy between belief and behavior is itself an important variable, for if it is great, cynicism is likely to become widespread (see Putnam, 1973a, pp. 232–233). Several methodological obstacles hinder efforts to test the link between elite attitudes and behavior: (1) difficulties of data gathering incline some investigators to rely on a leader's overt behavior as evidence for his beliefs, which risks circularity; and (2) when contradictory beliefs are ascribed to a single policy maker, they can explain anything, and hence explain nothing.

[89] Rosenau, 1963, p. 33.

ideologies among Third World elites increase the salience of certain issues, such as neo-imperialism, and reduce the likelihood of debate on others, such as genuine land reform. Other factors, too, influence the setting of the agenda —mass movements, crude self-interest, the evolution of science and technology, socioeconomic change of various sorts—but elite ideologies are an important part of the story.

Elite orientations also condition the nature and stability of patterns of governance. Although stable and effective democracy is generally more common among economically advanced nations, some developed countries, such as Germany, Austria, Argentina, and Italy, have historically found it hard to sustain democratic institutions. Part of the explanation for such cases is to be found in the beliefs and norms that guide their leaders.[90] Where the commitment of leaders to allow political competition and to accept the outcome of elections is feeble, where cognitive orientations either magnify or minimize conflicting interests, where hostility to one's opponents is virulent and endemic, open and responsive government is improbable.

[90] Dahl, 1971, pp. 124–188; Putnam, 1973*a*, especially pp. 154–156, 211–212, 229–236.

THE
STRUCTURE
OF
ELITES

5

The classical elite theorists, Mosca, Pareto, and Michels, treated the unity of the ruling elite as axiomatic, but the conceptual framework outlined in Chapter 1 makes the less restrictive assumption that the elite may be only an aggregate of powerful individuals, a statistical artifact whose members need have no more in common than their unusual involvement and influence in politics. The unity or disunity of this category, I argued, should be a matter for empirical investigation rather than definitional fiat. It is now time to redeem that promissory note—to examine some evidence on the integration of political elites.

Elite integration can be defined and measured in many ways, and thus our first task will be to examine several prominent *dimensions of integration,* including social homogeneity, recruitment patterns, personal interaction, value consensus, group solidarity, and institutional context. We must also face the following normative question: From the point of view of stable, effective, and democratic government, is elite integration desirable or undesirable? Although some social theorists argue that elite unity is a prerequisite for any high-performance political system, others claim that elite unity guarantees unresponsive, oligarchic politics. In the second part of this chapter, then, we will want to consider the *consequences of integration.*[1]

[1] Elite integration is the central feature of elite structure, but not the sole important one. Two other important structural dimensions treated elsewhere in this book are the permeability or ease of entrance into the elite (Chapters 3 and 7) and links between elites and nonelites (Chapter 6). I shall discuss only in passing the relative power of particular subelites —legislators, administrators, big businessmen, intellectuals, and so on. See Keller, 1963, Kadushin and Abrams, 1973, and Giddens, 1972, on this and other aspects of elite structure.

DIMENSIONS
OF
ELITE
INTEGRATION

One of the keys to the unity of the U.S. "power elite," according to C. Wright Mills, is its social homogeneity: "Insofar as the power elite is composed of men of similar origin and education, insofar as their careers and their styles of life are similar, there are psychological and social bases for their unity, resting upon the fact that they are of similar social type and leading to the fact of their easy intermingling."[2] Social origins constitute probably the most often discussed dimension of elite integration.

Bonds of kinship can provide a particularly intimate type of elite cohesion. Many traditional societies, from Tudor England to contemporary Morocco, are characterized by the politics of lineage. Occasionally, too, kinship links leaders in modern societies, particularly (but not only) where elements of a premodern aristocracy persist. One study of policy making in British public finance, for example, found that the intertwining branches of a few aristocratic family trees included a substantial number of the "top decision makers," and in America the tribal ties among the Rockefellers illustrate how members of a bourgeois elite can be linked by blood and marriage.[3]

Nevertheless, the political significance of family ties can easily be exaggerated, for lineage can divide as well as unite, as indeed the history of the Tudor family dramatically demonstrated. Moreover, family ties are less common and less significant among elective or administrative elites than within the economic elite. Finally, as we saw in Chapter 3, kinship has become a much less prominent credential for elite recruitment in modern political systems, and most leaders have no elite family ties. In general, kinship is much less important than other bases of elite integration.

In nearly every political system, as we saw in Chapter 2, the upper social strata supply a quite disproportionate share of the political elite. Moreover, this relative homogeneity extends beyond occupation and social status to include such traits as education, ethnicity, religion, geographic origin, and sex. The law of increasing disproportion guarantees a certain level of elite integration, for, as William B. Quandt has argued, "the integration of a political system may be

---

[2] Mills, 1956, p. 19.

[3] Waterbury, 1970, pp. 64, 94–110; Lupton and Wilson, 1959, pp. 38–43; Blondel, 1963, pp. 238–242; Domhoff, 1967.

viewed in terms of the degree to which members of the political elite share common socialization experiences."[4]

Elite educational institutions, exemplified by Tokyo University, Oxbridge and the English public schools, the Moscow Higher Party School, and the American military academies, foster elite integration by ensuring similar training for substantial numbers of elite members and by nurturing personal contacts and friendships. Three recent prime ministers of Japan had been school chums at Tokyo University, and nearly half of Sir Alec Douglas-Home's Conservative cabinet were (like him) Old Etonians.[5] The symbolic significance of the "old school tie" of the English public schools is matched by class rings among the American military elite; in Pentagonese, former West Point classmates are termed "ring-knockers."

But entirely apart from specialized elite schools, social homogeneity can further elite integration. As the new recruits to a national legislature or an administrative elite foregather, they inevitably discover more common entries in their social biographies than would a random sample of citizens. John Porter's conclusion about the Canadian elite applies much more widely: "Even if they have never met before, when they come into contact with one another as members of elites their identity of interests stemming from their common social characteristics and experience facilitates communication."[6]

In principle, the relative social homogeneity of national elites and of specific subelites could be easily compared by measuring the internal variance in their social profiles, but such studies are still very rare.[7] Other things being equal, we would expect an elite whose members are drawn predominantly from one niche of the social structure to be more cohesive than one whose members have highly diverse social origins, but other things are rarely equal. As we saw in Chapter 4, the link between social background and political behavior is often feeble, and, as we shall see later in this chapter, many other factors can intervene to strengthen or weaken cohesion. Social homogeneity is neither a necessary nor a sufficient condition for elite integration.

RECRUITMENT PATTERNS

One fundamental feature of any elite structure is the extent to which individuals hold key posts simultaneously in more than one organization or sector and can

---

[4] Quandt, 1970, p. 198.

[5] Langdon, 1967, p. 226. The content of an elite's education may also affect its integration, for leaders trained in various technical specialties probably have less in common than recipients of a "generalist" education. This proposition figures in some defenses of the generalist training of the higher British civil service.

[6] Porter, 1965, p. 528.

[7] Zapf, 1965, pp. 191–200, as cited in Dahrendorf, 1969, p. 258; Hacker, 1961; Quandt, 1970, pp. 184–185.

thus coordinate diverse activities. This mechanism is found in many contexts, from simple tribes in which the religious *shaman* also serves on the council of elders to complex capitalist economies in which interlocking directorates help sustain concentrations of corporate power. *Ex officio* appointments, formal or informal, often knit together otherwise distinct strategic elites. For example, the Central Committees of most ruling Communist parties include senior officials of the state administrative and economic bureaucracies, the military, the diplomatic corps, and the secret police, as well as the top members of the party apparatus itself. In Western systems a comparable integrating function is served by consultative committees and advisory boards, composed of leaders from government, business, labor, and other segments of society. However, holding executive (as opposed to consultative) posts in more than one elite sector simultaneously is less common, particularly as regards government officials. Indeed, such overlapping is sometimes formally barred—for example, by incompatibility regulations and conflict-of-interest laws—precisely in order to inhibit elite integration.[8]

Even more important than simultaneous overlap among elite positions is sequential overlap, that is, the successive holding of top posts in diverse sectors. C. Wright Mills was particularly impressed by such links among American business, government, and military elites. "The inner core of the power elite consists, first, of those who interchange commanding roles at the top of one dominant institutional order with those in another. . . . By their very careers and activities, they lace the three types of milieux together."[9] The archetype, of course, was Dwight D. Eisenhower, who moved from the post of Army chief of staff to the presidency of Columbia University, and thence to the top of the political hierarchy. This pattern of elite integration is associated with permeable recruitment channels, so that in-and-outers can rise rapidly. Career interchange is more pronounced in the United States, for example, than in contemporary Britain, where recruitment channels tend to be long, narrow, and impermeable.

British recruitment patterns, however, engender elite integration of a different sort. Within each institutional sector—politics, the civil service, finance, the universities, and so on—cohesion is generated by the long apprenticeships that leaders have served together. Members of a newly formed British cabinet see around the table men and women with whom they have worked closely for decades, whereas newly appointed U.S. cabinet officials often must be introduced to one another and to the president. Collectively, the career experiences of American political executives have given them greater familiarity with

---

[8] Cross-national data on overlapping and interlocking within elites are not available. On individual countries, see Welsh, 1973, pp. 5–6; Porter, 1965, pp. 215–216, 528–531; Guttman, 1963, pp. 359–367; Dye and Pickering, 1974; Barton, Denitch, and Kadushin, 1973, pp. 10, 261; Neumann and Steinkemper, 1973, pp. 30–40; Baylis, 1973, p. 15. Simultaneous incumbency in local and national elites may promote vertical elite integration; see Hancock, 1972, pp. 94–95; Pierce, 1973, pp. 256–258; Robins, 1975.

[9] Mills, 1956, pp. 288–289.

the people and the problems at the top of other institutions in society, but at the price of less intimate bonds with one another.[10]

This dilemma faces Communist elites, too. If the top leadership is drawn exclusively from lifelong party bureaucrats, internal cohesion is high, but links to (and control over) other elite sectors are weaker. On the other hand, recruitment of specialists from these other sectors into the top decision-making group may endanger the unity of the party elite itself. Significantly, as we shall see in Chapter 7, recent recruitment trends in the Soviet Union and Eastern Europe have favored "dual" executives, that is, officials with training and experience in specialized fields, but with a primary career commitment to the party apparatus itself. This pattern both broadens and deepens elite integration.

Sequential overlap among elite sectors may increase mutual understanding and coordination both in prospect and in retrospect. The present willingness of government officials to accommodate the wishes of business elites may be enhanced by the prospect of future retirement into a comfortable corporate job. This phenomenon, familiar to American observers of the Pentagon and various regulatory agencies, is also common in Japan, France, Turkey, and elsewhere.[11] (The apt French term for it, *pantouflage*, refers to the soft slippers [*pantoufles*] presumably donned by the administrator-turned-tycoon.)

Current behavior may also be affected by prior career experiences. Allen Barton reports that among Yugoslav elites, for example, "the influence of previous work in a sector is to socialize people to support the attitude now current in that sector, even when they move into other fields."[12]

Sequential overlap is no guarantee of elite integration, however, as is illustrated by the career of one of history's most renowned in-and-outers, Thomas à Becket. After diligent service as chancellor to Henry II, he was appointed Archbishop of Canterbury, but this dual career pattern did little to strengthen church-state elite integration. In his new post, Thomas became a staunch defender of the church, and his (ultimately fatal) opposition to the king is vivid testimony to the power of postrecruitment socialization to undermine elite integration.[13]

As a final illustration of the impact of the recruitment process on elite integration, we may hypothesize that the narrower and more unified the selectorate that reviews the credentials of prospective recruits, the more likely those recruits are to share perspectives and loyalties with one another and with the selectorate. In the Soviet case, for example, the ability of top party decision

---

[10] Dye and Pickering, 1974; Rose, 1974, pp. 212–215; Brzezinski and Huntington, 1964, pp. 160–161.

[11] Kubota, 1969, pp. 154–159; Ehrmann, 1971, pp. 154, 161; Roos and Roos, 1971, pp. 206–209.

[12] Barton, 1973, p. 259.

[13] On elite integration in the medieval church, see Robins, 1975, Chapter 4.

makers to control elite recruitment minimizes the likelihood of mavericks and limits the fragmentation that might otherwise be expected from an enlarged intake of specialists. In the case of the United States, Mills has hypothesized a similar mechanism, especially for business elites.[14]

PERSONAL INTERACTION

Elite integration is also enhanced by sociometric ties, that is, networks of personal communication, friendship, and influence. First, personal contacts facilitate coordination. To be sure, tacit coordination is always possible, as the behavior of some economic oligopolies illustrates, but antitrust laws and political scientists alike assume that overt contact is both more effective and easier to detect. Second, personal interaction is significant because, as social psychologists have shown, the link between interaction, friendship, and shared values is often close and reciprocal. "It seems reasonable to presume . . . that the greater the interaction among diverse types of leaders, the more they will comprehend each other's attitudes and thus the readier they will be to join together in support of a particular policy."[15]

We would expect elite members to have unusually high rates of personal interaction, for they are exceptionally involved in public affairs, and talking politics with one another is a job requirement. As Keith Legg has noted:

> Face to face interaction among the political, as well as economic and social, elites is quite probable in most countries. Whether or not recruitment patterns have thrown future members of the elite together, the mere fact of occupying the top roles in the system or having membership in the pool of eligibles is likely to [do so]. . . . [A]t the elite level, everyone is in a way a broker because connections are themselves major resources. It is through connections, through the maintenance of acquaintance networks, that access and information can be exchanged.[16]

Indeed, Michels' "iron law of oligarchy" was based in part on the hypothesis that communication networks are denser at the top of an organization than at the bottom.

Does this mean that Texas oilmen and Wall Street bankers and Minneapolis politicians and Washington bureaucrats—or bishops and generals and union leaders from Buenos Aires and cattlemen from the Pampas—all are close friends and frequent conversation partners? One student of "Top Leadership, U.S.A." claimed so: "The national power structure is held together, city by city,

[14] Fleron, 1969, p. 238; Mills, 1956, p. 348.

[15] Rosenau, 1963, p. 31. See also Homans, 1950, and McGuire, 1969, p. 191.

[16] Legg, 1972, pp. 9–10.

in large measure by a network of informal communications. . . . Those at the apexes of power in communities, states, regions, service organizations, and industrial complexes become generally known to each other."[17] However, because the "top leaders" in this study were identified in the first place by following chains of acquaintances, the finding that they were linked by those chains is methodologically circular.

Only two published studies of national elites, one on Venezuela, the other on Yugoslavia, have systematically examined ties of communication, friendship, and personal influence among independently identified leaders.[18] These studies support the following conclusions:

1. Personal ties are many times more frequent among members of the elite than would occur by chance in the population at large. Nevertheless, only a tiny fraction of all possible links are operative. Many leaders are isolated from one another and no single network includes more than a minority of the elite.

2. Ties within each sector of the elite are denser than cross-sector ties, so that businessmen talk mostly to other businessmen, party politicians to other pols, and so on. On the other hand, most networks include members from more than one sector, so that some leaders serve as linchpins between the sectors.

3. Interaction tends to be channeled by political factors, both ideological and institutional. Networks are largely, though not entirely, homogeneous in terms of party affiliation, and professional politicians have a wider range of contacts, both within their own sector and across sector boundaries, than do other elite members.

4. As Michels suggested, the density of sociometric ties is greatest at the top of the political hierarchy, implying "diffusion and dispersion of choices at low levels and a more closely and evenly knit network at the highest level."[19]

Until comparable data become available for additional countries, and particularly for larger countries, these generalizations must remain tentative. But they illustrate the importance of the sociometric basis of elite integration.

Bonds of communication and friendship are created and molded by many of the factors discussed elsewhere in this chapter—kinship, common social and educational backgrounds, recruitment patterns, ideological affinities, and so on. In addition, informal social activities and avocational associations can nurture politically relevant personal ties. The Georgetown cocktail circuit in Washington and the august London men's clubs provide congenial surroundings for interaction within the American and British elites, as do the Council on Foreign Relations in New York and the Nuffield College senior common room in Oxford.[20] The events of history, too, can forge enduring personal ties, even across ideological and organizational barriers. Mutual respect generated by years

---

[17] Hunter, 1959, pp. 8, 191.

[18] Bonilla, 1970, pp. 149–177; Kadushin and Abrams, 1973. See also Kadushin, 1968.

[19] Bonilla, 1970, p. 156.

[20] See Parsons and Barton, 1974; Domhoff, 1967.

spent together in exile or in Nazi concentration camps helped the leaders of postwar Austria to overcome deep prewar cleavages.[21] Survivors of revolutionary turmoil in China, Yugoslavia, India, Israel, Egypt, and elsewhere have felt a special kinship not shared with their younger colleagues.

Elite interaction can also be affected by geography and by the communications media. Most members of the British elite live and work in London, creating what Anthony Sampson in another context has called "the pressure of propinquity."[22] Paris, Buenos Aires, Tokyo, and Cairo each provides a similar locus for national elites, whereas in such countries as Brazil, Italy, and the United States the dispersion of national political and economic leaders across several major cities reduces personal contact among them. Elite integration is increased where intraelite communication is monopolized by a single newspaper, such as *The Times* of London, *Le Monde*, and (to a lesser extent) the *New York Times*. This century's technological revolutions in communications have almost certainly increased elite integration in those countries most touched by the newer media.

The numerical size of an elite also affects its level of integration. Experimental psychologists have established that smaller groups show greater interaction, solidarity, and consensus than do larger ones. Thus, William Quandt has argued that the fragmentation of the Palestine Liberation Organization, as contrasted with the unity of the Algerian National Liberation Front, can be traced in part to the larger size of the Palestinian leadership group. A study of California city councils found that larger councils and councils in larger cities displayed more internal fragmentation and conflict, and a survey of research on community power concluded that the smaller the city, the greater the overlap among personnel involved in different decisions.[23]

Cross-nationally comparable data on the size of national elites are not available, but in absolute terms the elite in populous countries such as West Germany, India, and the Soviet Union is doubtless larger than in smaller countries such as Sweden, Morocco, or Yugoslavia.[24] If size is related to integration, several interesting conclusions follow. First, elites of smaller countries should be more integrated, other things being equal. Second, as a nation grows, elite integration should tend to decline; it is widely accepted, for example, that the unity of the American elite declined during the course of the nineteenth century, and a similar phenomenon may occur in the rapidly growing countries of the contemporary Third World.[25] Finally, elite integration should be markedly greater in local communities than at the national level. If this is so, it is

[21] Steiner, 1972, pp. 172–173.

[22] Sampson, 1971, p. 10.

[23] Quandt, 1972, pp. 11–12; Eulau and Prewitt, 1973, pp. 187–188; Presthus, 1964, p. 408.

[24] Waterbury, 1970, pp. 86–87; Bellisfield, 1973.

[25] Mills, 1956, pp. 269–270; Dahl, 1961, pp. 11–24.

dangerous to infer the structure of a national elite from studies of community power.

<hr>

VALUE CONSENSUS

Perhaps the most central dimension of elite integration is the degree to which leaders agree on "what is to be done." Here we may distinguish *consensual, competitive,* and *coalescent* patterns, paying attention to agreements both about policy choices and about political procedures.

In the modern world, probably the best examples of consensual elites are in the Soviet Union and Eastern Europe. A wide range of socialization and recruitment devices—from the ubiquitous party schools and party cards to the *nomenklatura* and recurrent checks on ideological orthodoxy—ensure that leaders and activists are committed to Marxism-Leninism in theory and practice. Kremlinologists have alerted us to the inevitable personal, factional, and organizational disputes within Communist elites, but in rightly rejecting the notion that the Communist leadership is monolithic, we should not underestimate the breadth and depth of its ideological consensus.[26]

Among the communist nations, survey data on elites are available only in the case of Yugoslavia, which probably represents the most pluralist, least consensual of Communist elites. This evidence shows that Yugoslav leaders are consistently more committed to the regime and its goals of modernization and decentralization than are ordinary citizens. Moreover, the ethnic cleavages so apparent in the attitudes of the Yugoslav population as a whole have relatively little resonance within the elite. Not all Yugoslav leaders agree on the direction the society should take, but they are closer to consensus than is the Yugoslav public.[27]

In periods of rapid political change, value consensus is often more characteristic of elites than of mass publics. The Third World elites that led their nations to independence in the years after World War II were usually far more agreed on political and social objectives than were their followers. The leaders of the Indian Congress party, for example, shared a broad commitment to parliamentary democracy, socialism, socioeconomic modernization, and a secular state—values far from congenial to many ordinary Indians. In later years in India, as in most other nations of Asia and Africa, this idealistic elite consensus has progressively eroded, as the realities of self-government and domestic politics have superseded the shared experiences of the colonial period and the struggle for independence.[28]

---

[26] Brzezinski and Huntington, 1964, pp. 17–70.

[27] Zaninovich, 1970, 1973. Communist parties in the West display similarly high levels of elite consensus; the Italian Communist party, for example, is much the most cohesive party in Italy. See Barnes and Farah, 1972, pp. 9–11; Putnam, 1973a, p. 131; Putnam, 1975.

[28] Kothari, 1970, pp. 160–167; Weiner, 1965a. See also Chapter 7 of this book.

Political elites in the stable pluralist democracies of the West typically display high levels of consensus on what Kenneth Prewitt and Alan Stone have called "codes of conduct." Commitment to the politics of bargaining and compromise, tolerance for political opponents, and a willingness to abide by parliamentary and electoral decisions are widely shared norms, and there is broad agreement that "the acceptable way to conduct matters of state is negotiation among the leaders."[29]

Studies in several Western countries have shown that leaders are considerably more tolerant of political dissent and more committed to civil liberties and due process than are ordinary citizens. For example, whereas more than half of the American public agree that "a book that contains wrong political views cannot be a good book and does not deserve to be published," more than four-fifths of a sample of American politicians reject this point of view. In West Germany elites are more convinced than ordinary citizens that criticism of the government is a necessary part of democracy, that the general welfare is served by political conflict and compromise, and that unconventional social and political behavior must be permitted. And British members of Parliament support the procedural guarantees of democratic government more consistently than do British voters.[30]

Why should Western elites be more committed to the liberal democratic creed than nonelites? One reason is that leaders are more familiar with the game of politics, its rules and its players. They are thus more likely to understand those rules and to have reached consensus on how to apply them. Members of the elite are more sophisticated ideologically than ordinary citizens and are therefore more likely to see the connection between a widely endorsed principle, like "free speech," and a particular application of that principle, like "allowing Communists to speak here." Leaders' more extensive education has taught them to differentiate public and private worlds and has accustomed them to drawing consistent conclusions from abstract premises.[31]

Elite commitment to "the system" is doubtless also related to the gratifications the system gives them. Leaders are more likely to agree on the rules of the game, because it is fundamentally their game. They are, in fact, quicker to endorse political liberty than political equality, and the system within which they urge dissidents to work is one in which most important decisions are taken at the top.[32] Nevertheless, the relative tolerance and the commitment to political due

---

[29] Prewitt and Stone, 1973, p. 151.

[30] McClosky, 1964; Hedlund, 1973; Wildenmann, 1971, especially pp. 54–57; Wildenmann, 1973, p. 6; Budge, 1970, pp. 105–120, 142–147.

[31] Jackman, 1972, and Alford and Scoble, 1968, found that virtually all of the unusual tolerance of U.S. community leaders was traceable to their higher level of education.

[32] McClosky, 1964; Prewitt and Stone, 1973, pp. 151–156; G. Parry, 1969, p. 91.

process characteristic of most Western political leaders does distinguish them from elites in many other parts of the world.[33]

A shared commitment to "the system" in procedural terms need not preclude fundamental disagreement on issues of substance. Indeed, in terms of policy preferences elites in Western democracies are more competitive than consensual. Most national politicians in the West are, above all, party politicians. They are considerably more sensitive to ideological differences between the parties than are ordinary voters; for example, more than one British voter in three sees "not much" difference between the Labour and Conservative parties, as compared with fewer than one member of Parliament in ten.[34] Leaders' policy preferences, too, are more divergent than those of voters and are more closely tied to their party identification, as we noted in Chapter 4.

Elite polarization is perhaps not surprising in political systems like Britain or Italy, with their sharply divided political parties. But even in the United States and Canada, where the major political parties are often accused of offering echoes rather than choices, several studies have shown that party elites are in fact farther apart in their policy views than are their respective electorates. Democratic politicians are generally more liberal than Democratic voters, and Republican politicians more conservative than Republican voters. As one study concluded: "Little support was found for the belief that deep cleavages exist among the electorate but are ignored by the leaders. One might, indeed, more accurately assert the contrary, to wit: that the natural cleavages between the leaders are largely ignored by the voters."[35]

The particular pattern of elite-mass displacement along the Left-Right continuum seems to vary from time to time and from country to country, as is illustrated in Figure 5–1. In the Eisenhower era Republican leaders stood far to the right of their mass supporters, while Democratic leaders were slightly to the left of their electorate. In the 1972 presidential campaign, on the other hand, Democratic elites were far to the left of their supporters, while Republican leaders were only slightly to the right of theirs. Meanwhile, in Italy and Sweden, for example, every party elite stands to the left of its electorate, although this displacement is typically greater in left-wing than in right-wing parties. In each

---

[33] For evidence that Yugoslav leaders are more tolerant of dissent than other Yugoslav citizens, in part because of the former's higher level of education, see Zaninovich, 1973.

[34] Butler and Stokes, 1969, p. 466, and unpublished data from the study reported in Putnam, 1973a.

[35] McClosky, Hoffman, and O'Hara, 1960, p. 426. See also Shaffer, Weber, and Montjoy, 1973; Kornberg, Mishler, and Smith, 1975, pp. 32–34 and Table 5; Kirkpatrick, 1975; Budge, 1970, pp. 114–117. One important difference among community power structures in the United States lies precisely in the prevalence of party competition. Compare Hunter, 1953, on Atlanta and Dahl, 1961, on New Haven.

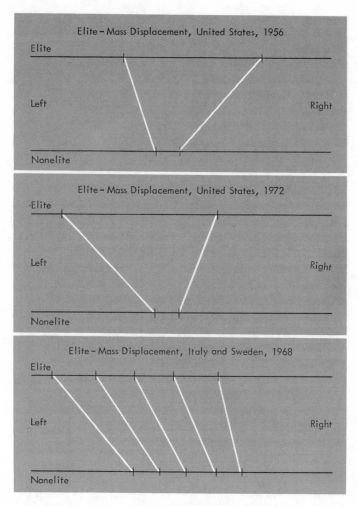

Figure 5–1   Elite-Mass Displacement Patterns: Some Examples

case, however, the basic generalization holds: Interparty distances are greater at the elite level than at the mass level.[36]

In addition to party-related cleavages, elites are also often divided along sectoral lines, for, as we saw in Chapter 4, in both capitalist and Communist countries a leader's views often depend on which strategic elite he belongs to. For example, a recent survey of American elites discovered two main lines of

[36] McClosky, Hoffman, and O'Hara, 1960; Kirkpatrick, 1975; Barnes, 1971; Holmberg, 1974.

cleavage. Domestic economic and social welfare policies pitted businessmen and Republican politicians against labor leaders and Democratic politicians. Defense and foreign policy and to some extent "youth and alienation" issues found hawkish Republican politicians at one extreme and the intellectual establishment at the other, with business, labor, administrative, and Democratic elites in the middle. Lack of consensus within the elite was not complete; most leaders in all sectors supported Keynesian economics and the welfare state, and virtually all opposed the nationalization of major industry. But this commitment to certain core values of "the American way of life," doubtless shared by most ordinary voters, should not obscure the sharp disagreements within the elite on many issues.[37]

On the other hand, many elites are not united by even this level of value consensus. In some societies intraelite competition and fragmentation reaches extreme levels. In particular, some countries are divided by deep cultural cleavages that are mirrored within the elite. After the Reformation, for example, religious divisions split many European societies from top to bottom. The Venezuelan and the Colombian polities and elites were violently divided along subcultural lines for several decades. And in many countries, from Belgium, Canada, and the United States to India, Malaysia, and Sri Lanka, politics and social relations are informed by ethnic and racial conflict.

Almost inevitably such cleavages rend the national political elite and raise the specter of civil war, as in America in the 1860s, Germany in the 1930s, and Nigeria and Northern Ireland in the 1960s. But occasionally top leaders of the hostile camps are willing and able to bridge the gulf separating them. Where elites fear social convulsion, where they are committed to the existing political system, and where followers are willing to defer to their respective leaders, a pattern of elite coalescence may emerge.

The sharpest example of this phenomenon is the case of postwar Austria, a country historically divided into two implacably antagonistic *Lager*, or armed camps, the urban, socialist, anticlerical "Reds" and the rural, conservative, Catholic "Blacks." In the 1930s, hostility between those two halves of the Austrian body politic led to the collapse of the First Republic in a bitter civil war, followed by the imposition of dictatorship. After World War II the leadership of the two camps agreed to put aside their historical differences, and for nearly two decades they governed together in a "grand coalition." Although middle-level elites on both sides continued to harbor deep suspicion and hostility toward their opponents, the top national leaders successfully resolved policy differences, divided government patronage between the two camps, and imposed a kind of rule by elite cartel.[38] In Figure 5–2 this pattern of coalescence is contrasted with the two previously discussed patterns, consensus and competition.

---

[37] Barton, 1974-1975.

[38] Steiner, 1972, pp. 172–175; Stiefbold, 1974.

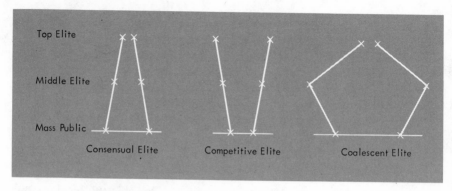

Figure 5–2   Consensual, Competitive, and Coalescent Elites

Elite coalescence has been noted in other so-called consociational democracies. In the Netherlands and (until recently) Lebanon, hostile and segregated religious communities have lived in uneasy truce under the auspices of coalescent elites. In Colombia, wracked for more than a decade by *la violenca*, a bloody, anarchic war between the two major political parties, leaders of the opposing parties agreed in 1958 to a 16 year truce, during which the presidency would be rotated between them every 4 years and government posts would be shared equally, regardless of electoral results. In neighboring Venezuela during the 1960s, party leaders achieved a less formal, but reasonably durable consensus on the rules of democratic competition, enabling them to avoid the twin traditional perils of civil strife and military dictatorship. Analogous arrangements have played an important role in the histories of Switzerland, Belgium, Uruguay, and Canada.[39] In fact, the behavior of American political elites in the years before the Civil War may be interpreted as an attempt to create the conditions for elite coalescence. The last major social institution to crack along regional lines was the party system, and when in 1860 Lincoln's election crystallized the failure of the party leaders to craft compromises acceptable to their constituents, war became inevitable.

Occasionally, a variant of coalescence appears in essentially competitive elites. Studies in France, Britain, and the United States, as well as Austria and Switzerland, have found a tendency for party activists and middle-level elites to disagree more sharply and to support the amicable give-and-take of practical politics less wholeheartedly than do the top national leaders.[40] Indeed, Giuseppe Di Palma has proposed

[39] Lijphart, 1968a, 1968b, 1969; Daalder, 1971, 1974; Levine, 1973, pp. 209–259; Blank, 1973, pp. 75–77, 271–272.

[40] MacPae, 1967, pp. 260, 322; Kornberg and Frasure, 1971, p. 703; Costantini, 1963; Stiefbold, 1974; Steiner and Lehnen, 1974. May (1973) argues that a "law of curvilinear disparity," equivalent to the pattern here termed coalescence, describes the relative policy preferences of top elites, intermediate elites, and nonelites in most Western party systems.

as a general sociological law that the acceptance and practice of the rules for conflict accommodation are most widespread at the upper level of elites. The organizational roles of these individuals are likely to expose them to the interests of diverse groups within society, and their constituencies are more heterogeneous than those of lower-level elites. Hence they are more likely to be attuned to rules that emphasize restrained partisanship, stress elite autonomy and expertise, and make possible the balancing of interests.[41]

Our evidence on patterns of elite consensus, competition, and coalescence is still too sparse and impressionistic for confident generalization, but it is quite likely that there are significant cross-national and cross-temporal differences.[42]

SOLIDARITY

One of the elements of elite integration most stressed by the classical theorists is a sense of mutual confidence among members of the elite—the "consciousness" of Meisel's three C's. "Nothing brings elites together so much as mutual respect which flows from sharing in the confraternity of power."[43]

Both those who condemn and those who praise elite integration agree on the significance of solidarity. Mills traces the unity of the American power elite in large part of the sense of fellowship among its members, to "the psychological affinities . . . that make it possible for them to say of one another: He is, of course, one of us. . . . Nowhere in America is there as great a 'class consciousness' as among the elite; nowhere is it organized as effectively as among the power elite."[44]

Ralf Dahrendorf, on the other hand, believes that contemporary West Germany needs a more integrated elite. He describes Germany's present leaders as a "cartel of anxiety," lacking solidarity and fearful of controversy that might overturn the fragile institutions through which they rule. "The elites lack the confidence needed for leadership or for conflict. If we ask why this is so, the answer must be that . . . [t]hey do not in fact form a group, but remain a mere category."[45]

Mills and Dahrendorf may or may not be empirically correct in their descriptions of the two elites. But they are correct in noting that mutual trust and solidarity is an important dimension of elite integration. As we saw in Chapter 4,

---

[41] Di Palma, 1973, p. 15.

[42] The International Studies of Values in Politics, 1971, pp. 139–168, found little variation in the degree of value consensus at the local level in India, Yugoslavia, Poland, and the United States.

[43] Porter, 1965, p. 532.

[44] Mills, 1956, p. 283.

[45] Dahrendorf, 1969, p. 256. For evidence contradicting Dahrendorf's characterization of the contemporary German elite, see Baylis, 1973, pp. 9–10, and Wildenmann, 1971.

in some countries rival leaders view one another as subversives and belligerents in a war of all against all. Elsewhere, partisan hostility and the "oppositional mentality" are less prevalent, and bonds of mutual confidence cross party and factional lines.[46] To be sure, conflict of one sort or another is probably endemic in any national elite. Indeed, some theorists have argued that intraelite conflict is the motor of history. The mark of a unified elite, therefore, is not the absence of disagreement, but rather sufficient mutual trust, so that its members will, if necessary, forego short-run personal or partisan advantage in order to ensure stable rule.[47]

INSTITUTIONAL AND SOCIAL CONTEXT

If the institutions whose command posts the elite occupy have overlapping interests, the elite incumbents may be led to take complementary actions, whatever their personal origins, contacts, and affinities. If, on the other hand, the institutions have conflicting interests, elite integration in terms of social background, sociometry, solidarity, and so on may have little impact on leaders' behavior.

Mills and other critics of capitalist elites believe that the structure of capitalism itself guarantees overlapping institutional interests.[48] The military-industrial-political complex that Mills described is based ultimately on the coincidence of interests between arms-producing big business, arms-procuring big government, and arms-employing big military. Ironically, a similar analysis may be applied to the military-industrial-political complex of the Soviet Union, in which the interests of the party apparatus, the managers of heavy industry, and the defense establishment overlap in roughly the same way and for roughly the same reasons as in the United States.[49] In short, interdependence among giant corporate and bureaucratic organizations seems a constant feature of modern society, so that with only a change in the proper nouns, the famed aphorism of a General Motors president turned secretary of defense might be repeated in any industrialized country: "What's good for the United States is good for General Motors and vice versa."

In several respects, however, the institutional context may also discourage elite integration. Functional specialization and organizational loyalties force leaders to view national problems from divergent perspectives. The evidence of Chapter 4 on postrecruitment socialization testifies to the power of each institu-

---

[46] Shils, 1962.

[47] See Field and Higley, 1973, p. 9.

[48] Mills, 1956; Miliband, 1969.

[49] Hough, 1972, especially p. 27.

tional sector to mold its leaders' outlooks in distinctive ways. Even in formally noncompetitive political systems, such as the Soviet Union or Nazi Germany, institutional rivalries provide the impetus for intense struggles behind the facade of unity. In formally competitive systems, these natural divisions are sometimes intensified by constitutional provisions—such as the separation of powers in the U.S. Constitution—that set ambition against ambition in a manner expressly intended to reduce elite integration.

In some circumstances elites are also fragmented by the necessity to be responsive to their respective constituencies. Business executives in capitalist economies must pay some attention to the desires of large shareholders and creditors, and elected politicians must occasionally respond to the wishes of voters, as we shall discuss in Chapter 6. Sometimes the interests of shareholders and voters overlap, as, for example, in districts with sizable defense-based employment. But in many other situations, constituency pressures will tend to draw elites in opposing directions.

Finally, institutional interests are not internally monolithic. In some instances what is good for General Motors is not even good for Ford, much less for other institutional sectors. Clearly, these are matters of degree, for all capitalist elites share certain common interests, for example, in avoiding widespread nationalizations. But in the finer grain of public policy, even straightforward economic interests can diverge markedly. One study of U.S. trade policy, for instance, found that the political impact of the giant DuPont chemical firm was blunted by the fact that while import-competitive divisions of the company had an interest in high tariffs, export-oriented divisions had an equal and opposite interest in free trade.[50]

Thus, the main theoretical dimensions of elite integration are multiple but reasonably clear. What is less clear is how they are related to one another. It is plausible to assume that the dimensions are positively intercorrelated so that an elite that is, say, small, socially homogeneous, and interlocked by recruitment patterns will also tend to be consensual, solidary, and sociometrically dense. But many interesting cases involve discrepancies in an elite's rankings on the several dimensions. The U.S. elite, for example, is probably more homogeneous than the Soviet elite in terms of social background and approximately as consensual on procedural matters, but probably less integrated by substantive consensus and recruitment patterns. And both are probably less integrated than the British elite in terms of size and sociometry. "Probably" is the operative word, however, for cross-nationally comparable evidence on these several dimensions, their interrelations, and the implications of contrasting patterns is at present very rare.

---

[50] Bauer, Pool, and Dexter, 1963, pp. 270–271.

CONSEQUENCES
OF
ELITE
INTEGRATION

One of the reasons for the interest of social scientists in elite integration is the widely shared assumption that a unified elite governs more effectively and more stably than a disunified elite. G. Lowell Field and John Higley point out that

> the evidence is overwhelming that politics, even in fully consolidated nation-states, normally approximates a fight to the death by mutually suspicious groups of activists struggling to defend or advance partisan interests with little regard for propriety or cost. . . . [But] the normal situation of political instability is abrogated in societies where a unified elite is present. [51]

Typically, elites are fragmented by the onset of socioeconomic moderniza-tion. Population growth and economic development foster a division of labor and produce a highly differentiated elite structure. New members, such as wealthy industrialists, for example, are added to the elite. Within the traditional elite itself, integration declines, as its members are differentially affected by social and economic change. Moreover, in the postcolonial epoch through which most of today's poorer nations are passing, centrifugal conflicts along generational and cultural lines threaten the fragile unity achieved during the struggle for inde-pendence. At the same time, increasing education, urbanization, commerciali-zation, the spread of mass media, and the growth of new political movements are all mobilizing masses of ordinary citizens into unaccustomed political participa-tion, releasing new energies and new pressures. [52]

In this situation political development is a contrapuntal interplay of in-creasing differentiation, which weakens established institutions and increases the complexity of political demands, and increasing integration, which creates new institutions and legitimates a single set of rules for allocating authority. Much depends on the emergence of strong and unified national leadership, but as the record of instability, coups, and political decay in much of the Third World suggests, elite integration is exceedingly difficult to achieve. [53]

---

[51] Field and Higley, 1973, pp. 12–13. For a useful discussion of stability and effectiveness per se, see Eckstein, 1966, especially pp. 228–230.

[52] Searing, 1971, p. 459; Ake, 1967, pp. 17–29; Deutsch, 1961; Keller, 1963, pp. 145–149.

[53] Kenworthy, 1970, pp. 105–107; Huntington, 1968.

An excellent example of the consequences of low elite integration in the new states is Nigeria, a country of several regionally and culturally distinct ethnic groups artificially joined in a single political unit by the accidents of European imperialism. Despite the federal structure bequeathed to the Nigerians by the departing British, ethnic particularism and mutual suspicion (and eventually, mutual aggression) have plagued Nigeria throughout its brief period of independence, so that "political competition in Nigeria has become a life-and-death struggle between the different tribes."[54]

In this context, only an exceptionally unified group of leaders could have provided stable, effective government. But the Nigerian political elite was itself fragmented along regional and ethnic lines; the two main groups were "characterized by almost totally different social background and political recruitment patterns" and held quite incompatible images of Nigeria's future.[55] Under the circumstances military coups and the bloody Biafran secession attempt that followed seem to have been inevitable.

For these reasons many scholars and practitioners of African politics believe that "the political stability (and to some extent the political integration) of the new state is greatly furthered by increasing the group-cohesiveness of its elites."[56] Many civilian leaders argue that only a single-party state can provide the necessary elite integration, and military leaders often justify their intervention in politics by the need to impose unity at the top. Neither one-party rule nor military rule, however, can guarantee elite unity; indeed, high-handed repression of potential competitors often encourages continued elite disunity. In a few countries, such as Tunisia and Tanzania, the single-party strategy seems to have succeeded in sustaining elite integration, but elsewhere the more familiar sequence of coup and countercoup testifies to the persistence of the underlying quandary.

Though less fragmented ethnically, the countries of Latin America are further along the road of socioeconomic development and have thus encountered still more sharply the dilemma posed by mass mobilization and elite disintegration. Argentina is perhaps the clearest example here of the consequences of elite disunity. Socioeconomically, it surpasses some European countries on statistical indices of modernity, and politically, many key sectors are well organized and mobilized. At the elite level, however, there is considerable disintegration, whether measured in terms of social background, recruitment patterns, sociometry, solidarity, or value consensus.[57] Most critically, there is little agreement on the rules of the political game, on what constitutes legitimate political currency. Votes count for party leaders, but not for the military. Armed

---

[54] Ake, 1967, p. 142.

[55] Kurtz, 1971, p. 15; see also Ake, 1967, pp. 144–149.

[56] Ake, 1967, p. 79.

[57] Imaz, 1970, especially pp. 242–276.

force counts for the military, but not for the union leaders. Strikes count for the unionists, but not for the economic elite.

The result, in Argentina as in most of Latin America, is the "praetorian society" described by Samuel Huntington, in which "social forces confront each other nakedly" and "no agreement exists among the groups as to the legitimate and authoritative methods for resolving conflicts."[58] Regardless of who is temporarily in control, the government reigns, but does not rule. The only certainty is that each group's reign will be brief. In the absence of an integrated elite the energies released by socioeconomic modernization are not harnessed for public purpose, but are dispersed in private battle and private gain. "In short, for all their differentiation, Latin American political structures do not do what most social theorists agree a political system is supposed to do: give binding and realistic decisions on controversial questions not resolved elsewhere in society."[59]

In some countries this dilemma of development has been resolved, at least temporarily, by the revolutionary advent of a unified counterelite. The most noted examples are the Communist revolutions of Russia, China, and Cuba, but effective elite integration sometimes springs from less totalitarian revolutions. For example, the leaders of contemporary India emerged from the Indian independence movement, "a small elite, homogeneous in social background, mainly upper caste, English-educated," unified by shared values and the solidarity of a successful conspiracy. Subsequent dissent and factionalism divided this elite, and socioeconomic development added new members to it, but until recently "the goals of dissenting and oppositional elements tend[ed] to be limited . . . directed not so much toward upsetting the old order as to finding an entry into it."[60] The unity of the independence movement long persisted, and Indian government remained surprisingly stable and effective. A similar analysis applies to the Mexican elite that captured power during the revolutionary period from 1910 to 1930, to the Israeli elite that created a new state after World War II, and to the English elite that emerged from the Glorious Revolution of 1688.

Revolutionary integration is not always successful or permanent, as recent events in India remind us. Similarly, the chronic instability of French governments can be attributed partially to the fact that the Revolution of 1789 left a divided, rather than a united, political class. Kemal Atatürk's revolutionary elite,

---

[58] Huntington, 1968, p. 196.

[59] Kenworthy, 1970, p. 115; see also Scott, 1967. Anderson (1967, especially p. 107) argues that there is often a minimal consensus in that new elites are admitted to the game on the condition that they challenge none of the existing players. But given the heterogeneity of the incumbent elites, this rule in effect precludes any positive action by government. Kenworthy's indictment obviously does not apply equally to all twenty Latin American countries. Scholars disagree, for example, about the degree of elite integration (and consequent effectiveness) in Venezuela. Compare Bonilla, 1970, pp. 315–320; Blank, 1973, pp. 75, 270–271; and Levine, 1973, pp. 231–259.

[60] Kothari, 1970, pp. 160–164.

integrated in terms of social background, recruitment patterns, solidarity, and value consensus, successfully ruled Turkey for nearly three decades, but in the years after World War II this Kemalist unity was fractured by "the resurrection of severe intraelite conflict" and by the irruption into the elite of new and quite heterogeneous elements. The result: decades of "simultaneous stagnation and instability."[61]

The leaders of the Meiji Restoration that thrust Japan into the modern world in the latter part of the nineteenth century were initially remarkably integrated, but this highly effective unity gradually declined with the differentiation of elites that accompanied Japan's rapid development. In the 1930s, cleavages among the political, administrative, economic, and military elites widened, and assassination and then military rule replaced the earlier consensual oligarchy. The Communist elite of Yugoslavia has achieved a remarkable rate of modernization in the face of severe ethnic fragmentation at the mass level, but whether the unity of this elite can survive Tito's departure is the central problem of contemporary Yugoslav politics. The continued stability, effectiveness, and possibly even the survival of the Yugoslav state depend on the answer to that question.

Elite integration also affects political performance and stability in societies more advanced socioeconomically. One important illustration is provided by the consociational democracies, "democracies with subcultural cleavages and with tendencies toward immobilism and instability which are deliberately turned into more stable systems by the leaders of the major subcultures."[62] Political stability in postwar Austria, for instance, has been attributed primarily to the high level of integration achieved by its leaders, chastened by their failures in the interwar period.

This example also illustrates that effective consociationism may eventually dissolve the social and cultural tensions that originally required it. In fact, in the years after 1945 the psychological barriers between the two Austrian *Lager* seem to have fallen rather quickly at the grassroots level, despite continued bitter partisanship among middle-level elites. In 1966 the "grand coalition" was replaced by a government composed only of the conservative People's party, and after the 1970 elections the Socialists in their turn formed a single-party cabinet, marking the return of the Austrian political elite to fully competitive politics, tempered only by an underlying procedural consensus. A similar evolution may lie ahead for some of the other consociational democracies I discussed earlier.[63]

Before the birth of survey research, theorists assumed that widespread popular commitment to the rules of the game was a precondition for stable and effective democracy. Studies of mass publics in liberal democracies, however,

---

[61] Frey, 1965, p. 391; see also Quandt, 1969.

[62] Lijphart, 1968b, p. 20; see also Daalder, 1974.

[63] See Stiefbold, 1974.

have largely disconfirmed the view that national electorates understand and support civil liberties and political equality. An amended theory emphasizes instead the importance of procedural consensus within the political elite.[64] In this sense there is an element of coalescence and consociationism in every successful democracy, indeed possibly in every stable political system.

Reflecting in 1965 on the tragic failure of the Weimar constitution and on the possibilities for a similar fate for the Bonn regime, the German sociologist Ralf Dahrendorf wrote, "If the political class . . . lacks those ties that transcend the common share in the exercise of power, then political conflict always involves the fear and the danger of jeopardizing the system of the constitution itself."[65] Fears about elite disintegration now seem unfounded in the West German case, but in contemporary Italy, lack of elite consensus continues to threaten the effectiveness and stability of constitutional government.[66]

In America and Britain, too, some observers have expressed concern that inadequate elite integration frustrates conflict resolution and inhibits policy coordination. Struck by the disparity in outlook between U.S. Senators and corporate executives, Andrew Hacker argued:

> *If the men who comprise the political and economic elites in a single society are markedly different in character and social background, then certain tensions are bound to arise in areas where their power and authority interact . . . even if the two sets of people profess to sharing a common ideology and even if they are ostensibly committed to working toward common objectives. . . . [In American society] there is, at base, a real lack of understanding and a failure of communication between the two elites.*[67]

The British elite analyst Anthony Sampson reaches a similar conclusion about his country:

> *My own fear is not that the Establishment in Britain is too close, but that it is not close enough, that the circles are overlapping less and less, and that one half of the ring has very little contact with the other half.*[68]

The argument that elite integration fosters political stability and effectiveness is very prevalent and very persuasive.[69]

---

[64] Key, 1961, pp. 536–539; Dahl, 1961, pp. 311–325; McClosky, 1964.

[65] Dahrendorf, 1969, p. 260.

[66] Putnam 1973*a*, 1973*b*.

[67] Hacker, 1961, pp. 539, 547.

[68] Quoted in Rose, 1974, pp. 214–215.

[69] See the International Studies of Values in Politics, 1971, however, for evidence that at the local level there is no simple link between elite value integration and policy output.

Equally prevalent and persuasive, however, is the argument that an integrated elite is likely to be oligarchic and that democracy can survive only where leaders are socially heterogeneous and politically divided. The authoritarian character of such diverse regimes as the Soviet Union and Franco's Spain has been attributed to the cohesive, interlocking nature of their elites. But the most theoretically significant work on oligarchy and elite integration has focused on the United States and Britain. If these countries, despite their historical, ideological, and institutional commitment to pluralist democracy, are made oligarchic by elite integration, then a fortiori we should expect less fortunate countries to be ruled by unresponsive elites.[70]

Both sides in the famous elitist-pluralist controversy accept the proposition linking elite integration and oligarchy.[71] Mills' argument for the power of the U.S. power elite consists of evidence about the several dimensions of elite integration, and W. L. Guttsman and Ralph Miliband adduce similar factors to support the claim that power in Britain is highly concentrated in a ruling class.[72] Critics of the elitist position concur that unified elites are potentially oligarchic: "The actual *political effectiveness* of a group is a function of its potential for control *and* its potential for unity."[73] But the pluralists deny that elites in Britain and America are actually unified and thus oligarchic.

The pluralists contradict some of the elitists' empirical assertions about elite integration, arguing, for example, that interlocking recruitment and sociometric interaction are not so widespread. They dispute the relevance of some of the elitists' evidence, denying, for example, that the political behavior of leaders is closely tied to their social origins. But the main force of the pluralists' counterattack is directed at two fundamental tenets of the elitists' case:

1. That a single, unified elite dominates decisions in all important issue areas. In Mills' words, "Insofar as national events are decided, the power elite are those who decide them."[74]

2. That political parties and elected officials are ultimately insignificant. As Jean Blondel writes of the British case, "If one holds the view that there is *a* ruling circle, one must

---

[70] Compare Michels' (1959) test of the iron law of oligarchy in an organization renowned for its formal commitment to democracy, the German Social Democratic party.

[71] My account here of the elitist-pluralist debate is very selective, concentrating only on the issue of elite structure. For useful anthologies of the debate, see Domhoff and Ballard, 1968, on the United States and Urry and Wakeford, 1973, on Britain. I have completely ignored the debate about community power, as tangential to our concern with national elites. For useful introductions to that debate, see Polsby (1968) and G. Parry (1969).

[72] Mills, 1956; Guttsman, 1963, especially pp. 319–362; Miliband, 1969.

[73] Dahl, 1958, p. 465.

[74] Mills, 1956, p. 18.

also assert that the opposition between the parties is, in some fundamental sense, irrelevant."[75]

On the first point, pluralists assert that different constellations of groups and elites are influential in each policy arena. Mills' triumvirate of big business, the administration, and the Pentagon may control military procurement, but an entirely different set of actors influences farm policy or race relations policy. Rather than a single, integrated elite, they claim, there are many distinct elites in shifting coalition with one another. Neither majority rule nor minority rule, but "minorities rule" is Dahl's characterization of American democracy.[76]

Secondly, the pluralists argue, professional party politicians cannot be dismissed as indistinguishable frontmen or brokers in trivia at what Mills calls "the middle levels of power."[77] Even in Britain and the United States, competing party elites hold different ideologies, are tied to quite distinct sociometric nets, and act on the basis of different priorities. The basic values shared by elites of both major parties—broad endorsement of free enterprise in America, for example—are shared as well by most ordinary citizens. Electoral competition allows voters to choose between distinct conceptions of the public interest, while it encourages the elites to conform to popular preferences.[78] In sum, the partisan cleavage among professional politicians is perhaps the most important fact about elite structure in Britain and America.

The elitists reply, first, that although American and British elites may be divided on minor questions such as farm policy or civil rights, they are united on the overriding issues of international affairs and political economy. Second, the elitists claim, the pluralists underestimate the integrating constraints imposed by the context of institutional interests, particularly the structural requirements of advanced capitalist economies. However, both these arguments turn on unresolved problems of definition and conceptualization. How are we to decide which issues are minor and which fundamental—by what criteria could we agree that farm policy or race relations policy is unimportant?[79] And how are we to determine where an institution's real interests lie—was the rejection of Keynesian economics by the Eisenhower Administration really in the interests of American capitalists, when that policy led to recurrent recessions?

But the elitists' most interesting argument reverts to Marx's concept of "false consciousness," the thesis that ordinary citizens may be so apathetic and

---

[75] Blondel, 1963, p. 236.

[76] Dahl, 1956, p. 128. See also A. Rose (1967) on the United States and Hewitt (1974) on Britain. On the general question of issue areas and elite structure, see Lowi, 1964b.

[77] Mills, 1956, pp. 254–255.

[78] On elections and elite-mass linkages, see Chapter 6.

[79] See Mills, 1956, pp. 253n, 261; Prewitt and Stone, 1973, pp. 114–115; McFarland, 1969, pp. 81–87.

uninformed politically as to be deceived about the real issues. Granted that the party elites offer the electorate a choice, nevertheless that choice may not be fair and free, for many options and indeed many fundamental issues may never be publicly articulated. The power and unity of the elite is revealed, not in overt decisions about issues already on the public agenda, but rather in the implicit "nondecisions" that keep sensitive topics from ever becoming matters of controversy at all. Thus, for example, it has been claimed that the issue of air pollution is kept from the agenda of many American communities by the silent but intimidating economic power of local industrial firms. The available empirical evidence, however, has been inadequate so far to resolve this dispute about issues and nonissues, and the matter remains on the agenda of scholars concerned with elites and policy making.[80] For our discussion of elite structure, the most relevant point to emerge from the debate between elitists and pluralists is the fundamental proposition accepted by both sides, namely, that elite integration, where it exists, encourages oligarchy, by limiting the ability of ordinary citizens to intervene in the policy-making process.

We should consider briefly the connection between the two propositions we have been discussing: (1) that elite integration increases political stability and effectiveness and (2) that elite integration increases oligarchy. Social theorists have emphasized one or the other of these consequences, according to their ideological predilections. Conservatives, who stress elites' service to society, emphasize the effectiveness and stability that flow from elite integration, whereas radicals, who stress elites' exploitation of society, emphasize the oligarchic consequences. But elite integration may in fact simultaneously both increase horizontal communication and coordination within the elite stratum and decrease vertical communication and coordination between that stratum and the mass public. Integration seems to be a necessary condition for efficiency and stability, yet a sufficient condition for oligarchy. As Raymond Aron writes, "A unified elite means the end of freedom. But when the groups of the elite are not only distinct but become a disunity, it means the end of the State."[81]

Empirical examples of this trade-off abound. Elite integration has given Mexico unusually stable government, but the Mexican elite remains essentially a self-recruiting oligarchy of professional politicians and technocrats. For many decades consociational democracy in the Netherlands stabilized a potentially chaotic society, but only by excluding most of the population from effective political participation. One vivid illustration was the Dutch election of 1917, in which all parties agreed not to contest seats held by incumbents, in order to safeguard a fragile agreement on sensitive religious and social issues that had been reached in negotiations among leaders of the various blocs.[82] Conversely,

[80] Bachrach and Baratz, 1962; Crenson, 1971; Cobb and Elder, 1972.

[81] Aron, 1950, p. 143.

[82] Lijphart, 1969, p. 214.

in Belgium in the 1960s the increasing responsiveness of linguistic elites to their divergent constituencies undermined consociationism and reduced government stability and effectiveness.

The normative implications of this dilemma are profound, for it calls into question the feasibility of stable democracy. The integration necessary for effective government precludes responsive government. Theorists who recognize the dilemma have responded in three different ways. Some argue for the possibility of a "golden mean," implicitly assuming that the empirical relationships of integration to effectiveness and oligarchy are nonlinear. In discussing a list of eight criteria for judging political systems, including effectiveness and responsiveness, Robert A. Dahl notes: "Like most standards of performance for complex achievements, they conflict with one another; . . . we cannot maximize one goal *beyond some range* without sacrificing another goal."[83]

A second group of theorists hypothesize that effectiveness and oligarchy are related to distinct dimensions of integration, so that it is possible (and desirable) that integration be high along one dimension and low along another. Ralf Dahrendorf, for example, concludes that "a democratic elite has to be united in its status, and divided in its politics," and others have suggested that while democracy excludes elite consensus on substantive issues, effectiveness requires merely procedural consensus.[84] On the other hand, if Peter Bachrach is correct that "procedural norms cannot realistically be dissociated from the political context in which they operate and the substantive values and interests which they affect," then this second resolution of the dilemma may be illusory.[85]

Finally, some theorists accept the logic that elite competition and elite integration are incompatible and conclude pessimistically that no government in a complex society can be both fully effective and fully democratic.[86] This is, of course, precisely the line of argument that led Michels to his iron law of oligarchy. To sort out this perplexing nexus between integration, effectiveness, and oligarchy, we need now to explore patterns of mutual influence between elites and nonelites. That is the task of Chapter 6.

---

[83] Dahl, 1966, p. 388 (italics added).

[84] Dahrendorf, 1969, p. 263; Porter, 1965, pp. 210–215; Aron, 1950. Lenin's prescription of "democratic centralism" for a revolutionary party is an attempt to resolve this same dilemma, by allowing dissent before decisions are taken, but demanding cohesion thereafter.

[85] Bachrach, 1967, p. 53.

[86] Field and Higley, 1973, p. 20.

ELITE-
MASS
LINKAGES
6

What is the nature of the relationship between rulers and ruled, between representatives and represented, between leaders and led? This question in both its empirical and its normative versions has perplexed philosophers and men of affairs throughout history. From Plato and Rousseau to Confucius and Mao, each of the giants of political thought has offered a distinctive interpretation of the respective roles of those who lead and those who follow. And in the aftermath of the great democratic revolutions of the last two centuries these issues have become matters of practical politics, as timely as the latest proposal for forcing decision makers in Washington or Paris or New Delhi or Peking to respond to sentiment at the grassroots.

In this chapter we shall consider two related sets of questions:

1. How does the elite influence the nonelite? What are the bases of elite power and authority? How does the elite mobilize and demobilize the masses in order to accomplish its purposes, while minimizing interference in its decisions?

2. How does the nonelite influence the elite? What are the bases of representation and responsiveness? Why and under what circumstances does the elite ever do what the nonelite wants done?

These pairs of questions derive from two different perspectives on society, the view from the top, so to speak, and the view from the bottom. Yet we shall see that the answers to these contrasting questions are closely intertwined, for the relationship between leaders and followers is always double-sided and interdependent. Both sets of questions must be asked about any sort of political system, for there are important elements of elite control in the most democratic of polities, and conversely, even dictatorial elites are subject to certain constraints from nonelites.

ELITE
CONTROL
OVER
NONELITES

COERCION

"Every state is founded on force," quoted Weber approvingly from Lenin.[1] One fundamental basis of elite power has always been violence or coercion. The stronger man or tribe or nation defeats the weaker, and victor becomes ruler. Particularly in simple, weakly institutionalized political systems politics is a game in which clubs are trump.[2] In today's world, military regimes are increasingly more common than parliamentary regimes. Even where civilian institutions are stronger, overt coercion is often an important technique of social control. During the turmoil of the Cultural Revolution, the elites of the Chinese Communist party were supplanted by the leaders of the People's Liberation Army, for only the soldiers had the arms to impose order. And the events of Watts and Belfast and Paris in the 1960s reminded us that coercive force can be employed by elites and counterelites in liberal democracies, too.

ORGANIZATION

The classical elite theorists were not blind to the coercive element in much elite power, but they emphasized other more subtle and more durable factors. In modern society, Michels argued, organization has become a technical and functional necessity. Inevitably, any organization of more than a few members develops some division of labor, assigning responsibility for coordination to a small group. It was Michels' central insight that power in this limited sense breeds broader, more lasting power. The larger and more permanent an organization, the more likely is the centralization of leadership and the longer the probable tenure of leaders. However democratic the formal rules are and however sincerely egalitarian the leaders, they acquire special skills, contacts, and other resources. Inadvertently, perhaps, they begin to monopolize the flows of information, and the structure of the organization becomes increasingly vertical rather than horizontal.

These traits are intensified when the organization interacts with other organizations. A trade union, for example, is typically more oligarchic than a camera club, because negotiations with management require that the union

---

[1] Weber, 1958, p. 78.

[2] Huntington, 1968, p. 196.

speak with a single voice. Armies are among the most oligarchic of organizations, for their raison d'etre is combat with opposing organizations. Lenin's main contribution to the theory of elite-mass linkages was based on this insight. To overthrow the tsar would require, he argued, a tightly organized, rigidly disciplined party of the revolutionary vanguard, not the flabby, decentralized, "democratic" organization favored by some of his less single-minded colleagues. To believe that leaders should be controlled by followers rather than vice versa was, according to Lenin, to commit the sin of "tail-ism." Michels was right: "Who says organization, says oligarchy."[3]

AUTHORITY

Unadorned power, whether based on force or organization, is neither the most efficient nor the most common means by which the elite can maintain its position and influence the nonelite. Every elite tries to transform coerced obedience into willing obedience, to convert its power into authority, by making its rule legitimate in the eyes of the nonelite. Mosca pointed to the importance of the *political formula*, those legal and moral principles on which the power of the elite rests, the political philosophy in terms of which might becomes right.[4] Monarchs in seventeenth-century Europe and the Meiji oligarchy in nineteenth-century Japan justified their rule in terms of divine ordination. The Communist leaders of contemporary Europe and Asia claim legitimacy by virtue of their commitment to achieving socialism. U.S. elites depend for their authority on the Constitution, a kind of social contract that "We, the people" did "ordain and establish."

Max Weber provided a classic typology of three kinds of political authority. *Traditional authority* derives from "an established belief in the sanctity of immemorial traditions."[5] This type of legitimacy is most prominent in preindustrial settings, but it is important everywhere. Every political community and every elite relies heavily on habitual, unreflective compliance, on citizens' respect for those they have been taught to believe are properly set above them. This is particularly so where upper-class leaders can tap reserves of social deference on the part of nonelites.

Weber's second type, *legal-rational authority*, is "based upon the belief in the legality of rules and on the right of those who occupy posts by virtue of those rules to issue commands."[6] Elites in all modern industrial societies derive at least part of their legitimacy from formally promulgated constitutions. The accusation of "unconstitutional" behavior is very threatening, whether hurled by Archibald

---

[3] Lenin, 1929; Michels, 1959, p. 401.

[4] Mosca, 1939, p. 70.

[5] Weber, 1947, p. 328.

[6] Willner, 1968, p. 2.

Cox or Alexander Solzhenitzyn, precisely because it directly questions the accused's right to rule.

Weber's third type, *charismatic authority,* "rests upon the uncommon and extraordinary devotion [of followers] to the sacredness or the heroic force or the exemplariness of an individual and the order revealed or created by him."[7] When older forms of authority crumble (under the impact of colonialism or socioeconomic crisis, for example), a legitimacy vacuum is created into which may step a charismatic leader whose rule is self-legitimating in the eyes of his devoted followers. The careers of such charismatic leaders as Hitler, Gandhi, Nkrumah, Mao, Atatürk, Nasser, and Peron illustrate that charismatic authority is inherently unstable. Charisma must be institutionalized, or "routinized," as Weber put it, if the legitimacy of the regime is to outlive its founder's initial successes. The postindependence history of Ghana illustrates the characteristic pattern: the weakness of traditional and legal-rational authority; the development of charismatic legitimacy focused on Nkrumah; an attempt at routinization in the form of his Convention People's party; the failure of routinization; and finally, the resort to coercive power, first by Nkrumah himself and then by the military who toppled his regime.[8]

Charisma, like beauty, exists in the eye of the beholder, for as Weber said, "What is alone important is how the individual is actually regarded by those subject to [his] charismatic authority."[9] Indeed, the rule of an elite is legitimate, in any of the senses used here, *if and only if* the nonelite believe it is. Thus, authority is to some extent a function of a leader's compliance with the expectations of his followers.[10] For this reason legitimacy can constrain as well as sustain elite power. Witness George Orwell's account of "Shooting an Elephant":

> *Here was I, the white man with his gun, standing in front of the unarmed native crowd—seemingly the leading actor of the piece; but in reality I was only an absurd puppet pushed to and fro by the will of those yellow faces behind. . . . A sahib has got to act like a sahib. . . . He wears a mask and his face grows to fit it.*[11]

Yet elites are not powerless to affect how nonelites will view their rule. In modern political systems legitimacy is influenced by the ability of the elite to produce outputs satisfactory to the nonelite, but performance legitimacy provides less security to elites than other forms of legitimacy.[12] Most political

---

[7] Weber, 1954, p. xl.

[8] Runciman, 1963; Apter, 1968. See also Dekmejian, 1971 and Rustow, 1968.

[9] Weber, 1947, p. 359.

[10] Barnard, 1947.

[11] Orwell, 1953, pp. 6–7.

[12] Baylis, 1974, p. 15.

systems are equipped with mechanisms to reinforce the political formula and the more enduring legitimacy it furnishes. Indoctrination may be overt and intensive, as in the mass propaganda, the study groups, and the "self-criticism" sessions of Communist China; or it may be more subtle and diffuse, transmitted through the familiar agencies of socialization—family, peers, schools, and so on. Mass acquiescence is often achieved by the manipulation of political symbols.[13] Symbolic reinforcement of the political formula rings out on the Fourth of July in America and on May Day in the Soviet Union. The authority of new leaders is often enhanced by the pomp and circumstance of coronations and inaugurations.

Marx stressed the importance of symbols and ideologies in sustaining established elites. For example, he described religion as the opiate of the masses, deadening their awareness of earthly exploitation by offering the misty hope of salvation in the world to come. But Mosca's concept of the political formula was more subtle. He was careful to deny that

> *political formulas are mere quackeries aptly invented to trick the masses into obedience. . . . The truth is that they answer a real need in man's social nature; and this need, so universally felt, of governing and knowing that one is governed not on the basis of mere material or intellectual force, but on the basis of moral principle, has beyond any doubt a practical and real importance.*[14]

His implication that elites, too, are subject to the influence of the political formula raises the interesting possibility that the legitimating myths of a political system may actually foster elite responsiveness to nonelites. This is a possibility we shall explore later in this chapter.

ELITE-MASS OPINION FLOW

Before considering how elites might be influenced by public opinion, we must first ask about the origins of public opinion itself. One image is that ideas about public affairs bubble up from the grassroots—that the common man articulates his political concerns, drawing on his practical experience with the problems of social life, and together with other like-minded citizens communicates his suggestions to decision makers. However, even in countries where levels of political sophistication are quite high, this "bubble-up" theory is less accurate than that Karl Deutsch has termed the "cascade" model.[15]

Imagine overlaid on the political stratification system a series of interconnected pools of opinion, as diagrammed in Figure 6–1. Information and persua-

---

[13] Edelman, 1964.

[14] Mosca, 1939, p. 71 (italics added).

[15] Deutsch, 1968, pp. 101–110.

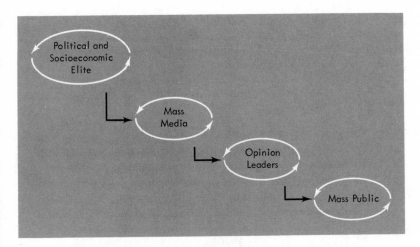

Figure 6–1   The Opinion Cascade
Source: Adapted from Deutsch, 1968, p. 105.

sion flow more freely within each level than between levels and more easily downward than upward. At the top are the political and socioeconomic elites. Just below is the pool of opinion represented by the mass media, sometimes generating political ideas autonomously, but more frequently merely retransmitting messages from the elite. Still lower is the stratum of "opinion leaders"—the 5 to 10 percent of the population who follow public affairs closely and who retail to ordinary citizens views usually acquired from the media wholesalers. Personal perceptions of social reality such as unemployment need not cascade down this spillway, but interpretations of reality typically do.

Some important qualifications must be added to this simplified model. First, none of these levels is likely to be internally homogeneous; different leaders and different media may offer different diagnoses of public problems. Second, in most societies information flows through multiple channels; workers are apt to get one interpretation of unemployment through the mass media and another from their union. Third, communication patterns are not identical in all societies. Even in a single society, political and socioeconomic development tends to remold patterns of communication over time. Finally, even though the main flow is downward, there is occasionally some capillary movement of information and opinion upward. As concern about medical costs, for instance, becomes more intense among ordinary citizens, this discontent is likely to be picked up and amplified by political leaders, for reasons we shall explore later in this chapter.

Nonetheless, as we discussed in Chapter 4, the elaboration and propagation of new political concepts is largely the province of elites. The translation of a private worry (How can I meet my medical bills?) into a public issue (How can we deliver medical care most effectively?) is normally performed by political leaders. Schattsneider was correct in stating, "He who determines what politics is about runs the country."[16] However, the converse is also true: "The political elite . . . mediate between the world of remote and complex events and the mass of the public. A great function of political leadership is the clarification of public problems and the presentation of courses of action."[17]

For this reason, leaders are often responding to demands they have themselves stimulated. Elite opinion is most apt to run ahead of mass opinion in periods of rapid change and on topics that are new to the national agenda. In the United States during the 1960s white support for civil rights legislation was much stronger within the political elite than among ordinary citizens; changes in mass opinion followed changes in public policy, rather than the reverse. Similarly, elite opinion seems more to be changing ahead of mass opinion on the issue of a guaranteed family income, favored in 1970 by less than half the mass public, but by two-thirds of the members of the House of Representatives and three-quarters of the Senate. In West Germany the improvement of relations with Eastern Europe undertaken by Willy Brandt was presaged by earlier changes in elite attitudes; mass support for these policies came only later. Modernization in such countries as India, Yugoslavia, and China was initiated by elites who then strove to mobilize mass support.[18]

ELITE **RESPONSIVENESS** **TO** **NONELITES**	Members of the political elite, by definition, have more influence over public affairs than do ordinary citizens. Why, then, would the elite ever do what the nonelite wants done? This is the central question with which theorists of representation and democracy have struggled. I want here to discuss four broad possibilities:

1. The elite may be like the nonelite in crucial respects.
2. Support from the nonelite may be an important resource or credential for members of the elite.
3. Influential intermediate groups or institutions may link elites and nonelites.
4. Members of the elite may believe they ought to be responsive to the needs and wishes of the nonelite.

[16] Schattschneider, 1960, p. 68.

[17] Key, 1961, p. 261.

[18] Dye, 1972, pp. 39–66; Wildenmann, 1973, pp. 6–9; Kothari, 1970, especially pp. 97–98; Zaninovich, 1970; Townsend, 1974. Compare Di Palma, 1973, pp. 7–10; Barton, 1973.

At the founding of the American Republic John Adams argued that a representative legislature "should be an exact portrait, in miniature, of the people at large, as it should think, feel, reason, and act like them."[19] If the elite were composed of people whose backgrounds, experiences, values, and needs were identical to those of the nonelite—if, in short, the elite were a microcosm of the nonelite —then leaders would only have to "be themselves" in order to ensure effective representation of nonelite desires.

The selection of such a microcosmic elite is technically simple. The laws of statistics guarantee that a random sample of the population will (within specifiable limits) be representative in this sense, with the correct proportions of (say) Republicans and Democrats, blacks and whites, men and women, rich and poor, hawks and doves, welfare mothers and corporate lawyers. Something like random sampling was involved in the lottery-based selection of leaders in ancient Athens.[20] But so far as I know, no modern state has ever employed this technique for linking elites and nonelites.[21]

The next best thing, some have argued, is that the composition of the elite should at least reflect the broad social groupings within the population. The English reformers Sidney and Beatrice Webb considered the House of Lords to be "the worst representative assembly ever created, in that it contains absolutely no members of the manual working class; none of the great class of shopkeepers, clerks, and teachers; none of the half of all the citizens who are of the female sex,"[22] and an English politician once observed that "ideally, the House of Commons should be a social microcosm of the nation. The nation includes a great many people who are rather stupid, and so should the House."[23]

In the case of the administrative elite, theorists of "representative bureaucracy" have held that "A civil service which includes members of all classes *therefore* ensures that all their different values and interests are articulated and hence brought to bear upon the decisions taken and policies formulated by it."[24] Critics of administrative recruitment in Britain, for example, have suggested that the middle-class servant, having no "memory of misery, hunger, squalor,

---

[19] As cited in Pitkin, 1967, p. 60.

[20] Krislov, 1974, pp. 42–46.

[21] But see Mueller et al., 1972.

[22] As cited in Pitkin, 1967, p. 61.

[23] Lord Booth, as cited in Birch, 1964, p. 232.

[24] Subramaniam, 1967, p. 1013; see also Kingsley, 1944, Krislov, 1974, and Meier, 1975.

bureaucratic oppression, and economic insecurity," is incapable of comprehending the needs and wants of the working class.[25]

"It is said to be necessary," wrote Alexander Hamilton in the Federalist Papers, "that all classes of citizens should have some of their own number in the representative body, in order that their feelings and interests may be the better understood and attended to. But . . . this will never happen under any arrangement that leaves the votes of the people free."[26] In fact, as we saw in Chapter 2, despite the occasional quotas and ticket balancing that derive from this theory of elite-mass linkage, elites are nowhere representative in this demographic sense.

However, the evidence of Chapter 4 on the weakness of the links between social background and political behavior among elite members suggests that demographic representativeness is neither necessary nor sufficient for responsiveness. Postrecruitment socialization implies that even a randomly chosen elite would, as its tenure lengthened, tend in outlook to diverge from the nonelite. Robert Michels complained that

> as the led becomes a subordinate leader, and from that a leader of the first rank, he himself undergoes a mental evolution, which often effects a complete transformation in his personality. . . . The permanent exercise of leadership exerts upon the moral character of leaders an influence which is essentially pernicious.[27]

One solution is rapid turnover, replacing leaders before they are perverted by the perquisites of power. But this strategy sacrifices the knowledge and expertise that come only with experience. The Chinese Communists have invented an intriguing alternative, the *hsia fang*, or "downward transfer" system. A 1957 directive decreed that in order to "change thoroughly the situation where those in leading positions are separated from the masses," the leading cadres of the party, the government, and the military should "devote part of their time to engaging in physical labor with the workers and peasants," so that they might "become closely knitted with the masses."[28] We have no reliable evidence on the actual impact of this system, but it is reasonable to suppose that several months spent by the minister of agriculture spreading dung in a rice paddy might well affect his outlook.

Elite actions might match nonelite desires, even without the measures so far considered, if elites and nonelites share in a broad consensus about public policy. In large, complex nation-states, universal agreement might seem elusive

[25] Kelsall, 1955, pp. 191–193.

[26] Cited in Kirkpatrick, 1975.

[27] Michels, 1959, pp. 205, 211.

[28] Lee, 1966, p. 44.

and illusory, but in relatively homogeneous communities, congruity between elite actions and mass preferences may be quite high even without institutional constraints. This may account for the otherwise surprising finding that U.S. congressmen from safe seats reflect their constituents' views more faithfully than do their colleagues from competitive districts.[29] Similarly, in subculturally divided countries, such as Austria or the Netherlands, subcultural leaders are likely to reflect their followers' views spontaneously on those issues on which opinion within the subculture is homogeneous.[30]

At the national level, too, consensus may link citizens and leaders on issues on which public opinion is stable and one-sided. For instance, in most industrial nations, support for free public education is continued by elites without overt pressure from nonelites. Rulers in noncompetitive political systems, such as the single-party states of Africa, often claim to be carrying out a broad national consensus. However, instances of dictatorship by plebiscite remind us that elite-mass consensus may be induced by the elite and may in that sense be counterfeit.

In sum, an elite may do what the nonelite wants done because the former mirror the latter in terms of background or experience or outlook. This type of congruence between elite actions and mass preferences does not actually involve mass influence on elites. Instead, the elites, in following their own preferences, merely act *as if* they were responding to nonelites. To discover genuine responsiveness we must turn to other mechanisms for linking leaders and led.

NONELITE SUPPORT AS AN ELITE RESOURCE

If getting into and staying in the elite were to depend, at least in part, on support from ordinary citizens, then aspiring leaders would have a powerful incentive to pay attention to the views of those citizens. For most of us, "effective access to elites depends more on the opportunity to influence the selection of members of elites than on the opportunity to enter elites."[31] The most prominent, though not the only, example of this type of elite-mass linkage is the competitive election.

---

[29] Miller, 1970; Kingdon, 1973, pp. 45–46; Fiorina, 1974. See also Prewitt and Eulau, 1969; Jennings and Zeigler, 1971, especially pp. 316–319; Eisenstein, 1973, pp. 149–156. Of course, homogeneous communities are less likely to sustain the sort of structured diversity and opposition that is associated with elite accountability. Thus, other forms of elite-mass linkage may suffer in such communities.

[30] Thomas Hare, an English electoral reformer of the last century, proposed an impractical but intriguing form of proportional representation in which voters would be able to create their own constituencies by voting for any candidate in the nation; any candidate receiving a minimum quota of votes would be elected. Each representative would thus speak for a unanimous constituency, at least on the dominant issues in his electoral appeal. See Birch, 1971, pp. 89–90.

[31] Kornhauser, 1959, p. 54.

Electoral Logic   As a means for elite recruitment, election is among the more remarkable of social inventions. Despite some limitations and imperfections that we shall discuss in a moment, competitive elections based on universal suffrage offer hope of mitigating the iron law of oligarchy. Election is sometimes thought important as a technique for choosing a leader who will be representative in the sense discussed in the previous section—who will represent the masses of ordinary citizens merely by being one of them. But elections may foster elite responsiveness for quite another reason—because they foster elite accountability to the nonelite.

Reflecting on the actual operation of liberal democracies, Joseph Schumpeter insisted that all that can reasonably be expected of ordinary citizens is that they periodically choose among competing teams of leaders. "The democratic method is that institutional arrangement for arriving at political decisions in which individuals acquire the power to decide by means of a competitive struggle for the people's vote."[32] Electoral competition, like competition between brands of toothpaste, tends to force the competitors to produce policies in accord with the desires of the voter. "Politicians subject to elections must operate within the limits set . . . by their expectations about what policies they can adopt and still be reelected."[33] And in politics, as in the marketplace, competitors have a strong incentive to introduce distinctive and popular (or at least popularizable) innovations—fluorides in toothpaste or social security legislation in politics.

This theory is neat and powerful. How accurately it describes politics in the real world is another question, however, for it makes several problematic assumptions about the behavior of elites and masses. I want to discuss three of these: the assumption of ambition, the assumption of competition, and the assumption of information.

Electoral Linkage and Ambition   First, the theory of electoral competition assumes that leaders are driven by ambition to seek reelection. A leader who is indifferent about, or precluded from, running again has no incentive to produce popular policies. "The desire for election and, more important, for reelection becomes the electorate's restraint upon its public officials. No more irresponsible government is imaginable than one of high-minded men unconcerned for their political futures."[34]

Some evidence for this theory has been offered by Kenneth Prewitt, who found that among California city councilmen, political ambition is associated with heightened sensitivity to voters' wishes. On the other hand, he also found a surprisingly high degree of "indifference to reelection." Roughly half the councilmen were unconcerned about reelection and hence felt themselves to be

---

[32] Schumpeter, 1950, p. 269; see also Downs, 1957, and Dahl, 1956, pp. 63–89.

[33] Dahl, 1956, p. 132.

[34] Schlesinger, 1966, p. 2; see also Mayhew, 1974.

—and in fact were—immune from electoral sanction.[35] Fortunately, however, in national politics most elected officials seem adequately ambitious. Over the last half century, for example, four-fifths of all U.S. senators have sought reelection.[36]

Electoral Linkage and Competition   Competition is a second important condition for electorally based responsiveness. In politics as in economics, monopolists are under little pressure to satisfy their customers. Leaders who face no credible electoral threat may be sincere and dedicated, but there is no gainsaying that single-party regimes—in Moscow or Mexico City, Cairo or Cape Town or Chicago—are under much less compulsion to conform to public sentiment than are their counterparts in competitive systems. "In the give-and-take between leadership echelons, with their intense policy drives and attachments, and the mass of people, the ultimate weapon of public opinion is the minority party."[37]

To be sure, even in multiparty systems like the United States, Britain, or West Germany, political competition is oligopolistic, with a few large "firms" dominating the political marketplace. Though producers in such a market are under some pressure to respond to consumers' demands, it is easier for them to disregard the preferences of certain groups and to limit the range of competition than it would be in a perfectly free market. Critics charge that parties in such systems offer voters little real choice and that unconventional alternatives are excluded from the political marketplace by an elite cartel. On the other hand, we saw in Chapter 5 that party elites usually diverge from one another in their policy preferences more, not less, than do their respective followers. Competition may be limited less by elite conspiracy than by nonelite moderation.[38]

---

[35] Prewitt, 1970, pp. 196–202; Eulau and Prewitt, 1973, pp. 444–462. Most empirical research on electoral representation has focused on the American case, and perforce most of the evidence presented in this section will be American. However, there is little reason to doubt that the generalizations I draw about ambition, competition, and information apply to most competitive electoral settings.

[36] Kostrowski, 1973; Erikson and Luttbeg, 1973, p. 265. At the summit of the American political elite, the Constitutional limit on presidential tenure formally constrains ambition. Whatever the possible benefits of the Twenty-second Amendment, it does mean that a second-term president has little electoral incentive to respond to public opinion.

[37] Key, 1961, pp. 555–556.

[38] Hansen (1975) reports persuasive evidence from American local politics that concurrence between leaders' and citizens' priorities is increased by a combination of electoral competition and active citizen participation. The logic of electoral competition might seem to imply that representatives from competitive districts should be more attentive to their constituents than representatives from safe seats, but as Miller (1970) and Fiorina (1974) have shown, the best available U.S evidence contradicts this proposition, partly because of the methodologically confounding effects of intradistrict and interdistrict homogeneity of voters' views. Similarly, the theory seems to imply that elite attentiveness to the welfare of the population should increase with competition, but studies of patterns of public policy have so far found little independent impact of electoral competition; see Hofferbert, 1972, Jackman, 1975, and the studies they cite.

Competition is also inhibited by the edge that incumbents often have over challengers in terms of resources and recognition. In the U.S. Congress in recent years, for example, four-fifths of all incumbents who run for reelection are successful.[39] To be sure, the victories of incumbents may simply reflect their success in satisfying constituents' desires. Yet as Prewitt has said of similar evidence at the local level, "If it is so atypical for the general election to eliminate incumbents, it is difficult to believe that the councilmen are restrained by 'their expectations about what policies they can adopt and still be reelected.' "[40]

Information is the third critical assumption of the theory of electoral democracy, as well as other theories of elite-mass linkage. Unless citizens have reasonably good information about leaders and their policies, and unless leaders have reasonably good information about voters and their preferences, even a perfectly competitive political marketplace is unlikely to generate policies in accord with the wishes of the nonelite. Consider the levels of information on each side of the political equation.

Information Flow: Elites to Nonelites   Two decades' worth of evidence about the levels of political information and attentiveness of mass publics around the world has shown that ordinary citizens know remarkably little about the activities of their leaders. For example, less than one-quarter of the U.S. electorate has read or heard something about both their congressional candidates.[41] Political ignorance may reflect citizen apathy, but it may also result from the deliberate obfuscations of leaders. Like their economic counterparts, political entrepreneurs often have an interest in providing misleading information to consumers. Herein lies the fundamental significance of freedom of the press, of information, and of political commentary.

On the other hand, we must not exaggerate the information requirements of this model. A rational voter need not understand macroeconomic theory in order to favor the party that more consistently provides full employment. One study of voting behavior in Britain concluded that "a government is credited or blamed for many things while it is in office without the public's having undertaken any serious analysis of the role of government policy in producing the conditions of which it approves or disapproves."[42] Unfair though it may be to a harassed government, this phenomenon does give leaders a powerful incentive to produce social conditions satisfactory to the electors, even when those electors are largely in the dark about what the government is actually doing.

Moreover, both voters and consumers can often rely on secondhand information and on mutual criticism by competing firms. A congressman's record

---

[39] Kostrowski, 1973; see also Mayhew, 1974, pp. 33–37.

[40] Prewitt, 1970, p. 211.

[41] Miller and Stokes, 1963, p. 54; see also Wahlke, 1971.

[42] Butler and Stokes, 1969, p. 182.

may have a very real bearing on his electoral success or failure without most of his constituents ever knowing what that record is. . . . [I]nformation about himself and his record may be considerably transformed as it diffuses out to the electorate in two or more stages. As a result, the public—or parts of it—may get simple positive or negative cues about the congressman which were provoked by his legislative actions but which no longer have a recognizable issue content.[43]

On the other hand, this diffusion process means that the information voters get will have been filtered (and in some ways biased) by opinion leaders in the constituency. Imperfections in the flow of information downward from elites to nonelites also put a premium on the techniques of public relations. David Mayhew points out that congressmen are led to emphasize "self-advertising," "position-taking," and "credit-claiming," especially for particularized benefits.[44] In politics, as in economics, poorly informed consumers are unlikely to get their money's (or vote's) worth.

Information Flow: Nonelites to Elites   Equally problematic is the flow of information in the opposite direction. Studies of U.S. congressmen, Iowa legislators, and Scottish local councillors have shown that except for highly salient issues such as race relations, politicians are as often wrong as right in guessing their constituents' policy preferences. British elites during World War II vastly overrated Churchill's popular appeal, and his landslide defeat in 1945 took them quite by surprise. Postwar Austrian party leaders misjudged the speed with which interparty hostility was dissolving at the mass level. Yugoslav politicians overestimate public satisfaction with the regime's policies.[45]

Such misperceptions derive from a fundamental asymmetry in social communication: "The number of people who can communicate directly with a single leader remains more or less fixed, whereas the number of people with whom a leader can communicate directly by radio and television has no theoretical limit."[46] Immersed in the pool of elite opinion at the top of the communications cascade, leaders must develop special strategies for gathering information about the preferences of ordinary citizens. American legislators, for instance, rely heavily on their mail, on sporadic personal contact with constituents, and to a lesser extent on editorial comment and communications from the party

---

[43] Miller and Stokes, 1963, p. 55.

[44] Mayhew, 1974, pp. 40, 49–83.

[45] Miller and Stokes, 1963, p. 52; Erikson and Luttbeg, 1973, pp. 276–278; Miller, 1970; Hedlund and Friesma, 1972; Brand, 1972, p. 261; Kavanagh, 1973; Stiefbold, 1974, pp. 144–146; Barton, Denitch, and Kadushin, 1973, pp. 277–279. On the other hand, at least in small group settings, leaders are better than nonleaders at estimating others' opinions. See Chowdhry and Newcomb, 1965.

[46] Dahl and Tufte, 1973, p. 75.

organization.[47] The representative's image of his constituency is focused on the foreground of letter writers, editorial writers, insistent constituents, and party activists, rather than on the average voter, standing quietly in the background.

Reliance on these channels would not matter much if this vocal public were representative of the rest of the electorate. But that is rarely so. Two-thirds of all letters to officials in the United States come from barely 3 percent of the public, and this "letter public" is quite idiosyncratic. Figure 6–2 shows that in 1964 the letter public on balance favored Barry Goldwater, while the electorate as a whole overwhelmingly favored Lyndon Johnson.[48] On tariff legislation, to take another example, protectionists are so much more likely than free-traders to write congressmen that one study concluded that the "body of citizens represented by our sample could appear to Congress to be two-to-one protectionist when we know they were more nearly three-to-one liberal traders."[49]

The personal contact channel is even more biased. Given the correlation between political participation and socioeconomic status, it is hardly surprising

[47] Erikson and Luttbeg, 1973, pp. 268–269; Kingdon, 1973, pp. 53–58.

[48] Converse, Clausen, and Miller, 1965, pp. 333–335.

[49] Bauer, Pool, and Dexter, 1964, p. 211.

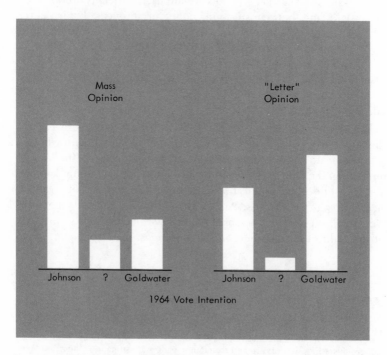

Figure 6–2   Public Opinion as Measured by People or Political Letters
Source: Adapted from Converse, Clausen, and Miller, 1965, p. 334, Figure 2(a).

that the priorities and preferences of the attentive public differ from those of less active citizens. The most salient personal and public problems for low participators in America are the bread-and-butter ones of housing and employment, while high participators are more concerned about such middle-class issues as education and air pollution. Activists are also ideologically more conservative than nonactivists on such topics as social welfare, income redistribution, and racial integration. And as we might expect, activists are more likely than nonactivists to have their priorities represented at the elite level, even controlling for the effects of socioeconomic status.[50]

Because a leader usually hears from constituents who share his social origins and political predilections and because his own public stands often evoke reinforcement from the grassroots, the flow of information to him magnifies public support for his views. Moreover, like most of us, he is usually selectively attentive to messages of agreement. Congressmen, one scholar concludes, hear mainly their own echoes.[51] One consequence is that (at least in the United States) elected officials overestimate their own public visibility. Ironically, this misapprehension may lead them to be more responsive to mass opinion than they really need to be.[52]

In addition to these distortions in elite-mass communications patterns, "information concerning the state of public opinion is filtered through the psychological and ideological screen of party leaders, and what parties will 'see' as mass demands will reflect the fact that party leaders differ from the electorate in their background, their role, their greater partisanship and ideological sophistication."[53] One celebrated example of the resultant message-garbling was the 1968 New Hampshire Democratic primary victory of Eugene McCarthy, widely interpreted—not least in Lyndon Johnson's White House—as evidence of grassroots dovishness on the Vietnam war. However, subsequent surveys showed that most of those who voted for McCarthy actually wanted a more hawkish policy than Johnson was then pursuing![54]

Despite these flaws in conventional communications channels, elites are often justly skeptical about scientifically accurate surveys of public opinion. First, leaders recognize that on detailed questions and evolving issues mass opinion is often imprecise, unstable, and even susceptible of leadership. "No congressman would long be re-elected who showed no more imagination in interpreting his constituents' needs than to vote at each point in time as his followers felt at that time. At the minimum, a political leader must guess where his followers are going and get there first."[55]

[50] Verba and Nie, 1972, pp. 267–285, 304–308.

[51] Dexter, 1963.

[52] Kingdon, 1967; Miller and Stokes, 1963, p. 54.

[53] Di Palma, 1973, p. 8, citing Hamilton, 1968, p. 132.

[54] Converse, Miller, Rusk, and Wolfe, 1969, pp. 1095–1096.

[55] Bauer, Pool, and Dexter, 1964, p. 452.

The leader's task is further complicated by the fact that groups within his constituency have differing priorities and preferences. If one group's views are particularly intense, he is likely to respond to those views, even if (as he may or may not be aware) they are not supported by a majority of the electorate.[56] Moreover, different leaders may represent the same constituency in quite different ways, depending on their particular electoral coalition. Such problems are eased in homogeneous districts, which accounts for the fact that U.S congressmen from safe seats are more accurate in their perception of constituency opinion, more confident of that perception, and more often vote in accord with it.[57] (Note that although the propositions of the last few paragraphs are stated in terms of the response of a single representative to his district, they also apply to the response of a political party to its national electorate.)

The flow of information between elites and masses is occasionally so obstructed that it is difficult to speak of elite-mass linkage at all. In 1940–1941 the central issue of American politics was whether or not to enter the war. Yet the best available evidence suggests that during this period nearly two-thirds of the American electorate did not know where their congressman stood on this issue. Conversely, while (according to contemporary survey data) nearly three-quarters of the public favored introducing the draft to prepare the country for war, senatorial mail was running nine-to-one against the draft.[58] In this game of blindman's bluff, it is hard to believe that electoral pressures—or any other mechanism—could have effectively linked elites and masses. Over the last three decades, the increasing use of scientific surveys and the rising levels of political sophistication at the grassroots have probably raised slightly the "signal-to-noise ratio" in elite-mass communications in America and a few other industrialized nations. But any assessment of the significance of electoral linkages between leaders and followers must reckon with the inevitable imperfections in the flow of information.

Elections and Elite Responsiveness   What are we to conclude about elections as a mechanism for linking elites and masses?[59] Some say elections produce *mandates*. For example, in 1906 a victorious British Liberal party pushed through the House of Commons a resolution "That this House, recognizing that in the recent general election the people of the United Kingdom have demonstrated their unqualified fidelity to the principle and

---

[56] For a discussion of the desirability of weighting preferences by intensities, see Dahl, 1956, pp. 90–123, 134–135.

[57] Miller, 1970; Fiorina, 1974.

[58] Key, 1961, pp. 492, 494.

[59] Elite-mass linkage is not the only significant political consequence of elections. See Rose and Mossawir, 1967.

practice of Free Trade, deems it right to record its determination to resist any proposal . . . to create in this country a system of Protection."[60] But in the light of modern survey research it is hard to believe that voters were demonstrating their "unqualified fidelity" to any position on tariffs at all. On specific issues a limited mandate theory may occasionally apply. "Nothing is more important in Capital Hill politics," reports David Mayhew, "than the shared conviction that election returns have proven a point."[61] Yet in general the mandate theory overestimates the importance of issues in determining votes and underestimates the range of decisions that elites must take without benefit of campaign debate.

Elections may, secondly, crystallize mass discontent and accelerate elite circulation. Students of American history have noted the importance of *critical elections*, such as the Roosevelt landslide of 1932, which are

> *short, sharp reorganizations of the mass coalitional bases of the major parties, . . . often preceded by major third-party revolts which reveal the incapacity of "politics as usual" to integrate, much less aggregate, emergent political demand, . . . closely associated with abnormal stress in the socioeconomic system, [and] marked by ideological polarizations and issue-distances between the major parties which are exceptionally large by normal standards.*[62]

Critical elections lead to high elite turnover and major change in the elites' social and generational composition. The new leaders bring with them new issues and new priorities, and they produce new policies.[63] Other examples of critical elections include the British Labour party's victory of 1945 and in the newly independent countries of the Third World the "ruralizing elections" that replaced Westernized elites with leaders more attuned to the newly enfranchised, largely rural electorates.[64]

But critical elections are relatively rare. Normally the significance of elections for elite-mass linkages derives instead from the *rule of anticipated reactions*. Rousseau believed that "the people of England . . . is free only during the election of members of parliament. As soon as they are elected, slavery overtakes it."[65] But he overlooked the subtle effects of the retrospective judgment that voters pass on the accomplishments of the party in power.

The elected official facing a policy decision must anticipate (1) the socioeconomic consequences of his decision; (2) how those consequences might

---

[60] Pomper, 1968, p. 247.

[61] Mayhew, 1974, p. 71.

[62] Burnham, 1970, p. 10.

[63] Brady and Lynn, 1973; King and Seligman, 1974; Brady, 1975.

[64] Elite circulation, both electorally and nonelectorally induced, is discussed in Chapter 7.

[65] Rousseau, 1913, p. 78.

be portrayed by his opponents; (3) how the decision could be defended; and (4) how voters would respond to reality, portrayal and defense.[66] Normally, he may be "free to act as he thinks best because the ordinary citizen is not pounding on his door with demands for action." But where elections are genuine, "his freedom to act is limited by the fact that he believes there *will* be pounding on his door if he does not act in ways that are responsive. . . . [Elected officials] act responsively, not because citizens are actively making demands, but in order to keep them from becoming active."[67] And this operating rule is occasionally confirmed by the unhappy fate of politicians who fail to anticipate voter reactions.[68]

Economic policy neatly illustrates the rule of anticipated reactions. Voters respond sharply to pocketbook issues, and politicians know it. By controlling fiscal and monetary policy and by writing checks for social security and similar programs, modern governments are able to affect the economic circumstances of ordinary citizens. Edward Tufte has shown that in the United States and most other democracies economic conditions pulsate to the rhythm of elections, with real disposable income usually accelerating and unemployment dipping just before the voters are due at the polls.[69]

The rule of anticipated reactions cannot guarantee that mass preferences always guide elite actions in detail. Rather, the electoral sanction undergirds what V. O. Key called the "dikes" of public opinion "which channel public action or which fix a range of discretion within which government may act or within which debate at official levels may proceed."[70] The rigor of this constraint varies from issue to issue and from time to time. When voters are inattentive, as is usually true in foreign affairs, for example, latitude for elite discretion is wide. On more salient topics, such as race relations, the constraints are tighter.[71]

To the immediate material interests of their constituents, most elected officials are exceptionally attentive. They engage in the politics of pork barrel, post office, and parish pump, hoping to win freedom of action where voters are more indifferent. The following description of Turkish politics, if modified only in detail (and perhaps in evaluative overtones), could apply to any electoral democracy:

> *The peasants have been given the vote, and the parties assiduously woo them to secure the award of that vote to their proffered candidates. The reaction of the villagers to variations in policy are elaborately discussed and estimated by political*

[66] Fiorina, 1974, p. 32; Kingdon, 1973, pp. 46–53.

[67] Almond and Verba, 1963, pp. 486–487.

[68] Miller and Stokes, 1963, p. 55; Davidson, 1969, p. 121.

[69] Tufte, 1974, and sources cited there.

[70] Key, 1961, p. 552.

[71] Miller and Stokes, 1963, pp. 51–52; Wildenmann, 1973, p. 7.

> *leaders. . . . There is a great temptation presented to all parties to pander to*
> *short-run peasant greed and political immaturity by promising tax reductions,*
> *fiddling with crop subsidies, incorporating many local potentates into top-level*
> *party and governmental positions, and so on. Fortitude to resist these temptations*
> *. . . has not so far been widely displayed.*[72]

Elections are, of course, *designed* to generate "great temptations" to mollify the masses. An election is like the classic weapon of detective fiction, a massive, blunt instrument. Much elite behavior is virtually unaffected by electoral considerations, but on the major issues of politics, at least in countries with genuine suffrage, "in the last analysis there is no substitute for victory in an election."[73]

Functional Equivalents of Elections   Mass support can be an important resource even in the absence of elections. One of the clearest illustrations is Trotsky's metaphorical analysis of revolution:

> *Only on the basis of a study of political processes in the masses themselves, can we*
> *understand the role of parties and leaders. . . . Without a guiding organization*
> *the energy of the masses would dissipate like steam not enclosed in a piston-box. But*
> *nevertheless what moves things is not the piston or the box, but the steam.*[74]

This dependence of revolutionary leaders on mass support constrains their strategy and tactics. In the apocryphal comment attributed to a French revolutionary, asked why he was chasing a crowd of angry citizens: "I'm their leader, and I must follow them."

Mass unrest and violence can generate powerful incentives for established leaders to respond. A study of the eighteenth-century origins of democracy in France and the United States concluded that "mob action provided the first concrete indication of the common man's claim to participate in the decision-making process which is government, of his demand for a share of political power."[75] During the last decade, mass violence has increased elite attentiveness to Catholics in Ulster, to Red Guards in China, to blacks in America, and to workers in Poland.

Sometimes this process is indirect and triangular, involving protesters, decision makers, and some powerful third party. Urban protesters in the United States in the 1960s tried to shift the balance of power in their favor by activating

---

[72] Frey, 1963, pp. 324–325.

[73] Schattschneider, 1960, p. 58.

[74] Trotsky, 1932, p. xix.

[75] Rudolph, 1959, p. 447.

upper-class sympathizers to whose views the city administration would be more sensitive. In Latin America the threat of strikes and mass violence sometimes forces civilian leaders to conciliate nonelites, not because the leaders fear overthrow by the masses, but because they fear that the military will intervene to restore order and in the process displace them.[76] In both examples, however, the interests of the protesters are not identical to those of the third-party interveners, and the outcome is seldom fully responsive to the protesters' demands.

Albert Hirschman has pointed out that withdrawal of cooperation is occasionally an effective alternative to overt protest—in his terms, *exit* and *voice* are both ways of making leaders respond.[77] Gandhi employed the boycott brilliantly against the British rulers of India. Peasant recalcitrance in the face of excessive demands from the government is common throughout the world. A decline in Communist party membership among students caused the Yugoslav elite to modify the party line. A fall in birthrates led East European governments to establish child-care centers.

These examples also illustrate that even a nonelected elite may sometimes be induced to respond to the nonelite. This fact is important, because in much of the world today the relative power of elected assemblies is declining vis-à-vis such nonelected elites as the senior civil service, the military, and various public and private economic elites. The impact of elections on the responsiveness of such elites is at best indirect, and it is attenuated by the inability of elected officials to supervise in detail all the activities of these other elites. Whether nonelites can influence nonelected elites depends significantly on the several other sorts of linkages to which we now turn.

INTERMEDIARY INSTITUTIONS AS LINKAGES

Most political systems have an array of formal and informal institutions that convey followers' wishes to leaders. Among the most prominent of these are political parties, interest groups, and patron-client networks.

Political Parties   Disciplined, well-organized parties can improve the effectiveness of the electoral linkage by mitigating problems of ambition, competition, and information. Where candidates run as party representatives, ambition is institutionalized, so to speak, because of the parties' permanent interest in electoral victory and hence in electoral credibility. Where disciplined parties confront each other in a single nationwide battle, rather than

---

[76] Lipsky, 1968; Payne, 1965. For a rather different example of how nonelite support can be a power resource in an authoritarian polity, see Tuohy and Ronfeldt, 1969.

[77] Hirschman, 1970.

in a series of constituency-by-constituency skirmishes, an absence of competition locally can be redressed nationally. Finally, party labels can simplify the voter's information processing. Where ideological cohesion and party discipline ensure distinctive electoral options and predictable legislative behavior, the citizen can vote for a party ticket with reasonable confidence that the candidate he has chosen will forward the program he prefers. In such a system leaders are selected by, and are responsive to, the party organization, which in turn is selected by, and is responsive to, its electorate. Responsiveness on a constituency-by-constituency basis is sacrificed in favor of national responsiveness and clear accountability. Politics in much of Western Europe is organized in this way.[78]

Elements of this theory of responsible party government apply even to the relatively disorderly American party system. Republican and Democratic elites diverge on many socioeconomic issues, and these differences are predictably reflected in their behavior when in power. Party platforms contain distinctive positions, and, historically, the victorious party has usually implemented most of its platform sooner or later. To some extent American voters, too, can reliably promote more conservative or more progressive government by their choice of party.[79]

The political party may also constitute a nexus of loyalty and communication that links leaders and followers independently of the electoral process. The mass parties of Western Europe promote elite-mass communication through party conferences, party newspapers, and organizational and informal contacts. As Michels stressed, information and persuasion flows more often downward than upward through these channels. But European party leaders are usually more exposed than are their American counterparts to pressure from party members at the grassroots. American parties once had a richer organizational life and a more important place in political recruitment, but throughout this century the role of party as a linkage between elites and nonelites in America has declined.[80]

Communist regimes often claim that the party is the main link between leaders and masses. Certainly it is true that officials in these countries are chosen by, and are accountable to, the party. We have virtually no microscopic evidence on the responsiveness, in turn, of the party to the grassroots. It seems doubtful,

---

[78] Barnes and Farah, 1972; Daalder and Rusk, 1972; Budge, Brand, Margolis, and Smith, 1972, pp. 80–124; Holmberg, 1974; Powell, 1974; Frasure, 1971; Schwarz, 1975.

[79] Sullivan and O'Connor, 1972; Erikson and Luttbeg, 1973, pp. 291–297; Pomper, 1968, pp. 149–203; Pomper, 1969. Miller and Stokes (1963) and Miller (1970) found evidence that party played a role in linking congressmen and constituents on issues involving socioeconomic welfare. On the theory of responsible party government, see Ranney and Kendall, 1956, and American Political Science Association, 1950.

[80] MacRae, 1967, pp. 322, 333–334; Steiner, 1972, pp. 258–271; Rose, 1962; Burnham, 1970; Seligman and King, 1970.

however, that an institution designed primarily for mobilization and even coercion of nonelites could also serve effectively to transmit information and pressure upward.[81] Certainly, the absence of electoral competition removes a prime sanction that inhibits oligarchy in Western political parties.

Communist parties are not all organized identically from the point of view of elite-mass linkages. The Leninist model heavily emphasizes centralization, discipline, and the role of the party elite. Mao's "mass line," on the other hand, reflects his commitment to peasant populism, his antipathy toward bureaucratic or intellectual elitism, and his belief that mobilization of the masses is a precondition for completing the revolution. The spontaneous articulation of demands by nonelites is more legitimate in Maoism than in Leninism, although in both systems the aggregation of those demands into policy remains in the hands of the elite.[82]

Interest Groups   Historically, this linkage evolved from the medieval institution of petitions to the monarch. A desire to safeguard this channel of access to the elite led the writers of the U.S. Constitution to provide that "Congress shall make no law . . . abridging . . . the right of the people . . . to petition the Government for a redress of grievances." In the modern world, organized interest groups have multiplied beyond measure —from Indian caste associations and the Federation of German Industry to the Catholic church and the Royal Society for the Prevention of Cruelty to Animals. Countless case studies have described the transactional relationship between interest groups and governmental elites, the groups providing information, cooperation, and political support, in return for more satisfactory public policy.[83]

Authoritarian regimes, too, often allow some leeway for organized public pressure, but only through "official channels." The corporatist regimes of the Mediterranean and of Latin America have conveyed mass demands through government-controlled agencies, leaving citizens little opportunity to express demands at odds with official policy. In Stalin's Russia, trade unions and other associations served, in his words, as "transmission belts," but they transmitted pressure mainly downward.

Recently, Jerry Hough has offered an alternative interpretation of contemporary Soviet politics that

> assumes that the institutional forces are at least somewhat responsive to broader societal forces. It includes an image of bureaucratic officials as men who are driven to represent many of the interests of their clientele and low-level subordinates, as

[81] On the inverse relationship between information and coercion in political systems, see Apter, 1965, p. 40.

[82] Townsend, 1974, pp. 75–77, 226–228, and works cited there; see also Schram, 1973.

[83] Beer, 1957; Truman, 1951; Wootton, 1969.

well as an image of politicians as men who take the danger of popular unrest into account as they mediate conflicts among the political participants.[84]

This model of institutional pluralism correctly recognizes that power in the Soviet Union today is not strictly monopolized by the elite in the Kremlin. But the closed character of bureaucratic politics inevitably limits the ability of private citizens to intervene.

Even in more open polities, interest groups may distort the flow of information and pressure from nonelites to elites. In the first place, many citizens and many interests are unrepresented in the world of pressure groups. Organizational membership is relatively rare among the poor and uneducated; this bias, though found in all countries, is particularly sharp in the United States.[85] In Schattschneider's famous barb at those who exalt this channel for elite-mass communication: "The flaw in the pluralist heaven is that the heavenly chorus sings with a strong upper-class accent. Probably about 90 percent of the people cannot get into the pressure system."[86]

Moreover, pressure groups, like parties, are subject to Michels' ubiquitous "iron law." The activities of organized groups are more likely to reflect the interests and preferences of the active minority directing the organization than of the membership at large. Although autonomous interest groups can provide an important auxiliary channel for nonelite influence, they cannot ensure an egalitarian distribution of that influence.

Patron-Client Networks   Whereas parties and pressure groups provide formally organized, impersonal links between elites and masses, the patron-client tie is based instead on a personal bond between two individuals.

The distinguishing feature of archetypal patron-client relationships is a broad but imprecise spectrum of mutual obligations consistent with the belief that the patron should display an almost parental concern for and responsiveness to the needs of his client, and that the latter should display almost filial loyalty to his patron.[87]

Clientelism originates in traditional, agricultural societies where physical and economic insecurity is very great. The patron-client tie is based on the feudal relationship of authority and exchange between landlord and tenant. In return for personal fealty to his patron, the client receives material benefits and protec-

[84] Hough, 1972, p. 29.

[85] Kim, Nie, and Verba, 1973.

[86] Schattschneider, 1960, p. 35.

[87] Landé, 1973, p. 105.

tion from a threatening outside world. Loyalty and obligation flow vertically rather than horizontally.

The rise of the modern state and the growth of mass suffrage modify, but by no means eliminate, clientelism. As the authoritative allocation of values becomes more centralized, patron-client pairs are chained together into networks linking the center and the periphery of society. During the late nineteenth century in Italy, for example, "the administration of the state became a gigantic spoils system for the benefit of political clientele."[88] The patron becomes, in the words of a study of American urban politics, "ambassador to the outside world."[89]

As the forms of electoral democracy appear, the ballot becomes part of the currency of the patron-client transaction. The party machine makes its appearance, and party boss replaces local notable as patron. National politics is organized around vertically structured clienteles, often institutionalized as factions within the dominant party, as, for example, the Liberal Democratic party of Japan, the Christian Democratic party of Italy, and the Congress party of India. Clientelistic and factional networks come to include members of parliament, civil servants, and members of the economic elite, so that the reciprocal flow of patronage and political support runs from the grassroots to the highest institutions of state and society. For the citizen, little may have changed from the traditional pattern when "the alternative to joining a clientele was to be totally powerless."[90]

Thus, the modern patron is essentially a broker between his clients and the larger political system—he trades blocks of votes for blocks of patronage in the national arena and distributes that patronage in the form of individual favors. The client continues to supply personal allegiance and political support, while the patron now mediates between his client and the anonymous state, obtaining for him jobs, licenses, welfare payments, and other material benefits, and providing protection from the apparently random depredations of officialdom. Figure 6–3, adapted from Blank's description of Venezuelan politics, is an apt summary of similar findings in Japan, Greece, Chile, the Philippines, Italy, and India, in addition, of course, to urban America in the late nineteenth and early twentieth centuries.[91]

Patron-client ties can sometimes provide personalized elite responsiveness to nonelites. However, this type of linkage has two grave deficiencies. First,

---

[88] Graziano, 1973, p. 15.

[89] Gans, 1964, as excerpted in Luttbeg, 1968, pp. 432–442; the Luttbeg book provides an excellent selection of readings on problems of elite-mass linkage in American politics.

[90] Graziano, 1973, p. 12; see also LaPalombara, 1964.

[91] Blank, 1973, p. 100 (illustration); Nakane, 1970; Legg, 1969; Valenzuela, 1976; Grossholtz, 1964; Graziano, 1973; Zuckerman, 1975; Bailey, 1963. For useful introductions to the rapidly growing literature on political clientelism, see Scott, 1969, and Lemarchand and Legg, 1972.

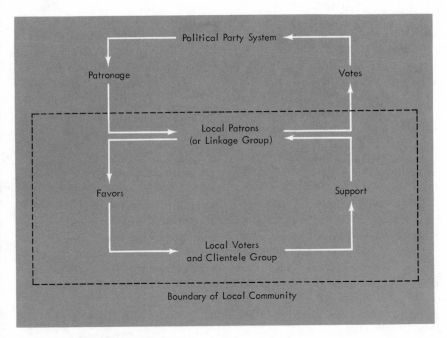

Figure 6–3   Patron-Client Linkages
Source: Adapted from Blank, 1973, p. 100. Copyright © 1973 by Little, Brown and Company, Inc.
Reprinted by permission.

whether in South America or South Chicago, the patron-client relationship is fundamentally asymmetric. The patron occupies a distinctly superior position, leaving the client in the role of supplicant. Second, patron-client transactions typically provide particularistic, rather than universalistic benefits. The patron offers favors, not policies. Indeed, clientalism may insulate elites from demands for programmatic changes that might benefit large classes of people and thereby threaten the political and socioeconomic status quo.[92]

Patrons, interest group leaders, and party militants are all "middlemen of politics."[93] Classical elite theorists noted the importance of this intermediate political stratum, "a bridge between the core of decision-makers and the rest of society, [mediating] between the rulers and the ruled by transmitting information in either direction and by providing explanations and justifications for elite

[92] Nakane (1972, pp. 103, 149–151) attributes both Japan's rapid, successful state-directed modernization and the conservative, oligarchic nature of contemporary Japanese politics to the vertical structuring of Japanese society. For an excellent comparison of dyadic networks and modern associations as elite-mass linkages, see Landé, 1973.

[93] Marvick, 1968b.

policy."[94] These theorists emphasized the downward flow of influence from elites to masses, and thus anticipated the so-called two-step-flow theory of interpersonal influence, according to which ideas flow from elites to masses via a layer of "opinion leaders."[95] However, there may also be a reverse two-step flow, for activists can transmit ideas upward as well. Leaders are often influenced by the demands and perspectives of the attentive public. Whether that relationship creates a linkage between elites and masses depends in turn on how well the activists represent the views of ordinary citizens.[96]

ELITE VALUES AND ELITE-MASS LINKAGE

As Mosca noted, elites need to believe that their political might is founded on moral right. Wherever the political formula refers to the welfare of the masses, leaders will feel psychological pressure to attend to the wants and needs of followers. Most forms of traditional legitimacy include some element of *noblesse oblige* or paternalism, even when the structure of rule was oligarchic; and some notion of popular sovereignty appears in the political formulas of most contemporary political systems.

The most persuasive application of this theory to liberal democracies was offered by V. O. Key:

> *The longer one frets with the puzzle of how democratic regimes manage to function, the more plausible it appears that a substantial part of the explanation is to be found in the motives that actuate the leadership echelon, the values that it holds, in the rules of the political game to which it adheres, in the expectations which it entertains about its own status in society, and perhaps in some of the objective circumstances, both material and institutional, in which it functions.*[97]

As we saw in Chapter 4, in the parliamentary democracies of the West these rules of the game require, above all, due regard for the wishes of the citizens and respect for the right to oppose incumbent elites.

This code of political ethics is diffused within the elite by a process of socialization.

> *These political actors constitute in effect a subculture with its own peculiar set of norms of behavior, motives, and approved standards. Processes of indoctrination*

[94] G. Parry, 1969, p. 33.

[95] Katz and Lazarsfeld, 1955.

[96] Compare Verba and Nie, 1972, pp. 332–333.

[97] Key, 1961, p. 537.

> internalize such norms among those who are born to or climb to positions of power
> and leadership; they serve as standards of action, which are reinforced by a social
> discipline among the political activists.[98]

A similar mechanism may operate in communist systems. For example, Mao's classic statement of the mass line explains that

> in all the practical work of our Party, all correct leadership is necessarily "from the
> masses, to the masses." This means: take the ideas of the masses (scattered and
> unsystematic ideas) and concentrate them (through study turn them into concen-
> trated and systematic ideas), then go to the masses and propagate and explain these
> ideas until the masses embrace them as their own, hold fast to them and translate
> them into action, and test the correctness of these ideas in such action. Then once
> again concentrate ideas from the masses and once again go to the masses so that the
> ideas are persevered in and carried through. And so on, over and over again in an
> endless spiral, with the ideas becoming more correct, more vital and richer each
> time.[99]

Such institutions as *hsia fang*, cadre schools, and mutual criticism sessions between leaders and masses are designed to perpetuate leaders' commitment to the mass line, but as Carl Riskin has pointed out, "the pressure to maintain mass-line relationships comes largely from above."[100]

The degree of concordance between mass preferences and elite actions is doubtless in part a function of elite values. But there are three difficulties with this account of elite responsiveness. First, the practical implications of values are almost always ambiguous. Mao inveighs against "commandism," "bureau-cratism," and "isolationism" (of elites from masses), but also against "tail-ism." Western political philosophy contains an analogous dilemma: Should a democra-tic leader act in accord with his constituents' expressed *wants*, or should he act on his own interpretation of their real *needs*? Liberalism generally assumes that wants and needs will coincide, because citizens normally know what is best for themselves. But theorists as diverse as Rousseau, Burke, and Lenin have denied this assumption.[101] Who is to judge what behavior is required in a particular case? If the answer is that the elite must decide, then the welfare of the masses remains, quite literally, at the mercy of the elite.

The second difficulty has frequently recurred in our discussion of linkages—the problem of information. Even if a leader is wholeheartedly com-

---

[98] Key, 1961, p. 537.

[99] Mao, 1965, p. 119.

[100] Riskin, 1971, p. 27; Pfeffer, 1972.

[101] Pitkin, 1967, pp. 144–208.

mitted to fulfilling the desires of his followers, his success can be no greater than the accuracy of his information on those desires. Reliance on the reverse two-step flow means responsiveness to a restricted constituency, whether organizational activists in America or party cadres in China.

Finally, in the absence of structured incentives for elite responsiveness, such as the electoral sanction, elite values seem a fragile link. John Stuart Mill put this point clearly:

> Rulers in the ruling classes are under a necessity of considering the interests of those who have the suffrage; but of those who are excluded, it is in their option whether they will do so or not, and however honestly disposed, they are in general too fully occupied with things they must attend to, to have much room in their thoughts for anything which they can with impunity disregard.[102]

In the short run, elite values can mean that elite responsiveness is not dependent on direct, immediate, and continuous sanction. Most British politicians, for example, believe that members of Parliament should help individual constituents with problems of housing, pensions, and so on. Support for this norm does not depend on the members' own electoral margin; those in safe seats are as committed to it as those whose seats are in jeopardy.[103] Elite values can thus serve as a kind of moral flywheel. Ultimately, however, unless torque is applied in the form of sanctions against unresponsive behavior, leaders are likely, when faced with a discrepancy between their own interests and those of their followers, to favor the former. Such is the melancholy lesson of history.

COMPARING LINKAGE MECHANISMS

As we have seen, if elites are to respond to nonelites, elites must know what nonelites want, and they must have some reason for responding. Moreover, if elite responsiveness is to be reasonably democratic, each citizen must have the same chance of being heard as any other. Linkage mechanisms differ in the extent to which they meet these three conditions of *information, incentives,* and *equality*.[104] For example, anomic rioting and some types of "exit" generate strong pressures for responsiveness, but relatively little information about what is wanted. On the other hand, patron-client ties and Mao's mass-line techniques often generate detailed information about the wishes of the nonelites, but relatively weak sanctions for conforming to them. Pressure groups can produce both copious information and intense incentives, but access to this mechanism is

---

[102] Mill, 1962, p. 144.

[103] Unpublished data from the survey reported in Putnam, 1973*a*.

[104] Compare Verba and Nie, 1972, pp. 323–333.

unequally distributed. Both opinion polls and polling booths are in principle egalitarian, but survey results bind no one, and electoral outcomes are notoriously uninformative. Other things being equal, a good elite-mass linkage will rank high on all three dimensions, but as these examples illustrate, other things are rarely equal.

MOBILIZATION AND THE ELITE-MASS GAP

Modernization universally requires the dissolving of traditional orientations and the mobilization of mass energies. Mobilization can occur from the bottom up or from the top down. In what J. P. Nettl terms "stalagmite mobilization," the primary initiative occurs at the nonelite level. On the other hand, top-down or "stalactite mobilization" is particularly common where leaders have firm notions about the proper direction for social change. But effective mobilization is always interactive, as suggested in Mao's maxim for party cadres dealing with peasants: "Listen-teach-listen-teach."[105] In many countries of the Third World, modernization is thwarted by the fact that the elite, though relatively immune from mass influence, is itself unable to mobilize its subjects in a process of controlled change, because of what is commonly termed the "elite-mass gap."

As we have seen in Chapters 2 and 4, elite-mass disparities in socialization exist in all societies. However, this elite-mass gap is particularly marked in less developed countries. Movements toward independence and modernization in these traditional, rural societies have usually been led by Western-educated, urban, upper-middle-class men and women. Formal education is most common among elites precisely in those countries in which formal education is least common among nonelites. In many of these countries, too, elites and masses are divided linguistically, the elites speaking English or French, the masses a babel of local languages.[106]

These disparities often result in distinctive elite and nonelite political cultures. Ordinary citizens tend to be traditional and parochial in outlook, while the elites are secular-minded, modernist, and cosmopolitan. Such leaders are ill equipped to respond to real problems at the grassroots, and politics tends to be court politics. The elite extracts taxes and services from the nonelite but does not attempt to mobilize them for collective goals. Intraelite conflict is personalistic and largely unrelated to broader social problems and tensions. Examples of this extreme pattern include Morocco, Ethiopia under Haile Selassie, and medieval Europe.[107]

This problem can be remedied at least in part by the emergence of

---

[105] Nettl, 1967, p. 271; see also Solomon, 1969.

[106] Weiner, 1965*b*, pp. 60–62; Shils, 1962; Kothari, 1970, pp. 40, 325.

[107] Waterbury, 1970; Jackson, 1970.

intermediary infrastructures that can transmit information and political pressures both upward and downward. In such countries as Japan, India, and Tunisia, effective modernization has been speeded by cadres of local politicians, less bound by tradition than the masses, but less alienated from local reality than the national leaders.[108] In addition, in many postindependence societies one consequence of this elite-mass gap is the progressive parochialization of national elites. We will examine this type of elite transformation in Chapter 7.

---

[108] Silberman, 1964; Kothari, 1970, pp. 127, 421; Quandt, 1970, pp. 186–187. See also Kornhauser, 1959, on the importance of intermediary structures between elites and masses.

ELITE
TRANSFORMATION
7

"History is the graveyard of aristocracies," wrote Pareto. In the long sweep of history nothing is more dramatic than the decline and fall of ruling groups and their replacement by new men of power. Elite transformation was of particular concern to the classical elite theorists, for they believed that the key to the riddles of historical change lay not in technological and economic trends (as their great antagonist Marx had argued), but rather in metamorphoses of the political elite. Indeed, Mosca claimed that "one could explain the whole history of civilized mankind in terms of the conflict between the attempt of rulers to monopolize and bequeath political power and the attempt of new forces to change the relations of power."[1] The link between elite transformation and broader social trends is complex, as we shall see, but most scholars agree that changes in the composition of political elites can provide a crucial diagnostic of the basic tides of history.

In principle one could examine change over time in each of the characteristics of political elites discussed in this volume—the shape of the pyramid of participation and power, the patterns of recruitment of political leaders, their beliefs and ideologies, their linkages to nonelites, and so on. In practice, however, most students of elite transformation have concentrated, first, on the social origins of elites and, second, on the skills of elites, for these seem the primary points of conjunction with broader historical change.

Methodological caution is especially necessary when studying elite transformation, for changes in the political process may alter the significance of institutionally defined roles. The House of Commons did not have the same significance under Elizabeth I and Elizabeth II, for example, and a heedless comparison of the changing characteristics of members of Parliament between the sixteenth century and the twentieth century might be misleading. Or again,

---

[1] Mosca, 1939, as cited in Dahrendorf, 1959, p. 198.

trade union leaders would not be counted among the top elites of nineteenth-century Western Europe, nor party bureaucrats in tsarist Russia, but these roles are obviously central in the maps of the respective national elites today. We must remain sensitive to the implications of such changes in the framework of politics.

How, then, does the composition of the political elite change? And still more intriguing, why? For if leaders are by definition more powerful than other groups in society, what could possibly explain their periodic displacement? This chapter begins with a brief review of several theories of elite transformation. We shall then turn to three historical case studies: (1) the impact of the industrial revolution on West European and American elites during the nineteenth and twentieth centuries; (2) the impact of nationalist and Communist revolutions on elites in this century; and (3) the impact of technology and bureaucratization on contemporary elites and the possible emergence of a technocratic, "post industrial" society.

THEORIES
OF
ELITE
TRANSFORMATION

SOCIAL PSYCHOLOGY

Pareto's theory of "elite circulation" rested on an analysis of the varying talents and psychological traits of leaders. Just as leading pickpockets are unusually light-fingered, he argued, members of the political elite are skilled in the techniques of power. But by a law of social decadence or entropy, elites tend to dissipate their talents, while at the same time a few forceful and talented individuals appear among the nonelite. Unless these gifted newcomers are allowed to displace "the degenerate elements" within the elite, accumulating tensions may lead to a violent revolution in which the decadent elite is entirely supplanted by a new, more vigorous group.

Pareto added another dynamic element to this theory. He distinguished two psychic types of elites—"lions" and "foxes"—and argued that they tend to alternate in power. The cunning foxes retain power for some time by their cleverness in forming and reforming coalitions, but "force is also essential to the exercise of government." Eventually a more forceful counterelite of lions, willing to use coercion and violence, capture power from the fainthearted foxes and impose order and discipline. In time, however, the intellectual incompetence and inflexibility of the lions lead to their gradual decline and infiltration by more imaginative foxes.

Pareto's theory has a certain plausibility. Something of the fox-lion-fox cycle seems exemplified in the displacement of the Greek parliamentary elite in

1967 by military strongmen and the colonels' subsequent fall in 1974, after a series of economic and diplomatic blunders. Moreover, the idea that revolution is born from a discrepancy between political skill and political status is strikingly confirmed by some evidence we will examine later.

Nevertheless, Pareto's theory of elite transformation is deficient in several important respects. First, it obscures the critical distinction between two quite different types of elite circulation—on the one hand, the rise and fall of individuals and, on the other hand, the rise and fall of social categories. Individual turnover is clearly an important issue, as we discussed in Chapter 3. But if incumbent and successor are basically similar, so that the social composition of the elite remains constant, we hardly want to speak of elite transformation.

Second, by emphasizing psychological traits and cyclical dynamics ("circulation"), Pareto's theory cannot account for historical changes in the sociological complexion of elites, particularly when these changes are acyclic. For example, the steady decline of the landed aristocracy in Western Europe over the last two centuries can hardly be explained in Paretian terms. Third, Pareto's theory risks violating the cardinal scientific principle of falsifiability. Because many key terms are vaguely defined, it is difficult to see what evidence could conceivably disconfirm this theory, and a theory which can explain anything really explains nothing.[2]

SOCIOECONOMIC FORCES

The links between elite transformation and social change are more directly traced in the theories of both Marx and Mosca. Marx argued that the composition of the political elite is a direct consequence of patterns of socioeconomic power. Those who own the means of production—land in an agricultural economy, machines in an industrial economy—constitute thereby a ruling class. Changes in the composition of the ruling class are a function of changes in the social structure, which, in turn, are determined by changes in the means of production. Inexorably, one ruling class is overturned by another, as technical and economic progress enfeebles the one and exalts the other. Thus, in its pure form the Marxist theory is remarkably parsimonious: technological change → economic change → social change → elite transformation.[3]

Like Pareto (and unlike Marx), Mosca believed that revolution could be forestalled by the timely admission into the elite of the ablest members of the

---

[2] On Pareto's theory, see Bottomore, 1964, pp. 42–48; G. Parry, 1969, pp. 60–63; and S. E. Finer's "Introduction" to Pareto, 1966.

[3] Classical Marxism also argued that with the advent of communism the political dominance of the few over the many ceases forever, but, as many subsequent theorists have noted, this more problematic thesis was not entirely consistent with Marx's fundamental theory of elite transformation. For a useful discussion of Marxism and elitism, see Bottomore, 1964, especially pp. 18–26.

lower classes. But like Marx (and unlike Pareto), Mosca found the origin of elite transformation (either evolutionary or revolutionary) not in elite psychology, but in the rise of new social forces:

> As soon as there is a shift in the balance of political forces . . . then the manner in which the ruling class is constituted changes also. If a new source of wealth develops in a society, if the practical importance of knowledge grows, if an old religion declines or a new one is born, if a new current of ideas spreads, then, simultaneously, far-reaching dislocations occur in the ruling class.[4]

By including intellectual and political influences, Mosca's theory is more eclectic and less crisp than Marx's economic determinism, but at the same time Mosca's theory more easily encompasses the diversity of elite transformations that history records.

SOCIAL NEEDS

An alternative perspective on elite transformation, to some extent complementary to the theories of Marx and Mosca, stresses the changing functional needs of society. According to this thesis,

> strategic elites move into ascendancy when their functions do likewise. . . . The rank order of elites, therefore, is generally determined by the types of problems confronting a society, the priority accorded to these, and the functional and moral solutions proposed to solve them.[5]

Functional explanations for elite transformation remain theoretically vacuous, however, without an objective specification of the needs of a particular society and a convincing explanation of how these needs change. Some versions of this thesis risk logical circularity, as in C. Wright Mills' suggestion that the relative importance of different elites in American politics "depends upon 'the tasks of the period' as they, the elite, define them."[6] Why this elite? Because this task. But why this task? Because this elite.

This logical trap can be avoided only if the functional theory specifies that the needs of a society respond to factors not directly controlled by the elite itself. One such theory has been offered by Joseph Schumpeter, who argued that "the

---

[4] Mosca, 1939, p. 65. On Mosca's interpretation of elite transformation, see Meisel, 1962, and Bottomore, 1964, pp. 26–27, 50–51.

[5] Keller, 1963, pp. 125–126; see also Mosca, 1939, pp. 65–66.

[6] Mills, 1956, p. 277.

position of each class in the total national structure depends, on the one hand, on the significance that is attributed to [its] function, and on the other hand, on the degree to which the class successfully performs the function." To illustrate, Schumpeter recalled the political preeminence of warriors in medieval Germany, when constant warfare and the need for physical protection put a premium on military prowess. Gradually, however, "physical, armed combat ceased to be a mode of life," and the emergence of an agricultural economy increased the functional importance of estate management. Consequently, power flowed from the warriors to the landed gentry.[7]

What of the staying power of older elites? Schumpeter recognized that "every class that has once enjoyed an elevated position is greatly aided in seizing on new functions, because the sources and gains of its prior function survive for some time." But he conceded that "this fact . . . constitutes a severe limitation on the explanatory value of the relationship between class and function," for it raises the possibility that functional changes will not invariably produce elite transformation.[8]

On the other hand, older elites may fail to respond to new circumstances. Henri Pirenne illustrated this possibility by the succession of economic elites in Europe from the eleventh to the nineteenth century:

> At every change in economic organization we find a breach of continuity. It is as if the capitalists who have up to that time been active recognize that they are incapable of adapting themselves to conditions which are evoked by needs hitherto unknown and which call for methods hitherto unemployed. . . . In their place arise new men, courageous and enterprising, who boldly permit themselves to be driven by the wind actually blowing and who know how to trim their sails to take advantage of it.[9]

If functional explanations of elite transformation are to meet the criterion of falsifiability, the "needs" of a given society must be specified rigorously and independently. This problem has severely hampered functional analysis in the social sciences, but it may be partially resolved by defining functions in terms of organizational or economic or technological requirements.[10] Despite their logical difficulties, functional explanations for elite transformation are extremely common, as our three case studies shall show.

[7] Schumpeter, 1951, pp. 176–208 (quotations from pp. 180, 194).

[8] Schumpeter, 1951, p. 198.

[9] Pirenne, 1914, in Bendix and Lipset, 1966, p. 97.

[10] On functional analysis, see Gregor, 1968, and Stinchcombe, 1968, pp. 80–101.

POLITICAL FACTORS

Some scholars have also suggested that political factors can have a direct impact on elite transformation. Modifications in recruitment channels, selectorates, and credentials can influence the composition of political elites independently of changes in socioeconomic forces or functions. Mass suffrage and competitive elections, for example, appear often to have a "democratizing" effect on the characteristics of elected elites. One dramatic illustration, outlined in Figure 7–1, is the emergence of a black political elite in the American south in the 1970s,

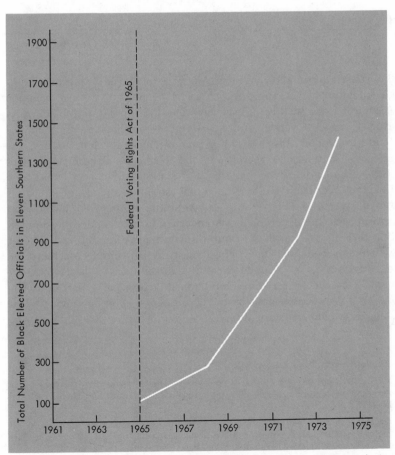

Figure 7–1   The Extension of Suffrage and Transformation of Elites: The Case of Blacks in the American South
Source: Joint Center for Political Studies, 1975, and earlier volumes in that series.

following the extension of voting rights to previously disenfranchised black voters.[11]

In nonelectoral contexts, too, elite transformation can sometimes be traced to political factors. The changes embodied in the Communist and nationalist revolutions discussed later in this chapter are explicable more easily in political than in socioeconomic terms. Another example: For more than five centuries in Ming and Ch'ing China (1368–1912), the social composition of the Mandarin elite was closely tied to the dynastic cycle. During the war and turmoil surrounding the collapse of one dynasty and the emergence of another, the rate of upward mobility of commoners into the elite rose sharply, even though the socioeconomic structure remained essentially unchanged.[12]

A GLOBAL TREND?

Students of elite transformation have long sought some simple uniformity underlying the kaleidoscopic complexities of social change. The most common hypothesis postulates a worldwide, secular trend from tradition to modernity, from particularism to universalism, from ascription to achievement. Evidence can be found to support this thesis. For example, over the last century, the significance of kinship for elite recruitment has steadily declined in such countries as the Netherlands, France, the United States, Turkey, Sri Lanka, and Japan.[13] On the other hand, we have seen that ascription and achievement are blended in all systems of elite recruitment, from the most ancient to the most modern. Moreover, the experience of Mandarin China calls into question any assumption that history can flow in one direction only, for during the three centuries before the collapse of the Ch'ing dynasty in 1912, intellectual merit was increasingly replaced by parental wealth and status as a basis for elite recruitment.[14] The theory of a single grand transition from particularistic ascription to universalistic, achievement-based recruitment is at best a rough guide to the parameters of elite transformation.

---

[11] See also Campbell and Feagin, 1975.

[12] Marsh, 1961, pp. 160–164; Ho, 1962, pp. 215–219. On the relation between political and socioeconomic determinants of elite transformation, see Prewitt and Stone, 1973, pp. 178–182.

[13] Dogan and Scheffer-van der Veen, 1957–1958, pp. 114–123; Dogan, 1961, pp. 83–85; Clubok, Berghorn, and Wilensky, 1969; Szyliowicz, 1971, pp. 391–397; Singer, 1964, especially pp. 8–21, 35–47, 148–149; Silberman, 1964, especially pp. 108–117.

[14] Ho, 1962, pp. 107–125, 262–266; Marsh, 1961, pp. 160–162.

LONGER
WAVES
OF CHANGE:
THE CASE
OF
INDUSTRIALIZATION

THE INDUSTRIAL REVOLUTION AND EUROPEAN ELITES

During the nineteenth and early twentieth centuries Western Europe and the United States experienced the most thoroughgoing socioeconomic transformation in world history—the transition from an agricultural to an industrial society. The impact of the industrial revolution was felt on nearly every aspect of social, cultural, and political life, but not least significant among its consequences were changes in the character of national political leadership.

Social scientists since Marx have sought to understand the general impact of industrialization by examining its impact in Great Britain, its country of origin. Preindustrial Britain was ruled by an aristocratic oligarchy rooted in the land. Agriculture formed the basis of the English economy into the eighteenth century, and possession of the land was astonishingly concentrated. As late as 1873 just 4,217 proprietors—0.23 percent of the agricultural work force—owned nearly 60 percent of the arable land of England and Wales.[15] The economic strength of this landed elite was buttressed by its legitimacy as the traditional ruling class—"the chain that connects the ages of the nation," declared Edmund Burke.

With the onset of the industrial revolution in the late eighteenth century the economic importance of agriculture began a long, slow decline. After a brief burst of rural prosperity during the Napoleonic wars, this descent would continue virtually unbroken for the next 100 years. By 1830 barely one-quarter of British national income derived from agriculture. These economic changes and their consequences for the political role of the landowning aristocracy are traced statistically in Figure 7–2.

Large landholders had by tradition virtually monopolized positions in the House of Commons (and, of course, in the House of Lords as well). This monopoly had been marginally eroded by the entrance of merchants and lawyers throughout the eighteenth century. Nonetheless, at the passage of the First Reform Bill in 1832, granting the vote to the upper middle classes, three-quarters of the members of Parliament were landed gentry. Their numerical

[15] Guttsman, 1963, pp. 128–129.

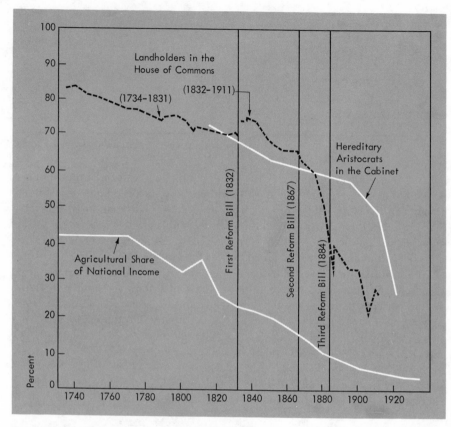

Figure 7–2   The Decline of Landowning Elites in Britain
Sources: Judd, 1955, pp. 71, 88–89; Jennings, 1940, p. 37; Thomas, 1958, pp. 14–15, 28–30; Laski, 1928, pp. 16–21; Deane and Cole, 1967, pp. 156–157, 166; Mitchell and Deane, 1962, p. 366. The graph for the House of Commons is broken at 1832 because two different statistical series must be joined at that point.

importance continued to decline steadily but slowly. Yet in 1867, when the Second Reform Bill extended suffrage to the urban artisan class, still nearly two-thirds of the House of Commons were large landowners, and, conversely, more than half of the nation's largest landowners sat in the House of Commons.[16]

During the next two decades, however, the landowners' share in the elite plummeted. By 1884, when virtually universal manhood suffrage was introduced, they constituted barely one-third of the House of Commons. (By this time, however, agriculture provided less than one-tenth of British national

[16] Guttsman, 1974, p. 25.

income.) Thereafter, the landowners' decline continued more slowly, interrupted only occasionally by the swings of the party pendulum between the Conservative party (where the landowners were concentrated) and the Liberal party (where the industrial classes found readier acceptance). By World War I landowners constituted roughly a quarter of the House of Commons.

At the top of the political hierarchy the social composition of the cabinet, too, showed the much delayed effects of the industrial revolution. The hereditary aristocracy—a still smaller socioeconomic elite within the landowning class—had supplied three-quarters of the cabinet in the years before the First

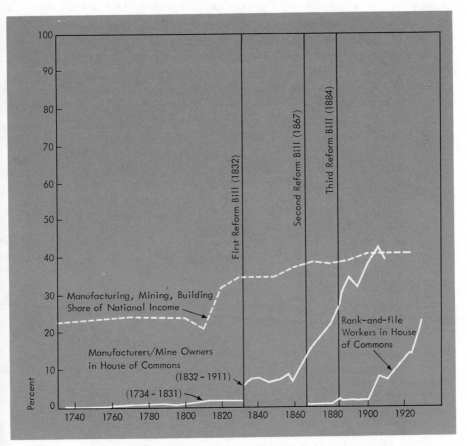

Figure 7–3   The Rise of Industrial Elites in Britain
Sources: Deane and Cole, 1967, pp. 156–157, 166; Mitchell and Deane, 1962, p. 366; Judd, 1955, pp. 71, 88–89; Jennings, 1940, pp. 37, 41; Thomas, 1958, pp. 14–15, 28–30. The graph for the House of Commons is broken at 1832 because two different statistical series must be joined at that point.

Reform Bill.[17] Their share drifted slowly downward during the next half century, reaching 60 percent in 1885. Only then began the plunge in aristocratic domination of the cabinet, nearly a quarter century after the comparable drop in landed representation in the House of Commons. After World War I the aristocracy's average share of cabinet seats leveled off at approximately 20 percent.

This century-long decline of elites rooted in preindustrial institutions was paralleled by the rise of new elites whose power was founded in the factories and mines of industrial Britain. As shown in Figure 7–3, the importance of mining and manufacturing to the British economy surged upward in the decade after the Napoleonic wars, and by 1830 this sector had achieved a clear and widening lead over agriculture. Nevertheless, for the next three decades manufacturers and mine owners constituted a virtually invisible 5 to 8 percent of the political elite in Parliament. Beginning with the election of 1859, however, and continuing for the next half century, their share in the House of Commons skyrocketed, passing the landowners in the election of 1900 and reaching a peak of 42 percent in 1906. The numbers of industrialists in Parliament then drifted lower for at least the next seven decades.[18]

The appearance of cloth-capped industrial workers in the House of Commons was delayed until the 1880s, and their share of elite posts increased more slowly than had that of their bosses. But the growth in working-class representation accelerated after World War I, as the recently founded Labour party rapidly expanded its share of the electorate. Coupled with the continued decline of landowners and the postwar stagnation in the industrialists' share of the elite, this trend seemed to bode well for the future of the working class. The emergence of industrialists within the elite had lagged 40 years behind the onset of industrial growth, and the emergence of the working class had been delayed for four more decades. But perhaps the twentieth century would belong to the proletariat, just as the eighteenth had belonged to the aristocracy, and the latter half of the nineteenth to the bourgeoisie.

Before examining the socioeconomic, cultural, and political factors that underlay this remarkable transformation of the British political elite during the nineteenth century, let us extend our view in time and space by comparing the changing social origins of several European cabinets over the last 70 to 100 years. In part this evidence (see Table 7–1) confirms the general tendencies we have noted: the sharp decline in the number of aristocrats in the elite during the

---

[17] During most of the nineteenth century almost all members of the aristocracy were large landholders, though the reverse was not true. Hence, data on aristocrats provides a conservative estimate of the numbers of landowners in the cabinet. See Guttsman, 1963, pp. 37–38, 83, 117. For evidence on the declining numbers of hereditary aristocrats in the House of Commons, see Cole, 1955, p. 134. More generally, see Arnstein, 1973.

[18] Jennings, 1940, p. 41; Ross, 1955, p. 433.

Table 7-1   Social Origins of European Cabinets During the Nineteenth and Twentieth Centuries

I. Britain

	1868–1886	1886–1916	1916–1935	1935–1955	1955–1970
Aristocracy	55%	49%	23%	21%	13%
Middle class	45	49	57	58	72
Working class	—	3	19	21	14

II. France

	1870–1899	1899–1940	1945–1958
Nobility	14%	4%	3%
Upper middle class	52	38	13
Middle class	26	34	60
Lower middle class	4	17	17
Working class	4	7	7

III. Germany

	1890–1918	1918–1933	1933–1945	1949–1960
Aristocracy	65%	11%	27%	—
Middle class	35	78	70	89%
Working class	—	11	3	11

Sources: R. W. Johnson, 1973, pp. 36, 50, 52; Dogan, 1967, p. 471; Knight, 1952, p. 33; Schmidt, 1963, p. 176.

period from 1890 to 1920, the rise of the bourgeoisie, and (later) of the working class.[19] These similarities are all the more striking, given the dramatically different texture of politics in these three countries over this span: Britain's steady constitutional evolution, France's succession of unstable parliamentary regimes, Germany's experimentation with monarchy, unstable democracy, Nazism, and stable democracy.

[19] See also Holmberg, 1974, Chap. 9, on Sweden; Dogan and Scheffer-van der Veen, 1957–1958, pp. 104–107, on the Netherlands; Sartori, 1963, pp. 168–169, and Lasswell and Sereno, 1965, p. 184, on Italy; Sheehan, 1968, on Germany.

THE END OF INDUSTRIALIZATION'S IMPACT?

One further cross-national regularity must be noted in Table 7–1. In each
country the middle-class share of cabinet seats has risen steadily, reaching clear
numerical predominance in the most recent period. By contrast, in each case
growth in working-class representation in the cabinet has halted at or even below
the high points of the interwar years. Moreover, at the parliamentary level in
these and other European nations, the working-class contingent has been stag-

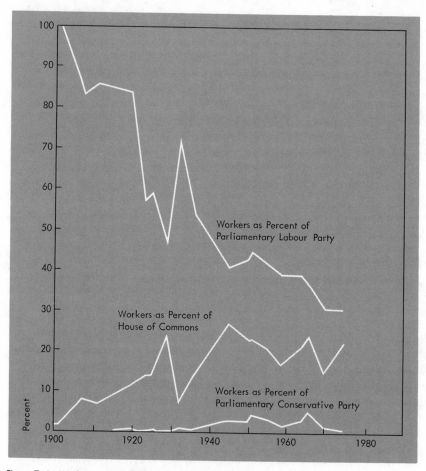

Figure 7–4   Workers in the House of Commons, 1900–1975
  Sources: Jennings, 1940, p. 41; R. W. Johnson, 1973, pp. 40, 46. Compare Guttsman, 1974, p.
  33.

nant or declining throughout the postwar era. The tide of democratization of elite composition that followed the industrial revolution is ebbing.[20]

The origins of this remarkable reversal are explored in Figure 7–4. The data presented there show, first, that the entrance of the working class into the House of Commons in the first half of this century was due almost entirely to the Labour party, for virtually no workers were to be found on the Conservative benches. On the other hand, the data vividly portray the *embourgeoisement* of the Labour party leadership, the decline in the proportion of workers on the Labour benches from 100 percent in 1901 to 31 percent in 1975. Similar findings have been reported for the Labour party leadership outside Parliament, as well as for socialist and communist parties in other industrial nations.[21]

Thus, while on the Conservative side the aristocrats and industrialists of the turn of the century have been increasingly replaced by men and women of the professional and administrative classes, in the Labour party, rank-and-file workers have given way to intellectuals and professional politicians.[22] These convergent trends suggest that the changes wrought on the European political elites by the industrial revolution of a century and more ago have finally been played out.

THE LAGGED RESPONSE OF ELITE COMPOSITION TO INDUSTRIALIZATION: SOME EXPLANATIONS

The industrial revolution brought in its train "the bourgeois revolution . . . [whose] chief impact [in elite terms] was the decline of feudal aristocracy and the rise of the businessman."[23] On this central point, Marx's theory was accurate.

But elite transformation followed economic change only after several long and theoretically significant lags. As Reinhard Bendix has noted:

> *The changes of social stratification in the course of industrialization do not present the simple picture of a declining aristocracy and a rising bourgeoisie. In most European countries the social and political preeminence of pre-industrial ruling groups continued even when their economic fortunes declined, and the subordinate social and political role of the "middle classes" continued even when their economic fortunes rose.*[24]

[20] For evidence of analogous historical trends in income distribution and socioeconomic equality, see Goldthorpe, 1964, in Bendix and Lipset, 1966, pp. 651–655; Jackman, 1975.

[21] Guttsman, 1974, p. 33; Hanby, 1974; Charlot, 1973, especially p. 82; Holmberg, 1974, Chap. 9; Hancock, 1972, pp. 181–183; Childs, 1966, pp. 31–36; Parkin, 1971, pp. 150–151.

[22] R. W. Johnson, 1973; Guttsman, 1974, especially p. 35.

[23] Lasswell in Lasswell and Lerner, 1965, p. 79.

[24] Bendix, 1970, p. 302.

Though it is difficult to be precise in these matters, our evidence from Britain suggests that the lag between economic change and elite transformation was about a half century at the parliamentary level and about three-quarters of a century at the level of the cabinet. Few people born at the height of the industrial revolution lived to see its impact on the composition of British political leadership.

Part of the explanation for this lag is cultural, for the aristocrats' rule was legitimized in the eyes of both rulers and ruled by a traditional political formula that was much slower to change than were older economic patterns. Only in the latter half of the nineteenth century did both aristocracy and bourgeoisie come to accept fully the right of the latter to participate in governing the nation. Moreover, local selectorates continued thereafter to prize candidates from the older ruling classes.[25]

In addition, in Britain and throughout Europe the rise of the bourgeoisie and later of the proletariat was closely tied to the emergence of essentially new political parties. Businessmen found it much easier to enter politics through the Liberal party, and the socialist parties of Europe were founded as vehicles of the working-class movement. To be sure, the socioeconomic changes were eventually reflected in the leadership of other parties as well, but the changes there were slower still.[26] The rise of new elites required a lengthy process of organizing or reorganizing political parties and winning adherents to the new formations.

The timing of shifts in elite composition also suggests the importance of institutional factors, including, above all, the extension of the suffrage. As we have seen, the first tentative electoral reform of 1832 had little impact on the relative numbers of landowners and industrialists in the House of Commons. However, the Second Reform Act of 1867 virtually doubled the size of the electorate by adding nearly a million urban voters, and the effect of this reform on the social composition of Parliament seems to have been almost immediate.

But at the cabinet level, nearly another quarter century was required before the newly elected industrialists began to displace the landed aristocrats. This further lag was due in part to the informal rules that required several decades' seniority in Parliament before advancement to the front benches. Throughout the entire period upper-class politicians entered Parliament younger and stayed longer. Consequently, they were much more likely to reach the cabinet, to stay there longer, and to occupy the most august posts, such as foreign secretary. Those who had made a career in industry rarely had time to complete this parliamentary obstacle course, and as a result industrialists never entered European cabinets in numbers proportionate to their power in legislative and other arenas.[27] Another institutional factor in several countries was the

---

[25] Guttsman, 1963, pp. 53–61; Guttsman, 1974, p. 41.

[26] Thomas, 1939, pp. 3–21; Jennings, 1940, pp. 37–43.

[27] Guttsman, 1963, pp. 77–78, 95, 201–202; Laski, 1928, p. 28; Lasswell, Lerner, and Rothwell, 1952, pp. 15, 30.

continuing, though declining, proportion of the cabinet drawn from nonelected bodies, such as the House of Lords in England and the higher civil service in Germany and Sweden.

Thus, changes in both economic and political institutions had a pronounced impact on elite composition, but neither repealed the law of increasing disproportion. Transformation of the European elites followed the same pattern of "capillary action" that Frederick Frey found characteristic of twentieth-century Turkey: "The lowest levels of formal power are affected first. If the pressure continues, the middle leaders are then altered, and only after a noticeable time lag is there a seepage into the highest levels of leadership and the cabinet."[28] Those seeking early indications of elite transformation should look not at the highest levels of power, but at the lowest.

Though important, the vote itself was not the key to the entire process of elite transformation, for the composition of nonelected elites displays much the

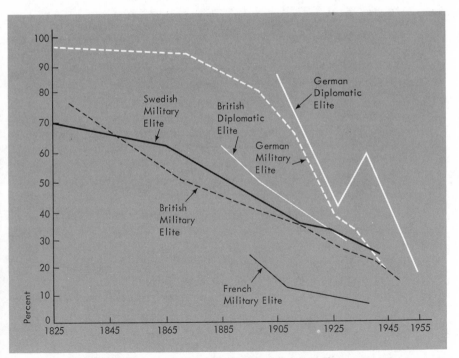

Figure 7–5   The Decline of Aristocrats in European Military and Diplomatic Elites
Sources: Edinger, 1961, p. 28; Nightingale, 1930, pp. 320–321; Kourvetaris and Dobratz, 1973, pp. 234–235. British diplomatic data corrected for date of senior incumbency.

[28] Frey, 1965, p. 282.

same pattern that we have noted in the case of elected politicians. European military and diplomatic elites, traditionally well-insulated from electoral politics, show the same slow slump in aristocratic membership, roughly synchronized with (though perhaps slightly later than) the decline we noted earlier in the case of the cabinets (see Figure 7–5). Broadly similar, though less uniform, changes have also been noted in the composition of civil service and even religious elites.[29]

If changes in the social origins of elites lagged behind socioeconomic change, elite political culture responded even more slowly. In Britain, for example, aristocratic values and political style have lingered on in the parliamentary milieu long after the landed gentry lost their numerical superiority. To some extent this cultural lag is the consequence of postrecruitment socialization within the House of Commons. Keir Hardie, founder of the Independent Labour party, complained in 1887:

> *The working man's representative (in Parliament) thinks more of his own reputation in the eyes of the House than of the interests of his suffering brethren in mill and mine. He desires to be reckoned a gentleman, fit to take his place as a member of the "finest club in the world."*[30]

One early Labour party member of Parliament reminisced:

> *In my young and callow days I was probably a little prejudiced in favour of my class and hot with resentment against those whom I regarded as their oppressors. But experience teaches and I now know that a gentleman is a gentleman whatever his rank in life may be and always will be trusted as such.*[31]

Among middle-class elite recruits aristocratic values were also perpetuated by the Victorian public school. Soon after the onset of the industrial revolution these previously exclusively aristocratic schools opened their gates to the sons of the rising middle classes and inculcated in them the political values and style that had been characteristic of the traditional elite. Rupert Wilkinson concludes: "The public schools . . . perpetuated the political supremacy of the landed

---

[29] Armstrong, 1973, pp. 73–92, especially p. 91; Thompson, 1974, p. 200. There is some evidence that among civil service and military elites, as among political elites, the trend toward democratization of social composition has recently slowed or even reversed. See Armstrong, 1973, especially p. 82; Putnam, 1973*b*, pp. 268–269; Kourvetaris and Dobratz, 1973, p. 233.

[30] Quoted in Guttsman, 1963, p. 247.

[31] Robert Smillie, quoted in Guttsman, 1963, pp. 248–249.

classes by 'capturing' talent from the rising bourgeoisie and moulding that talent into 'synthetic' gentlemen."[32]

I have so far emphasized how the British experience is typical of the elite transformation that follows the industrial revolution. In some respects, however, the British case was quite atypical. Marx himself, writing from the British Museum at about the midpoint of this elite transformation, recognized its peculiar character. He described the British ruling class as an "antiquated compromise"—the aristocracy "ruled officially," while the bourgeoisie ruled "over all the various spheres of civil society in reality."[33] But as Anthony Giddens has commented: "The 'antiquated compromise' . . . lasted considerably longer than Marx foresaw. . . . The relatively amicable interpenetration of aristocratic landowners and wealthy industrialists remains one of the striking facts of British history in the latter half of the nineteenth century."[34]

British aristocrats came. to show less disdain for mere commerce than did continental nobility. Many younger sons of the British aristocracy entered the world of business. In turn, increasing numbers of the newly enriched bourgeoisie were allowed to buy their way into the social establishment. Indeed, by 1922 company directors outnumbered landowners in the House of Lords.[35] This social accommodation was mirrored in politics. As we have seen, the middle classes adopted many traditional aristocratic values. For their part, the British aristocracy—in marked contrast with their French counterparts, for example —accepted the rules of the new game of democratic politics. In return, the aristocracy retained more enduring political influence in Britain than in France (see Table 7–1). Mosca noted the significance of this Victorian compromise:

> In the course of the nineteenth century England adopted peacefully and without violent shocks almost all the basic civil and political reforms that France paid so heavily to achieve through the Great Revolution. Undeniably, the great advantage of England lay in the greater energy, the greater practical wisdom, the better political training that her ruling class possessed. . . .[36]

A comparison with Germany illuminates other peculiarities of the British experience. In 1848–1849, as British industrialists were beginning their success-

[32] Wilkinson, 1964, p. 4; see also Cole, 1955, and Rex, 1974.

[33] As cited in Giddens, 1972, p. 357.

[34] Giddens, 1972, pp. 357–358.

[35] Guttsman, 1963, p. 134.

[36] Mosca, 1939, p. 119.

ful climb to power, the weaker German middle class failed in a revolutionary attempt to establish a liberal nation-state. When Bismarck succeeded in creating a nation-state under authoritarian auspices two decades later, he left political power firmly in the hands of the landed aristocracy (see Table 7–1).

Bismarck's solution to the problems of power posed by the industrial revolution was to tame the bourgeoisie with economic aid and protection from the working class. In return, the bourgeoisie left the political power of the traditional ruling class unchallenged: "Imperial Germany absorbed industrialization quickly and thoroughly. But she assimilated this process to the social and political structures by which she was traditionally [governed]. There was no place in these structures for a sizeable, politically self-confident bourgeoisie."[37]

The tormented history of Germany from 1918 to 1945 revealed the tragic long-term costs of this Bismarckian bargain.[38] Surprised by the collapse of the empire in 1918, middle-class and working-class elites nominally collaborated in founding the Weimar Republic. But history had denied them political experience and mutual trust. When, from the economic chaos of the 1930s, Hitler forged a cynical alliance between elements of the traditional elite and the traumatized middle classes, the feeble orphan of a republic died defenderless. The human costs of the Nazis' bizarre political experiment were staggering. In the end only the very universality of the *Zusammenbruch* ("collapse") in 1945 cleared the way for the Bonn attempt to reconcile German elite politics with the realities of industrial society.

Both rising and declining elite groups had played important roles in the British version of the drama of industrialization. Potentially explosive discrepancies between socioeconomic status and political power were minimized throughout. The relatively easy adaption of the British bourgeoisie and aristocracy to their changing roles helped forestall the emergence of reactionary movements such as Nazism. The willingness of these elites in turn to coopt working-class leaders (and the willingness of those leaders to be coopted) helped forestall the emergence of revolutionary socialism such as appeared elsewhere in twentieth-century Europe. For good or for ill, the high degree of elite integration maintained in Britain during this century-long transformation greatly reduced chances for instability and radical change.

THE AMERICAN EXPERIENCE

Many images have been sketched of the changing composition of American elites during the last two centuries. "Turning-point" theories indicate some particular epoch (such as the Jacksonian period) as the point at which the doors to power

---

[37] Dahrendorf, 1969, p. 44; but see also Sheehan, 1968.

[38] Rintala, 1968.

were thrown open to the common people. "Waxing-and-waning" theories ascribe to transient phases of American history (such as the opening of the frontier) temporarily greater opportunities for upward mobility into the elite. "Linear" theories hypothesize long-term trends toward steadily increasing (or steadily decreasing) elite openness.[39] But despite this covey of conjectures, there is remarkably little consensus about the facts.

Scattered evidence has been gathered. Family ties among congressmen seem to have become rarer since the earliest years of the Republic.[40] In business, diplomacy, and the military, it appears, "the trend is toward expanding opportunities for lower class and lower status aspirants."[41] At least one community study suggests that the patrician elites of the postcolonial period were succeeded by a generation of self-made businessmen, who in turn gave way to more plebeian professional politicians supported by the votes of working-class immigrants.[42] Scholars have described the political ascent of successive ethnic groups, of which blacks are a belated example.

Yet at the national level, unexpectedly little evidence exists about elite transformation in America. Still more surprisingly, this evidence strongly suggests that two centuries of economic, social, demographic, and geographic expansion have produced remarkably little change in the aggregate socioeconomic characteristics of the American elite. In particular, four independent studies—of presidents, vice-presidents, and cabinet officers from 1789 to 1934; of cabinet secretaries from 1789 to 1972; of U.S. senators in 1820, 1860, 1900, and 1940; and of public officials born between 1736 and 1876 and recorded in the *Dictionary of American Biography*—support the following generalizations.[43] (See Table 7–2 and Figure 7–6 for illustrative evidence.)

American national political leadership has remained largely the province of men from the middle and upper middle classes throughout the last two centuries. No trends are evident that bear comparison with those we have noted in the European cases. There is some evidence of a tendency toward greater openness in the decades prior to the Civil War, but this tide seems to have ebbed before the greatest surge of the American industrial revolution in the last decades of the nineteenth century. Access to elite positions for citizens from ordinary backgrounds seems to have been stable or declining from at least the 1880s, just as the industrial revolution was reaching its peak.

[39] Harris, 1969, pp. 165–184.

[40] Clubok, Berghorn, and Wilensky, 1969.

[41] Keller, 1963, p. 210.

[42] Dahl, 1961, pp. 11–51.

[43] Anderson, 1935; Witte, 1972; Hoogenboom, 1968; Harris, 1969; see also Seligman and King, 1970. Harris finds in addition a cyclical pattern of increased openness roughly every two decades and traces these brief bursts of upward mobility to a pulsating rhythm in demographic growth. Though intriguing, this pattern is not immediately relevant to our concern with the effects of the industrial revolution. In Table 7–2 I have grouped Harris' data to smooth out these short-term cycles and to emphasize long-term tendencies.

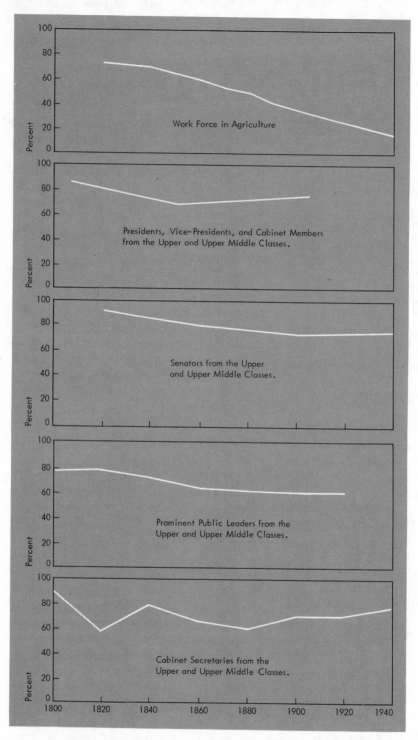

Figure 7–6   The Social Origins of American Elites, 1800–1940: Stability amidst Change
Sources: See Table 7–2.

Table 7–2   Social Origins of American Political Elites*

I. Presidents, Vice-Presidents, and Cabinet Members

	1789–1824	1825–1876	1877–1934
Initial Occupation			
Professionals	77%	89%	81%
(Lawyers)	(69)	(82)	(69)
Proprietors and Managers	13	8	13
(Manufacturers)	(0)	(2)	(3)
Farmers	10	2	2
(Large landowners)	(8)	(2)	(0)
Clerical and manual workers	0	1	3
	100%	100%	99%
Parental Social Status			
Professionals and managers	86%	69%	76%
Farmers	14	28	21
Clerical and manual workers	0	3	3
	100%	100%	100%

II. U.S. Senators

	1820	1860	1900	1940
Occupation†				
Law	42%	38%	42%	41%
Other professions	5	11	13	17
Business	9	27	34	27
Agriculture	44	24	11	10
Labor	—	—	—	4
Housewife	—	—	—	1
	100%	100%	100%	100%
Social Origins				
Elite	73%	36%	23%	24%
Substantial	20	45	52	53
Subsistence	7	19	25	23
	100%	100%	100%	100%

III. Men Recorded in the Dictionary of American Biography with Principal Careers in Government, Law, and the Military

Years of Birth	Years of Maturity	Percent from Lower-Middle-Class Homes or Below
1736–1756	1786–1806	25%
1757–1777	1807–1827	22
1778–1798	1828–1848	27
1799–1819	1849–1869	35
1820–1840	1870–1890	37
1841–1861	1891–1911	38
1862–1876	1912–1926	38

* Percentages are calculated after excluding missing data; in almost all cases this amounts to less than 10% of the total.

† Lawyers with other interests, such as agriculture, business or labor, have been allocated to those categories.

(cont.)

Table 7–2 (cont.)

IV. U.S. Senators and Other Government Officials Recorded in the Dictionary of American Biography

Years of Birth	Years of Maturity	Percent from Lower-Middle-Class Families or Below
1796–1816	1846–1866	40%
1817–1837	1867–1887	47
1838–1858	1888–1908	45
1859–1873	1909–1923	41

V. Cabinet Members' Socioeconomic Class of Origin

	Lower	Lower Middle	Upper Middle	Upper	Total
1789–1809	5%	5%	10%	80%	100%
1810–1829	16	26	5	53	100
1830–1849	6	14	19	61	100
1850–1869	12	21	24	43	100
1870–1889	22	17	17	44	100
1890–1909	13	15	28	44	100
1910–1929	19	9	24	48	100
1930–1949	5	16	37	42	100
1950–1972	8	13	32	47	100

Sources: Anderson, 1935, pp. 514, 517; Hoogenboom, 1968, pp. 54, 63; Harris, 1969, pp. 198–199; Witte, 1972, p. 13.

Most of the limited upward mobility into the American political elite has been among the sons of modest farmers, using the avenue of professional (especially legal) training. The proportion of elite members from agricultural backgrounds declined during the nineteenth century, but less sharply than the changing work force composition would have implied. The proportion of businessmen (or sons of businessmen) entering the political elite has remained relatively small and essentially unchanged throughout the period during which America moved from an overwhelmingly agricultural to an overwhelmingly industrial society.[44] Rank-and-file workers in business and industry (and their children) have remained virtually excluded from the peaks of American political power throughout this period.

Of course, neither the structure of power nor the skills and outlooks of the

---

[44] Witte (1972) does find some increase in the numbers of businessmen holding cabinet posts after 1890.

powerful have remained unchanged during these two centuries. The number of strategic elites has expanded, as the industrial revolution spawned concentrations of corporate power and, later, influential labor and professional organizations. George Washington could not have conceived the constellation of socioeconomic forces that would face Teddy Roosevelt a century later, nor would Roosevelt easily recognize the complex force field within which a contemporary president must act. The ideologies and professional skills of American leaders have also undergone several profound transformations. Yet in comparison with the soaring swoops and stunning plunges in graphs of European elite composition in this era, the American elite has been strikingly stable. As one perplexed scholar of the American case concluded, "the impact of industrialism has been remarkably small."[45] What are we to make of this American anomaly?

First, the transatlantic contrast underlines the importance of the social context within which industrialization takes place. The grand planters of the American colonies were but a pale reflection of the European aristocracy. With the temporary regional exception of the southern plantation owners, power in America passed permanently from patrician hands shortly after 1789. By the time Alexis de Tocqueville arrived in the 1830s to observe the American experiment with democracy the nation was ruled by the middle classes. The industrial revolution could hardly undermine the power of a landed aristocracy that no longer existed.

Second, the American case highlights the significance of historical sequences. Almost all white male Americans had the vote decades before the industrial revolution created a substantial urban working class. America missed that critical conjuncture of economic *and* political change that sparked elite transformation in Europe. Probably the single most important differentiating factor was the absence of a working-class party in American politics. The socialist parties that thrust working-class representatives into the European elites had no counterpart in this country. Any explanation for this decisive difference must include the early extension of mass suffrage, a relatively fluid social structure, the massive infusion of immigrants into the American proletariat, and a political culture that emphasized individual self-improvement rather than collective advance.

CONCLUSIONS

I have restricted this discussion to Western Europe and the United States. The impact of industrialization on elites in Eastern Europe and the Third World is still incomplete and is complicated by trends to be discussed later in this chapter.

---

[45] Hoogenboom, 1968, p. 72.

Yet are there lessons relevant to the future of Latin America, for instance, that are implicit in this account of the European and American past?[46]

The European experience confirms the basic thesis, shared by Marx, Mosca, and Schumpeter, that fundamental socioeconomic change creates strong pressures for elite transformation. When the industrial revolution occurs in an essentially feudal society and is carried forward under capitalist or semicapitalist auspices, the long-term consequence seems to be the coexistence of three fairly distinct class structures.[47] The oldest, based on agriculture, is presided over by the landed aristocracy. The second, centered on industry, finds the capitalists in command, occasionally challenged by representatives of the working class. The third, to be discussed in the final section of this chapter, arises out of the growth of technology and bureaucracy and is headed by a highly educated professional and administrative elite.

Our comparisons of Britain, France, and Germany have illustrated that the interplay among these three class structures and their associated elites powerfully conditions national politics. But in both Europe and America political and cultural factors have been important independent and intervening variables, affecting the relationship between socioeconomic change and elite transformation. Marx was wrong and his elitist critics right (at least in this): Even in the long run, the industrial revolution does not completely democratize politics, and neither traditional nor emergent elites are mere spectators of an economically determined drama.

SHORTER WAVES OF CHANGE: THE CASE OF REVOLUTION

We turn now from elite transformations that require a century and more to complete to the compressed changes embodied in successful revolutions and, in particular, to the nationalist and Communist revolutions of the twentieth century. I intend no complete account of the origins, course, and consequences of revolution. Thus, we can adopt Friedrich's simple definition of revolution as "a sudden and violent overthrow of an established political order."[48] Every revolution is directed at distinctive ends and is conditioned by unique social and historical circumstances. Nevertheless, revolutions always involve, in Harold Lasswell's phrase, "rapid and extensive change in the composition and the vocabulary of the ruling few."[49] I shall discuss the characteristics of both those who lead the revolution and those who inherit it.

---

[46] On the possible consequences of incipient industrialization for Latin American elites, see Cardoso, 1967, and Scott, 1967.

[47] Cole, 1955, pp. 106–107.

[48] Friedrich, 1966, p. 5. Elite transformations of the fascist variety display distinctive dynamics, and for the most part I shall ignore fascist revolutions here.

[49] Lasswell and Lerner, 1965, p. 279.

THE SOCIAL MATRIX OF REVOLUTIONARY LEADERSHIP

What manner of men and women become successful revolutionaries? Chapter 2 noted that revolutionary leaders are broadly middle class in origin. But most members of the middle classes do not become revolutionaries. One answer to this puzzle is suggested by Pareto's theory that revolutionary discontent arises out of a discrepancy between political skill and political status.

Henry Kissinger once pointed out that "a revolutionary must possess at least two qualities: a conception incompatible with the existing order and a will to impose his vision."[50] Revolutionary leadership demands great ideological and organizational ability. Such skills often require a degree of education not available to the exploited masses. On the other hand, the intense commitment demanded of a revolutionary is likely to derive from perceived deprivation or discrimination. Simply put, revolutionary leadership seems to presuppose both high education and low social status. Figure 7–7 may help to clarify the inconsistency between this pair of requirements.

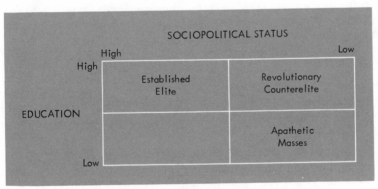

Figure 7–7   Education, Status, and Revolutionary Activism

Because of the virtually universal correlation between education, social status, and political power, most people have either low education and low status (and are hence unlikely to participate in politics at all) or high education and high status (and are hence likely to stand within the established elite). Few have the discrepant status called for by my prescription for revolutionary leadership. However, successful revolutionaries are drawn disproportionately from precisely this quarter. Let me offer some evidence.

[50] Kissinger, 1968, p. 891.

Well-educated members of deprived ethnic minorities have been prominent among Communist revolutionaries in Eastern Europe. The Jewish ghettos, where discrimination and intellectualism were peculiarly conjoined, produced an exceptional number of Communist leaders, joined in the Russian case by unusual numbers of Georgians and Armenians.[51] R. V. Burks has concluded, "All our Communist-producing social groups . . . combine in an unusual degree personal insecurity and better than average perception of the greater world."[52]

The nationalist revolution that in 1868 brought Japan into the modern world, the Meiji Restoration, was led by lower *samurai* from the bottom of the traditional gentry class, whose relative socioeconomic position had deteriorated steadily in the years before the revolution but who (significantly) were unusually well-educated.[53] The nationalist revolutions that overturned colonial regimes in the Third World were also led by men whose educational, social and political statuses were discrepant. John McAlister describes the Vietnamese revolutionaries:

> *Through education they got the opportunity for some upward mobility and some economic rewards, but their mobility into a potentially modern world was limited by the narrow contours of colonial society. Most of all, they got the chance to develop skills that made them significant competitors for political influence. But in colonial Viet Nam there were no legitimate means by which emergent groups of Vietnamese could use their political skills to compete for influence over governmental decisions. Only by organizing themselves into a revolutionary movement could they share in the governing of the country—a role which they felt their political strength entitled them to and which French intransigence prevented.*[54]

A similar portrait of an educated, but socially and politically frustrated, counter-elite could be painted for the initial stages of most anticolonialist movements, from India to Algeria.[55]

Nearer home, discrepancy between educational and socioeconomic status is characteristic of the leaders of the Women's Liberation Movement.[56] Another example: in the American urban upheaval of the 1960s, "the rioters were . . . among the more intellectually oriented and politically sophisticated of the black community."[57] More generally, "status inconsistency"—a discrepancy among a person's ranks on the several dimensions of social status—is predictive of dissatis-

[51] Rigby, 1971, pp. 425–426; Schueller, 1965, p. 107.

[52] Burks, 1961, p. 71; see also Moskos, 1965, p. 215.

[53] Silberman, 1964, pp. 108–109.

[54] McAlister, 1969, pp. 327–328.

[55] Crane, 1959; Quandt, 1969.

[56] Stiehm and Scott, 1974.

[57] Dye and Zeigler, 1972, p. 190.

faction with the existing distribution of power and privilege.[58] In sum, potential revolutionary leaders are typically found neither in the mansions of the establishment nor in the hovels of the dispossessed, but rather among overeducated outgroups.

In most societies only a small minority of the population falls into this quadrant, and not everyone of these persons becomes a revolutionary. Some retreat into apathy or piety, and others try to "pass" into the establishment. Other things being equal, however, the number of potential revolutionaries increases as a function of the proportion of the total population that is educated, but socioeconomically or politically deprived. A society in which the level of education is rising more rapidly than the opportunity for social mobility is particularly liable to revolutionary discontent, unless extraordinary efforts are made to coopt the newly educated groups into the established elite. Precisely this dilemma now faces many of the developing nations, given their surfeit of unemployed graduates. Mosca saw this point clearly:

When the aptitude to command and to exercise political control is no longer the sole possession of the legal rulers but has become common enough among other people; when outside the ruling class another class has formed which finds itself deprived of power though it does have the capacity to share in the responsibilities of government—then that [regime] has become an obstacle in the path of an elemental force and must, by one way or another, go.[59]

REVOLUTIONARIES AS COSMOPOLITAN INTELLECTUALS

Another common characteristic of revolutionary elites is the prominence of cosmopolitan intellectuals. Most of the top leaders of the Russian Revolution had attended university, most had lived and studied abroad, and several were distinguished writers.[60] The Communist revolutionaries of Eastern Europe were drawn from the tiny minority of their societies who had been exposed to Western education. Even in primitive Albania a majority of the leading Communists had studied abroad and were drawn from the more Western oriented of the two major ethnic groups.[61]

---

[58] Lenski, 1966, pp. 86–88, 409–410; see also Galtung, 1964, and Gurr, 1970.

[59] Quoted in Bottomore, 1964, p. 49. Despite the generally middle-class origins of top revolutionary elites, the net effect of most leftist revolutions is to expand access to elite positions for social groups previously excluded from such posts. See Rigby, 1971, p. 436; Cohen, 1973, pp. 63–64; Moskos, 1965, pp. 210–212; North and Pool, 1965, pp. 377, 387–406.

[60] Schueller, 1965, especially, p. 131.

[61] Burks, 1961, pp. 63–64, 191; Moskos, 1965, pp. 213–215.

On the other side of the world, a study of Nationalist and Communist elites in China between 1910 and 1930 concluded:

> *In both parties, the leaders have been drawn most frequently from a relatively thin upper layer of the Chinese population. In both parties these men were often the sons of landlords, merchants, scholars, or officials, and they usually came from parts of China where Western influence had first penetrated and where the penetration itself was most vigorous. All of them had higher educations, and most of them had studied abroad. . . . The majority were alienated intellectuals, men and women whose Western educations isolated them from the main currents of Chinese society.*[62]

With the adoption of Mao's strategy of peasant revolution, persons of more plebeian origins began to enter the Communist elite, but the members of the Central Committee of 1945 were still characterized by "relatively high education and extensive foreign travel."[63]

Western-educated intellectuals were also prominent leaders of the nationalist revolutions elsewhere in Asia and Africa. The leaders of the Meiji Restoration came from the small segment of the traditional Japanese ruling class that had had Western contacts or education. Throughout the Middle East from Morocco and Egypt to Lebanon and Turkey, this century's nationalist revolutions have been spearheaded by intellectuals educated in Western Europe, who seized the initiative from their less cosmopolitan compatriots.[64] A study of thirty-two revolutionary leaders throughout Asia, Africa, and Latin America concluded:

> *While only a very small fraction of the total population of underdeveloped countries has received a higher education, has lived or traveled extensively abroad, or has served in a modern institution or profession, all or virtually all of the top revolutionary leaders in such countries have done one or more of these things.*[65]

One classic study of world revolutionary elites suggested that "the most significant fact of our time is the *rise of the intellectual whose capital is his knowledge.*"[66] Intellectuals are particularly suited as leaders of revolutionary movements, for they are apt to be sensitive to discrepancies between distant ideals and contemporary realities. Equally important, they are skilled in for-

---

[62] North and Pool, 1965, pp. 376–377; see also Rejai, 1973, p. 32.

[63] Barnett, 1967a, pp. 74–76.

[64] Silberman, 1964, pp. 57–64; Cheng, 1974; Moore, 1970, pp. 47–52; Frey, 1965, p. 70; Dekmejian, 1975.

[65] Kautsky, 1969, p. 446. See also Shils, 1960, Benda, 1960, and Huntington, 1968, p. 290.

[66] Lasswell, Lerner, and Rothwell, 1952, p. 18.

mulating alternative futures and in communicating the excitement of these dreams. A study of the American revolutionary elite—itself an extraordinarily intellectual group—points out that "When elites come to power in periods of crisis, they do so in part by their ability to rally the community around a drive for new goals and by their skill in propounding a new value system acceptable usually to a majority of the community."[67]

Yet why should those most divorced from the cultural mainstream of their native lands be so prominent among revolutionary leaders? Part of the explanation lies precisely in their cultural marginality. Social scientists have often noted that culturally marginal individuals frequently take the lead in social and economic innovation.[68] Less secure in their identity, they are driven to seek respect and influence, and less bound to cultural orthodoxies, they are open to novel ideas.

Travel broadens. It provides an external vantage point from which to judge one's own society. For the student returned from abroad, the tension between his foreign experiences and the realities of his homeland often prove a revolutionizing force. Burks' description of future Albanian revolutionaries in the 1930s is broadly applicable: "The youngster, fresh out of lycee, approached the village and its backward ways as something to be changed, root and branch. When village tradition and village superstition and suffocating village poverty proved obdurate, conversion to apocalyptic Communism might follow."[69] Education and foreign exposure have this crucial point in common—they both foster subversive visions of a different and possibly better world.

THE YOUTH AND AGING OF REVOLUTIONARY ELITES

Revolutionary leaders are generally much younger than established elites. Three-quarters of the founders of the Chinese Communist party were 30 years old or younger at the time. The average age of delegates to the Soviet Party Congress in 1917 was about 30. Leaders of the Irish revolutionary Sinn Fein, the Meiji Restoration, the Algerian national liberation movement, and Atatürk's early National Assemblies were all unusually young. Even the Nazi elite was more than 10 years younger than the Weimar elite it ousted, the Bonn elite that succeeded it, and the average for comparable American, British, and French elites.[70]

Part of the explanation for the youthfulness of revolutionary elites is

---

[67] Lamb, 1952, p. 34; see also Geertz, 1964. My discussion of revolutionary intellectuals has benefited from an unpublished seminar paper by Fritz Gaenslen.

[68] Hagen, 1962; Park, 1950, pp. 345–392, as cited in Hoselitz, 1960, pp. 66–67.

[69] Burks, 1961, p. 64.

[70] Lee, 1968, as cited in Rejai, 1973, p. 31; Rigby, 1971, p. 423; Cohan, 1973, p. 218; Silberman, 1964, pp. 95–97; Cheng, 1974; Quandt, 1969, p. 151; Frey, 1965, p. 171; Lerner, Pool, and Schueller, 1965, p. 291; Edinger, 1961.

institutional. Establishment figures have generally had to climb a well-defined, time-consuming career ladder, whereas the less bureaucratic organization of a revolutionary movement facilitates the rapid rise of youthful talent. In addition, having been more recently socialized, youths are less tied to older ways of thought, more competent in nontraditional skills, and thus more suited for revolutionary leadership than older generations.

Because revolutionary leaders are typically young when they capture power, the revolutionary generation tends to monopolize power for many years. Even when the initial revolutionaries are purged, their successors tend to be older, for the institutionalization of the new regime recreates lengthy career ladders and apprenticeships. The consequent aging of the postrevolutionary elite is marked and portentous. The average age of the Russian Politburo has risen steadily from 39 in 1917 to 61 in 1971, and Figure 7–8 shows that older cohorts have claimed a steadily growing share of the seats on the Central Committee over this period. The proportion of the Japanese cabinet taking office before the age of 50 fell from 78 percent in the Meiji period to 36 percent in 1913–1945 and to 17 percent after World War II. Aging postrevolutionary elites have been noted in the Irish Republic, the Communist countries of Eastern Europe, and many developing nations, including Tunisia, the Ivory Coast, Turkey, Lebanon, Israel, and Egypt.[71]

The leaders of an aged revolutionary elite are sometimes drawn from a remarkably narrow birth cohort. During the entire period from 1960 to 1972, for example, all top seven posts in the North Vietnamese elite (excepting Ho's unique position) were held by men born between 1908 and 1912. The classic aging revolution is the Chinese Peoples' Republic. The youthful group that founded the revolutionary movement in the 1920s was to lead the party for the next half century. The party leadership aged more rapidly than the party membership; in 1956, 92 percent of the members, but only 16 percent of the leaders, had been born after 1910. Nor did the Cultural Revolution much rejuvenate the highest echelons of the party. By 1969 more than half of the members of the Central Committee were in their sixties and only 17 percent were under 55, this being the elite of a movement begun by men in their twenties. By 1975 the Chinese Communist elite, once among the youngest in the world, was among the oldest.[72]

Several important consequences follow from the persistence of the revolutionary generation. Confining leadership to men and women who share personal loyalties and a common outlook forged during the revolution may provide an important element of stability to the precarious new regime. On the other hand, blocking oncoming generations may create severe tensions, as

---

[71] Schueller, 1965, p. 111; Rigby, 1972, p. 15; Hough, 1972, p. 37; Nagle, 1975; Cheng, 1974; Cohan, 1973, p. 218; Beck, 1973, p. 135; Cohen, 1973, p. 56; Zartman, 1976; Frey, 1965, p. 170; Dekmejian, 1975.

[72] Chau, 1972, p. 773; Waller, 1973a, pp. 162, 171; Donaldson and Waller, 1970, p. 630; Waller, 1973b, p. 8; North and Pool, 1965, p. 383; Barnett, 1967b, p. 434.

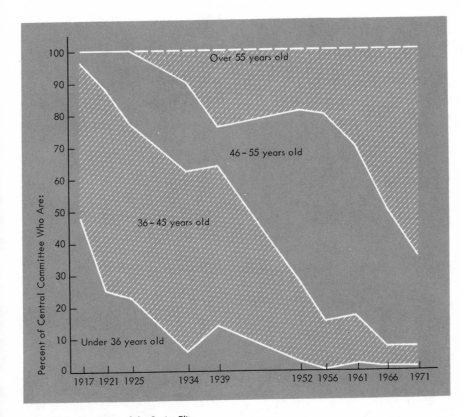

Figure 7–8   The Aging of the Soviet Elite
   Source: Nagle, 1975, p. 8.

potential successors jockey for position. This conflict is exacerbated by discontinuities in socialization, for the rapid change of the postrevolutionary era creates a compressed sequence of distinct political generations. Rapid economic development can ease the blockage problem by increasing the number of challenging and remunerative jobs. Nevertheless, the successful institutionalization of a revolutionary regime is closely tied to its ability to resolve these dilemmas.[73]

THE PAROCHIALIZATION OF POSTREVOLUTIONARY ELITES

The most striking pattern in the evolution of postrevolutionary elites is the gradual replacement of cosmopolitan intellectuals by more parochial types who are less intellectual and often less educated and who have closer ties to the

---

[73] See Zartman, 1976, and Quandt, 1969, especially p. 14. On generational blockage in the contemporary Soviet elite, see Hough, 1967b, and Lewytzkyj, 1967.

indigenous culture and to the rural heartland. Let us examine some evidence of this development and then explore its causes and effects.

The transformation of the Russian elite in the decades after 1917 may be symbolized by the transition from the cosmopolitan Lenin to the parochial Stalin and may be measured by the changing composition of their Politburos. By 1951 most of the earlier middle-class, urban-born intellectuals, often from ethnic minorities, had been replaced by village-born Slavs, from peasant or working-class families, having little formal education and less foreign experience. Under Khrushchev and Brezhnev the educational level of the Politburo rose sharply, as we shall see later, but in other respects there was no reversal of the trend toward men from plebeian, parochial backgrounds.[74]

In China the long turmoil from the fall of the imperial dynasty in 1912 to the Communists' seizure of power in 1949 blurred the distinction between revolutionary and postrevolutionary elites, but the basic pattern of increasing parochialism applies. During the protracted struggle between Nationalists and Communists, each group's leading cadre was composed increasingly of less educated individuals of lower-class origins from the rural hinterland. This tendency was especially marked in the victorious Communist elite, and after 1949 the trend toward a more parochial, less formally educated elite continued. The Cultural Revolution accelerated the eclipse of the remaining cosmopolitan intellectuals. By 1975 the predominance of leaders from plebeian, heartland origins was well established.[75]

In new nations the emergence of a vernacular-speaking, rural, less educated elite is common in the postindependence period. India's fight for independence was led by English-speaking intellectuals. In the first years of the new state a cosmopolitan elite, typified by the upper-class, Oxford-educated Nehru, dominated politics. In later years, however, "with each election, there has been a decline in the number of M.P.'s who command English and in their average level of education."[76] Rajni Kothari has distinguished between earlier "modernists" and more recent "modernizers." The modernists were urban and Brahminic in origin, urbane and ideological in orientation, committed to the abstract ideal of modernity. The "modernizers" are modest merchants and peasant proprietors by background, rooted in rural politics, closely tied to local interests, speaking and acting in a traditional idiom, but more practical and more effective in bringing change to the grassroots of Indian society. Similar transitions have been traced in the postindependence political elites of Sri Lanka, the Philippines, Ireland, Tanzania, and—in the form of Jacksonian Democracy—

---

[74] Scheuller, 1965, and Rigby, 1972, pp. 9–12. At lower levels in the party elite, "Russification" and "plebeianization" began immediately after the revolution; see Rigby, 1971, pp. 424–432.

[75] North and Pool, 1965, pp. 387–405; Klein, 1966, pp. 75–77; Donaldson and Waller, 1970, p. 650; Scalapino, 1972.

[76] Hardgrave, 1970, p. 60.

the United States.[77] The replacement of the urbane Milton Obote by the rustic Idi Amin epitomizes the transition in the Ugandan case.

Frederick Frey found that the transformation of the Turkish revolutionary elite after Atatürk's seizure of power in 1920 followed a curvilinear pattern, as outlined in Figure 7–9. During the transition from the still partially traditional elite in the early 1920s to the fully Kemalist revolutionary elite of the mid-1930s, indicators of localism (such as personal ties to a local constituency) declined and indicators of cosmopolitanism (such as knowledge of foreign languages) rose. Thereafter, as the tendency toward parochialism took hold, these indicators reversed direction. Similarly, Charles Moskos' study of Albanian elites before and after the Communist victory in 1945 found that indicators of cosmopolitanism (such as college education and membership in the most Westernized ethnic minority) were highest among the last generation of the prerevolutionary monarchists and the first generation of the postrevolutionary communists. Evidence for this curvilinear model of revolutionary and postrevolutionary elite transformation has also been found in such countries as Japan and Sri Lanka.[78]

Why does the tide of cosmopolitan intellectuals ebb? One explanation, modeled on Mosca's theory that elite transformations are determined by social forces, emphasizes the breakup of the revolutionary coalition and the resurgence

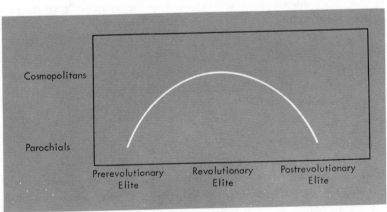

Figure 7–9 Parochials, Cosmopolitans, and Revolutions

[77] Kothari, 1970, p. 138, 237; Shils, 1961; Singer, 1964; Grossholtz, 1964, pp. 223–233; Cohan, 1973; McGowan and Bolland, 1971, p. 66. For somewhat contrary evidence on the Jacksonian elite, see Aronson, 1964. For a discussion of the emerging southern black political elite in these terms, see Salamon, 1973.

[78] Frey, 1965, pp. 196–197, 388–389; Tachau and Good, 1973; Moskos, 1965, pp. 214–217; Kuroda, 1974; Singer, 1964.

of prerevolutionary ethnic and geographic cleavages. Cosmopolitan rule is seen as a passing aberration. The victory of the heartland is the inevitable reassertion of an underlying social equilibrium.

In competitive regimes this theory underscores the importance of electoral pressure, as the still mostly rural and traditionalist electorate supports elites more congenial in background and idiom. This trend is often fostered by remnants of the prerevolutionary elites, striving to regain at least a share of national power by rallying mass support. Often in so-called ruralizing elections an urban, upper-middle-class, modernist elite is ousted by a rival party drawing both its leaders and its electoral support from the more parochial segments of society. Such elections have transformed elites in Sri Lanka, Turkey, the Philippines, the United States, and (though in a less concentrated way) India. Analogously, some analysts have in part traced the Chinese Communists' victory over the Nationalists to the more rapid and extensive parochialization of the Communist elite.[79]

A second explanation of parochialization, akin to Schumpeter's functional theory of elite transformation, distinguishes two needs that must be met during a successful revolution: (1) the germination of new social ideals and (2) the rooting of those ideals in local soil. Thinking new thoughts is the province of cosmopolitan intellectuals, but expressing those thoughts in the language of the hinterland requires different skills. Consolidation of the new regime demands leaders who can embody the parochialism of the heartland and thus reintegrate the national community around the ideals of the revolution. This theory underlies Kothari's distinction between modernists and modernizers. The need to reaffirm an indigenous sense of identity helps account for the tendency even of revolutionary cosmopolitans to don more traditional garb (sometimes literally) in the post-revolutionary era.

The emergence of parochial elites can have several important consequences for politics and government. Industrialization and centralized planning are likely to be higher on the agenda of cosmopolitans. Parochials are usually more attentive to the immediate needs of their rural constituents. Policy on education and language may be treated differently by leaders whose reference groups are provincial and local rather than national and international. The resurgence of parochialism is likely to exacerbate traditional ethnic or regional hostilities; the deadly communal riots that followed Sri Lanka's ruralizing election are a lesson in point.

Because parochialization is usually more marked in the political or elective elite than in the civil service, tensions endemic in relations between administrator and politician are exacerbated. Politicians appear petty, provincial, even corrupt to the cosmopolitan administrators, while the latter seem impractical

---

[79] Huntington, 1968, pp. 443–461; Rosenthal, 1970, pp. 194–195; North and Pool, 1965, p. 417; see also Quandt, 1969, pp. 159–161.

and unresponsive to mass demands. If the functionalist argument is correct, the exit of the cosmopolitans may signal a movement from a command polity toward a consent polity. Stalin to the contrary notwithstanding, parochial politicians may adopt a more responsive (if technically less efficient) decision-making style than their cosmopolitan predecessors and thereby help to overcome the elite-mass gap.

FROM IDEOLOGUES TO BUREAUCRATS?

Some scholars have hypothesized that in the postrevolutionary period ideologues are progressively displaced by bureaucrats, agitators by *apparatchiki*, revolutionary modernizers by managerial modernizers, specialists in ideas by specialists in control and coercion. The thesis is plausible, for once power is achieved, propagandizing becomes less crucial, managing more crucial.[80]

This thesis fits the Soviet case, as typified by the victory of Stalin, the coercive organization man, over Trotsky, the brilliant ideologue. In fact, the hypothesis simply describes in more general terms the process of Stalinization. But it accommodates other cases less easily. Coercive specialists controlled the Nazi party from the outset. During the Chinese civil war, power on both sides did flow into the hands of the military, but most scholars agree that coercion has played a less important role than propaganda and indoctrination in postrevolutionary China.

The distinction between revolutionary and managerial modernizers finds some echo in China, for Mao himself distinguishes between revolutionary "Reds" and managerial "experts." He appears to fear that, without special precautions, some "natural" postrevolutionary dynamic would elevate bureaucratic and technical criteria over political and ideological criteria—the experts over the Reds. Mass campaigns and such exercises as the Cultural Revolution are designed to "put politics in command." On the other hand, systematic analysis of the Chinese elite has so far disconfirmed the hypothesis that managerial modernizers have in fact displaced revolutionary ideologues.[81]

The theory is further weakened by severe difficulties in distinguishing operationally between ideological and managerial types. As leader of the People's Liberation Army, Lin Piao was occupationally a manager-bureaucrat, but ideologically he appears to have been a member of Mao's Red faction, at least until personal intrigue hopelessly confused factional alignments. After attempting to classify thirty-two top leaders in Asia, Africa, and Latin America, a one-time proponent of the theory conceded that "it would appear that we cannot

---

[80] Kautsky, 1968, p. 165; Lasswell, Lerner, and Rothwell, 1952, p. 32.

[81] Waller, 1973*a*, p. 189; Scalapino, 1972.

distinguish sharply between revolutionary and managerial modernizers in terms of their experience and training, their attitudes, or even their policies."[82]

The theory also blurs the distinction between bureaucrats and technicians, and it confuses postrevolutionary elite transformation with changes that accompany technological progress. Admittedly, these distinctions are obscured in Russia and the more advanced countries of Eastern Europe, where rapid technological development coincides with the later postrevolutionary period. In these countries, three separate stages of elite transformation can be distinguished:

> *Ideologues with revolutionary experiences have given way to party apparatchiki with administrative skills, and the ability to use or effectively threaten coercion. These* apparatchiki, *in turn, are yielding to somewhat younger, nonrevolutionary, technically trained bureaucrats, who tend to rely on persuasive techniques for maintaining social control.*[83]

But the cases of China and the United States remind us that political revolution and technological revolution are distinct phenomena, both logically and empirically.

The change from ideological activists to managerial bureaucrats is probably better conceived in terms of role change rather than personnel change. After the revolutionaries capture power, more of them work in offices and fewer on street corners. But this change in roles need not imply change in ideological orientation or in personnel. Trotsky, the archetypal ideologue-agitator, successfully organized and managed the Red Army during the chaotic civil war. If we hold role constant and look at the changing characteristics of incumbents, we find, for example, in Turkey that the number of civil and military officials holding political posts, though initially high, declined steadily after the revolution.[84]

Roles in the postrevolutionary elite tend to become functionally differentiated and bureaucratically organized. Social management requires specialized officials, and government agencies proliferate. But whether these changes inevitably mean less zeal and more coercion is far from certain on the evidence now available. There is little corroboration that Stalinism is a universal stage in postrevolutionary elite transformation.

The new regime's urgent need for bureaucrats and specialists does have one virtually invariant consequence: Postrevolutionary transformation of the administrative elite is almost always slow. In the short run the skills of the specialists from the old regime are irreplaceable:

---

[82] Kautsky, 1969, p. 189.

[83] Welsh, 1969, pp. 325–326.

[84] Frey, 1965, pp. 181–183, 208–211.

Once it is fully established, bureaucracy is among those social structures which are the hardest to destroy. . . . [The bureaucratic machine] makes "revolution," in the sense of the forceful creation of entirely new formations of authority, technically more and more impossible.[85]

All revolutionaries have faced this problem—Hitler and Mussolini no less than Lenin, Mao, and Nyerere. Each tried to train specialists committed to the revolution, but for years each had to rely on prerevolutionary experts—Prussian and monarchist administrators in Germany and Italy; tsarists, "Whites," and Englishmen in Russia, China, and Tanzania. After each regime change in Germany in this century, turnover has been much lower in the economic and administrative elites than in the political elite. The Italian higher civil service has shown remarkable endurance in the face of political revolution. Fifteen years after Mussolini's march on Rome every top official in the all-important Ministry of Corporations was still a pre-Fascist entrant, and a quarter century after the revolution that expelled Mussolini 95 percent of the administrative elite were still Fascist-era recruits.[86] The inability of revolutionary politicians to replace prerevolutionary administrators powerfully constrains the new regime.

WAVES **OF THE** **FUTURE?** **THE CASE** **OF TECHNOCRACY**	How are elites being transformed today and by what social, economic, and political trends? This final case study will assess one prominent hypothesis—the emergence of a managerial or technocratic elite in postindustrial society.

SOME THEORETICAL CONJECTURES

Predictions about postindustrial elite transformation have been derived from many theoretical bases. The first theorist of technocracy, the nineteenth-century Frenchman Henri de Saint-Simon, relied on a *functional* argument. In a famous pair of mental experiments he imagined, first, the disappearance of France's nobles, ministers, public officials, clergy, and wealthy rentiers and, second, the elimination of her leading scientists, engineers, economic managers, and technicians. An industrial society could survive the first of these experiments, he argued, but hardly the second; therefore, the future belonged to the technical and managerial experts.[87] The century and a half since Saint-Simon's prophecy has witnessed a series of technological revolutions almost unimaginable in his time. From the assembly line to the computer and from the automobile to the

[85] Weber, 1958, pp. 228, 230.

[86] Dahrendorf, 1964, p. 308, citing Zapf, 1965; Edinger, 1960; Putnam, 1973*b*, pp. 279–280.

[87] Saint-Simon, 1952, pp. 72–75.

rocket, each innovation has increased the technical and managerial skill required to run society. The functional theory of elite transformation argues that those who possess the new skills are destined to inherit political power.

James Burnham's theory of the "managerial revolution" links elite transformation to *the changing mode of production.* Like Marx, Burnham argued that social and political power derives from control over the means of production. But unlike Marx, Burnham distinguished between ownership and control. Control over the productive process, he argued, is passing from capitalists, who nominally own the enterprises, to technical managers, who actually run them. Whether ownership is formally public or private is of secondary importance. Indeed, in Burnham's view the worldwide tendency toward state control over the economy is both symptom and accelerator of the managerial revolution. The distinction between private managers and public bureaucrats is of vanishing significance. Burnham's theory was echoed by the heretical Yugoslav Communist Milovan Djilas, who denounced the growing power of a "new class" of party bureaucrats in Eastern Europe.[88]

John Kenneth Galbraith has also traced elite transformation to the changing character of the productive process. To the classic economic triad of land, capital, and labor, Galbraith adds technology and organization. Just as the suppliers of the earlier factors of production—landowners, capitalists, and labor leaders—gained political power as a function of their economic roles, Galbraith foresees growing influence for those who control technological and organizational assets. "Effective power of decision is lodged deeply in the technical, planning, and other specialized staff"—the "technostructure."[89]

Others have suggested that contemporary political elites are being remolded by the explosive growth of *scientific and technical knowledge* and by the consequent expansion of professional and technical occupations. Students of both the Soviet Union and the West have argued that these trends have "created a new constituency—the technical and professional intelligentsia." Thus, "in the post-industrial society, technical skill becomes the base of and education the mode of access to power."[90]

Recent political trends, too, seem to foster technocracy. According to Max Weber, rapid, almost universal growth in *the scope of government* has made bureaucratization inevitable and thereby enhanced the role of professional experts. Noting the "ever-increasing complexity of the administration of state

---

[88] Burnham, 1941, pp. 71–111; Djilas, 1957, pp. 37–54. Burnham borrowed the distinction between ownership and control from Berle and Means, 1932. Although most observers now concur that decision-making discretion in most contemporary capitalist enterprises has passed from shareholders to managers, there is much debate about how distinct these groups are empirically in terms of motivation, outlook, and social composition. See G. Parry, 1969, pp. 77–80.

[89] Galbraith, 1969, pp. 77, 80, 405–406.

[90] Bell, 1973, pp. 358–364; Fainsod, 1963, p. 282. For an interesting Marxist treatment of this phenomenon, see Klein and Zeleny, 1970.

services," Jean Meynaud concludes that "as the Executive's responsibilities increase, technocratic influence penetrates into most sectors of state activity."[91]

Thus, economic, social, and political trends in advanced industrial societies seem to portend a technocratic or managerial transformation of political elites. This transformation might manifest itself in two ways. First, there might be changes in the composition of institutionally defined elites. For example, the training, the skills, the career patterns, and the outlooks of members of the Central Committee or of the House of Commons may be changing in ways that suggest the emergence of a new type of elite. Second, and more subtly, the structure of power itself may be shifting, so that the influence of the Central Committee or of the House of Commons is declining, say, relative to that of state bureaucrats or industrial managers.

In principle, the technocracy thesis should apply to all modern societies, regardless of political regime or ideology. Let us explore some evidence of contemporary elite transformation, first in the capitalist West and then in the Communist East. Finally, we shall examine the assumption that the putative elite of technocrats and managers is homogeneous and unified.[92]

CONTEMPORARY TRENDS IN WESTERN ELITES

One of the most striking features of elite transformation in contemporary Western societies is the increasing importance of educational credentials. For example, in the House of Commons, university graduates have comprised a steadily growing fraction of each party's delegation since the end of World War I. This trend has been so marked within the Labour party—from 4 percent in 1918 to 57 percent in 1975—that most of the earlier interparty disparity has been wiped out (see Figure 7–10).

University education has also become ever more common among administrative and economic elites throughout the West. Studies of business leaders in the United States, Britain, France, Sweden, and Germany have shown that a college degree, particularly in a technical field, has become increasingly crucial throughout this century. Indeed, this trend seems to have accelerated in recent decades. And for civil servants, too, "the school is replacing the family as an avenue to the top."[93]

---

[91] Weber, 1958, pp. 196–244; Meynaud, 1969, pp. 72, 95.

[92] The theory that Communist and non-Communist systems should show similar types of elite transformation in the postindustrial era is related to, but distinct from, the theory that both are converging toward a single type of society. On the so-called convergence theory, see Brzezinski and Huntington, 1964, especially pp. 9–14, and Meyer, 1970. Note that our primary focus in this final case study is the changing skills and roles of elites, rather than their social origins, which was the focus of our discussion of the impact of the industrial revolution.

[93] Dahrendorf, 1964, p. 306; Newcomer, 1965; Stanworth and Giddens, 1974, pp. 89–91; Granick, 1962; Myers, 1959, p. 292; Hartmann, 1959, p. 279; Dahrendorf, 1959, p. 46.

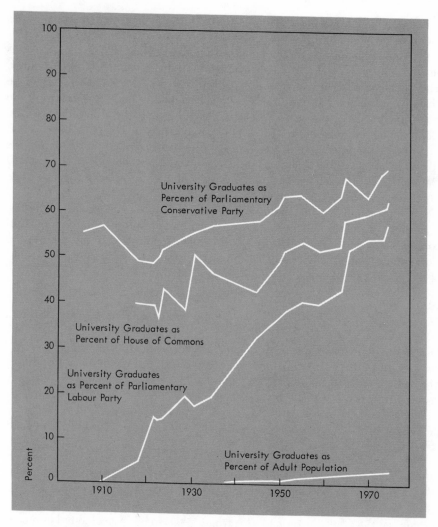

Figure 7–10   The Growth of University Education in the British Elite
Sources: Ross, 1955, pp. 424–425; R. W. Johnson, 1973, p. 46; Butler and Pinto-Duschinsky, 1971, and other books in that series.

Occupationally, political elites in the West are drawn in ever greater numbers from the professional and administrative classes. In particular, those whom Harold Lasswell termed "symbol specialists" are increasingly numerous and prominent—journalists, teachers, publishers, technologists, accountants, social scientists, administrators, and public relations experts.[94] We seem to be

[94] Lasswell, 1961, p. 267. However, relatively few natural scientists and engineers have entered Western party or parliamentary elites.

witnessing the ascent to political power of the professional intelligentsia, in the broad European sense of that term. As noted earlier, these educational and occupational trends are producing a steady convergence toward a middle-class predominance in most major European political parties.

In one sense, however, the prepolitical occupations of political leaders are increasingly misleading, for another marked trend is the professionalization of the career of politics itself. Among the indications of this trend are the growing tendencies for aspiring politicians to enter politics early, to make their career almost entirely within that sphere, and to seek the autonomy and the material perquisites characteristic of the older liberal professions. Evidence of the professionalization of politics as a specialized, middle-class, education-based, economically secure, lifetime career has been discovered in such countries as Britain, Italy, Japan, Sweden, and West Germany.[95] Careers in public affairs may be spent partly in official roles, such as legislator or administrator, and partly in semiofficial or unofficial roles, such as political consultant, interest-group representative, or party official. As Max Weber predicted more than a half century ago, the professional politician, for whom politics is a permanent vocation rather than a temporary avocation, has emerged as the central figure of modern democratic politics.[96]

Weber also foresaw another significant aspect of contemporary elite transformation—the steady rise in the power of bureaucrats. Controllers of the means of administration are succeeding controllers of the means of production as the rulers of a bureaucratized world, he argued. To be sure, not all bureaucrats are technocrats, and not all technocrats are bureaucrats. Yet as Reinhard Bendix points out:

> *Modern bureaucracy is characterized by the development of administrative autonomy due to the importance of technical skills. In the sense that these skills make the higher administrative personnel irreplaceable, a modern governmental bureaucracy holds a monopoly of skill.*[97]

Trends in the institutional balance of power constitute one aspect of the increasing importance of bureaucratic elites. The older constitutional theory that the executive branch simply executes what the legislature legislates is clearly unrealistic. Key decisions are increasingly preformed by bureaucrats. Most laws are crafted not on the floor of the legislature, but in the offices of the bureaucracy. Administrators increasingly control the public agenda, monopolizing as they do much information about how current policy works, as well as much of the

---

[95] R. W. Johnson, 1973, pp. 75–76; Sartori, 1967, pp. 169–173; Cheng, 1974; Holmberg, 1974; Hancock, 1972, p. 181; Baylis, 1973.

[96] Weber, 1958, pp. 77–128.

[97] Bendix, 1945, p. 118.

expertise necessary to design alternatives. Each day's headlines also record the growing importance of semipublic agencies, such as the U.S. Federal Reserve Board, the Bank of England, and the public enterprises of Western Europe. Moreover, in market economies the emergence of powerful public bureaucracies has been bound up with the simultaneous concentration of economic power in the private bureaucracies of a few large firms.

The power of bureaucrats is, of course, restrained by many factors—by the greater legitimacy accorded in constitutional democracies to decisions taken by elected officials, by the countervailing power of other political institutions, such as parties and pressure groups, by conflicts among the bureaucrats themselves and alliances cutting across the conventional distinction between politicians and bureaucrats, occasionally even by the bureaucrats' own code of self-restraint and neutrality. Nevertheless, in historical perspective the institutional power of bureaucracy has grown significantly in recent decades.

Changing elite career patterns also reveal the increasing significance of bureaucracy. Most nineteenth-century American cabinet secretaries had had prior legislative experience, but this pattern has become much rarer in this century, whereas previous administrative experience has become more common.[98] As noted in Chapter 3, in many countries the bureaucracy is an ever more frequent path to national elective office. Increasingly, too, posts in the private economic elite are filled by persons drawn from officialdom; France and Japan provide perhaps the best examples of this phenomenon.

Within the executive branch itself technical expertise is an increasingly crucial credential. Among American senior civil servants "a considerable number are lawyers, [but] an even greater number are engineers and natural scientists."[99] Posts in the French administrative elite are virtually monopolized by graduates in engineering and administrative science.[100] Even in the determinedly "amateurish" British civil service several postwar reforms have been designed to improve the standing of professional, technical, and scientific specialists. In 1964 Jean Meynaud argued that the influence of technocrats was most pronounced on national defense, economic planning, and scientific research, but technological experts have become equally influential on the newer issues of the 1970s, such as energy and environmental protection.[101] Monks, mistresses, and seers, prominent among the privy counsellors of rulers in a simpler age, have been succeeded everywhere by scientists, economists, and management consultants.

[98] Witte, 1972; Huntington, 1973, p. 14. For a similar trend in local government, see Lowi, 1964a, pp. 10, 60.

[99] David and Pollock, 1957, p. 92.

[100] Ridley, 1966; Suleiman, 1974.

[101] Meynaud, 1969, pp. 95–107.

The theory of technocracy seems to have special applicability to Communist elites. As the revolutionary tumult fades, as the new regime becomes institutionalized, as the complexities of running a modern society multiply—the theory argues—power shifts inexorably from the ideologues and party organizers toward the managers and technicians. This trend might manifest itself in either (or both) of the following ways: (1) technical and managerial qualifications might become more important than political and ideological credentials for recruitment to the party elite; and (2) managerial elites in technical and economic sectors might gain increasing autonomy from the party and its leaders. In either case the Reds give way to the experts. Let us examine the evidence.

In recent decades educational levels have risen sharply among both national and local elites, among both party bureaucrats and economic managers, and in nearly every country of Eastern Europe.[102] The importance of educational credentials within the Soviet elite has increased even more rapidly than among British members of Parliament over the past quarter century (compare Figures 2–3 and 7–10). Moreover, the education of the newer recruits is concentrated in technical fields, particularly agronomy and engineering. During the 1950s and 1960s, for example, the rates of technical higher education both among Soviet regional party secretaries and among Politburo members rose from 45 percent to 80 percent.[103] Few of the transformations noted in this chapter are so marked and well documented as the rapid and virtually universal rise in the significance of technical training as a prerequisite for elite recruitment in industrialized Communist societies.

Occupationally, the number of party leaders without specialized technical or managerial experience has declined in recent decades. Men and women who made their mark first in such endeavors are increasingly represented within the party elite.[104] However, while technical and managerial backgrounds are becoming more common, this trend has *not* come at the expense of experience and training within the party organization. Rather, in both the Soviet Union and Eastern Europe positions at all levels within the party leadership are held increasingly by "dual executives" whose careers combine specialization in a particular branch of the economy and long service within the party apparatus.[105]

[102] Fischer, 1968; Farrell, 1970a, pp. 96–98; Gehlen, 1970, pp. 144–145; Baylis, 1974, pp. 208, 210; Bauman, 1964.

[103] Blackwell, 1972, pp. 135–137; Rigby, 1972, p. 11.

[104] Gehlen and McBride, 1968, p. 1240; Fleron, 1973, pp. 57–59.

[105] Fischer, 1968; Blackwell, 1972; Rigby, 1972; Gehlen, 1970; Hough, 1967a, p. 35; Beck, 1973, pp. 124–129; Beck, 1970, especially p. 192. Farrell, 1970b, and Beck et al., 1973, are useful collections on the general topic of elite transformation in contemporary Communist societies.

Among elites of the industrialized Communist world, technical expertise has become more significant—thus far is the theory of technocracy substantiated. But this transformation has not created a new elite of pure technocrats in place of the older, more "political" party elite. Scaling the path to the top now requires technical skills and managerial experience, but the path itself still lies within the party apparatus. Commitment to the party's purposes is still a condition for success. The reality of recruitment fits well the dialectic ideal enunciated by Communists from Mao to Ulbricht—neither Reds nor experts, but Red experts.

What are the implications of this shift in the kind of men and women who lead modern Communist societies? It is sometimes said that the party is coopting the technical and managerial elites, but as we noted in Chapter 3, cooptation is ambiguous. Will the coopted technicians and managers feel more loyalty to their old colleagues in the "technostructure" or to their new colleagues in the party apparatus? Has the party captured the managers, or have the managers begun to capture the party? Each interpretation has exponents among Western observers, and the evidence now available does not allow a neat answer.[106] But the question itself leads naturally to a consideration of the second broad way in which technocracy might make itself felt—greater institutional influence and autonomy for technical and managerial elites.

Some scholars have suggested that a kind of interest-group politics is now emerging in which technical elites will play an increasing role in Communist decision making. Industrial managers in the Soviet Union have apparently tried recurrently to influence party policy, occasionally with success.[107] One systematic analysis of the professional journals of the party *apparatchiki* and of the economic, legal, military, and literary subelites between 1952 and 1965 found that the specialist elites displayed growing self-consciousness, growing aspiration for autonomy and influence on policy making, and growing divergence from the policy views of the party officials.[108] Day-to-day decisions on issues within the specialists' areas of competence are likely to reflect their professional predilections. Such a political system, though not pluralistic, is also not totalitarian; Ludz in his study of East German elites terms it "consultative authoritarianism."[109]

On broader questions involving the direction and control of social change, however, the party remains in command. The more crucial a decision, the more likely it is to be made by central party officials. In the face of party power "collective action on the part of the managers has been a high-risk enterprise."[110]

---

[106] Compare Gehlen, 1970, p. 149, and Fleron, 1973, p. 48.

[107] Azrael, 1966, 1970; see also Skilling and Griffiths, 1971.

[108] Lodge, 1969.

[109] Ludz, 1972.

[110] Azrael, 1970, p. 247.

Many organizational and ideological factors reinforce the party's preeminent position. The role of the party apparatus as the system-wide selectorate is particularly significant. *Nomenklatura* means that party officials screen recruits to both party and specialist elites. Jerry Hough has described the process in practice:

> *If the local party officials normally apply rational-technical criteria in personnel selection, it is because the factor of loyalty seldom needs to be taken into account. . . . If an administrator needs to be reminded of some basic "truth" as the party defines it, the party secretaries have the possibility of reminding him. If he persistently ignores such reminders, the party secretaries are in a position to apply nontechnical criteria in personnel selection.* [111]

Against this background it seems plausible that rising levels of technical expertise within the party apparatus facilitate party supervision of specialized elites. Yet this formulation assumes that policy disputes in Communist elites follow (rather than cross) occupational and organizational lines. Are technocrats and party *apparatchiki* really politically distinct and internally homogeneous groups?

The answer is probably no. More likely, the *apparatchiki*, like regulatory officials in America, share interests and perspectives less with one another than with the specialized subelites each are supposed to control. [112] Similarly, among the specialized elites, apart from a shared desire for more autonomy, "on power-political issues and matters of non-economic policy, it seems unlikely that the managers have been united, and they have probably been divided on a number of critical economic issues as well." [113]

TECHNOCRATS AS PHILOSOPHER-KINGS

Hopes for rule by a wise, disinterested, and unified elite are at least as old as Plato's utopian *Republic*, where power was placed in the hands of philosopher-kings. The theory of technocracy echoes these hopes. Technocracy's proponents believe (and its critics fear), not merely that the new elite will share certain educational and occupational characteristics, but that they will share a common outlook and will act cohesively. However, we have just seen that this assumption is debatable in at least one case. Now at last we must face this issue squarely.

Will the rise of a new political class based on technical skill and expertise

---

[111] Hough, 1969, p. 284.

[112] Hough, 1971.

[113] Azrael, 1970, p. 242.

mean the end of ideological politics, perhaps even of politics altogether? In the case of Western Europe some observers rejoice that

> the "technocrats" are those who deal with issues of public policy in a manner of social scientists rather than political ideologues. They identify the values to be maximized, estimate the probability of success for the available policy alternatives, and weigh the ratio of costs to benefits of each alternative. . . . The ascent of the technocrats to top levels among the elites—their designation as a meritocracy based on skill by contrast with an aristocracy of birth or a plutocracy of wealth— represents the new pragmatism at work among the peoples of postwar Europe.[114]

In the case of Eastern Europe, too, it is supposed that the technocratic transformation of elites will alter elite political culture. Dogmatism will give way to pragmatism, coercion and authoritarianism to decentralization and pluralism, socialist idealism to economic growthmanship. Technocrats, East and West, are said to believe that efficiency is more important than morality, "that politics can and ought to be reduced to a matter of technique, that is, that political decisions should be made on the basis of technical knowledge, not the parochial interests or untutored value preferences of politicians."[115] Engels (echoing Saint-Simon) wrote that communism would bring "the transformation of political government over men into the administration of things and the direction of production processes."[116]

Political scientists have gathered remarkably little evidence to test these speculations empirically. A survey of Yugoslav elites found that industrial managers were distinguished by their commitment to economic development and their skepticism about egalitarian ideals.[117] A study of Polish local elites found a trend from traditional, political thinking toward rational, managerial analysis. Respondents in the study were asked

> what they would do if there were only one unoccupied dwelling left and two families asking to be accommodated in it: a poor widow with two small children and a young engineer who will not want to stay and work in the town if the opportunity to bring his wife is not soon guaranteed. Most of the older type of elite members decided in favour of the widow, while representatives of the new echelons voted for the engineer (several of them commented: "the engineer will build a house for the widow").[118]

[114] Lerner and Gorden, 1969, pp. 205–206.

[115] Baylis, 1974, p. 2.

[116] Engels, 1939, p. 283.

[117] Barton, 1973, pp. 254–257.

[118] Bauman, 1964, p. 540. See also Lane, 1971, p. 128, and Lodge, 1973.

But my own research on politicians and bureaucrats in Western Europe casts doubt on simple hypotheses about the end of ideology and politics. Today's younger politicians are less hostile and dogmatic than their older colleagues, but they are no less prone to analyze policy in terms of ideological and moral principles, no more addicted to mere administrative and technical efficiency. Among high-ranking bureaucrats, the younger generations are more (not less) politically sensitive, more (not less) sympathetic to social pressures and ideological concerns and political democracy.[119] Hopes or fears that politicians of passion and principle will soon be outnumbered by antiseptic social engineers are at least premature.

What happens to elite integration in postindustrial society? Theories differ. Some hold that "as elite occupations become more functionally specific, they become more *interdependent* and *interchangeable*."[120] Across society's nominally separate institutional hierarchies, lateral mobility and mutual awareness increase. As leaders become professional generalists, an increasingly homogeneous social and political outlook emerges.

Other theorists (with somewhat better evidence) reply that occupational specialization and organizational differentiation tend to reduce elite integration. Postrecruitment socialization and patterns of personal interaction foster divisions within the elite along institutional lines. Data on legislative, administrative, and business elites in America and Britain suggest that "it is becoming more and more difficult to move from one elite sphere to another."[121] Longer, more specialized apprenticeships imply less permeable recruitment channels. Careers become compartmentalized. Loyalties and outlooks diverge.

The cohesiveness of the technocratic elite, more narrowly defined, is equally dubious. Technicians and managers may share common social, educational, and occupational backgrounds, but the ethos and camaraderie sometimes nurtured by these shared experiences barely conceal important cleavages within the technocratic elite. Conflict between specialist experts (technicians) and generalist administrators (managers) is endemic in most large organizations. Distinctive experiences and loyalties divide public bureaucrats from private managers, and within each category are found both conservatives and progressives.[122] The spectrum of views among "symbol specialists" is very wide, ranging from humanists and social scientists on the left to engineers and agronomists on the right.[123] Some technocrats bolster the socioeconomic status quo, while others promote innovations that would undermine it. Technocrats may

---

[119] Putnam, 1973*a*, pp. 64–74; Putnam, 1973*b*, pp. 278–286.

[120] Searing, 1971, p. 463.

[121] Keller, 1963, p. 213. See also Guttsman, 1974, p. 24; Stanworth and Giddens, 1974, pp. 86, 94; Rubinstein, 1974, pp. 168–169.

[122] Barton, 1974-1975.

[123] Ladd and Lipset, 1972.

agree that "politics" should be replaced by "rationality," but on most practical issues they rarely agree which policy is uniquely "rational." Political coalitions are as likely to cross as to follow any formalistic line between technocrats and nontechnocrats.[124]

How shall we assess the technocratic revolution? The power of technocrats to resist political direction may be enhanced by a vacuum of political leadership; Fourth Republic France illustrates this phenomenon, as do many Third World countries. But we have seen that in most industrial nations of both East and West, bureaucrats and technicians are faced by increasingly well-trained professional politicians. Indeed, in both East and West the emergence of the hybrid figure of the politician-technician may be the most significant trend in elite composition. One study of modern management concludes, "the managers are a *part* of the ruling elite, but they are not *the* elite."[125]

Political elites will continue to be affected by contemporary economic, social, educational, and political trends. Science, technology, and bureaucracy will set new public problems. Scientists, technicians, and bureaucrats will play new public roles. The emergence of technocratic elites may modify the terms of public debate and private deliberation, as the assumptions and the criteria guiding policy makers are subtly remolded.[126]

Yet the abolition of politics and conflict is chimerical. Daniel Bell, the most renowned contemporary prophet of postindustrial society, points out that

> *Technical knowledge—the administration of things—is a necessary and growing component of many kinds of decisions, including political and strategic ones. But power—the relations between men—involves political choices that are a compound of values and interests and cannot always be "ordered" in a technical way. The technocrat in power is simply one kind of politician . . . no matter how much he employs his technical knowledge.*[127]

Immersed in today's history ourselves, we cannot now know the final contours of this elite transformation. But for good or ill, we can be sure that should technocrats come to rule in the years ahead, they will not be—cannot be—Platonic philosopher-kings. The end of politics is not at hand.

---

124 Suleiman, 1974, pp. 374–383.

125 Kerr, Dunlop, Harbison, and Myers, 1960, p. 145.

126 Baylis, 1974, pp. 13–14.

127 Bell, 1973, p. 79.

BIBLIOGRAPHY

ABEGGLEN, J. A. and HIROSHI MANNARI. 1960. "Leaders of Modern Japan: Social Origins and Mobility," *Economic Development and Cultural Change*, vol. 9, no. 1 (October), 109–134.

ABERBACH, JOEL D., and BERT A. ROCKMAN. 1976. "Clashing Beliefs within the Executive Branch: The Nixon Administration Bureaucracy," *American Political Science Review* (forthcoming).

ABRAMS, MARK. 1965. "British Elite Attitudes and the European Common Market," *Public Opinion Quarterly*, vol. 29 (Summer), 236–246.

AGOR, WESTON. 1971. *The Chilean Senate*. Austin: University of Texas Press.

AKE, CLAUDE. 1967. *A Theory of Political Integration*. Homewood, Ill.: Dorsey.

AKZIN, B. 1967. "The Knesset in Israel," in *Decision-Makers in the Modern World*. Paris: UNESCO, pp. 144–146.

ALFORD, ROBERT R. and HARRY M. SCOBLE. 1968. "Community Leadership, Social Status, and Political Behavior," *American Sociological Review*, vol. 33 (April), 259–271.

ALLISON, GRAHAM. 1970–1971. "Cool It: The Foreign Policy of Young America," *Foreign Policy*, no. 1 (Winter), 144–160.

ALMOND, GABRIEL A., and SIDNEY VERBA. 1963. *The Civic Culture: Political Attitudes and Democracy in Five Nations*. Princeton, N.J.: Princeton University Press.

American Political Science Association, Committee on Political Parties. 1950. "Toward a More Responsible Two-Party System," *American Political Science Review*, vol. 44 (September), Supplement.

ANDERSON, H. DEWEY. 1935. "The Educational and Occupational Attainments of our National Rulers," *The Scientific Monthly*, vol. 40 (June), 511–518.

ANDERSON, C. A. 1956. "The Social Status of University Students in Relation to Type of Economy: An International Comparison," *Transactions of the Third World Congress of Sociology*. London: International Sociological Association, vol. 5, 51–63.

ANDERSON, CHARLES W. 1967. *Politics and Economic Change in Latin America*. Princeton: Van Nostrand.

APTER, DAVID E. 1965. *The Politics of Modernization*. Chicago: University of Chicago Press.

———. 1968. "Nkrumah, Charisma, and the Coup," *Daedalus*, vol. 97 (Summer), 757–792.

ARIAN, ALAN. 1968. *Ideological Change in Israel*. Cleveland: Press of Case Western Reserve University.

ARMSTRONG, JOHN A. 1973. *The European Administrative Elite*. Princeton, N.J.: Princeton University Press.

ARNSTEIN, WALTER L. 1973. "The Survival of the Victorian Aristocracy," in *The Rich, the Well Born, and the Powerful: Elites and Upper Classes in History*, ed. Frederic Cople Jaher. Chicago: University of Illinois Press, pp. 203–257.

ARON, RAYMOND. 1950. "Social Structure and Ruling Class," *British Journal of Sociology*, vol. 1 (March and June), 1–16, 126–143.

ARONSON, SIDNEY H. 1964. *Status and Kinship in the Higher Civil Service.* Cambridge, Mass.: Harvard University Press.

ARORA, SATISH K. 1972. "Social Background of the Indian Cabinet," *Economic and Political Weekly* (India), 7(31–33), Special Number (August), pp. 1523–1532.

AUSTIN, LEWIS, 1975. "The Political Culture of Two Generations: Evolution and Divergence in Japanese and American Values," in *Japan: The Paradox of Progress*, ed. Lewis Austin. New Haven, Conn.: Yale University Press.

AZRAEL, JEREMY R. 1966. *Managerial Power and Soviet Politics.* Cambridge, Mass.: Harvard University Press.

———. 1970. "The Managers," in *Political Leadership in Eastern Europe and the Soviet Union*, ed. R. Barry Farrell. Chicago: Aldine, pp. 224–248.

BACHRACH, PETER. 1967. *The Theory of Democratic Elitism: A Critique.* Boston: Little, Brown.

BACHRACH, PETER and MORTON S. BARATZ. 1962. "Two Faces of Power," *American Political Science Review*, vol. 56 (December), 947–952.

BAILEY, FREDERICK G. 1963. *Politics and Social Change: Orissa in 1959.* Berkeley: University of California Press.

BALTZELL, E. DIGBY. 1966. " 'Who's Who in America' and 'The Social Register': Elite and Upper Class Indexes in Metropolitan America," in *Class, Status, and Power*, ed. Reinhard Bendix and Seymour Martin Lipset. New York: Free Press, pp. 266–275.

BARBER, JAMES DAVID. 1965. *The Lawmakers.* New Haven: Yale University Press.

———. 1972. *The Presidential Character.* Englewood Cliffs, N.J.: Prentice-Hall.

BARGHOORN, FREDERICK C. 1970. "Trends in Top Political Leadership in USSR," in *Political Leadership in Eastern Europe and the Soviet Union*, ed. R. Barry Farrell. Chicago: Aldine, pp. 61–87.

———. 1972. *Politics in the USSR*, 2nd ed. Boston: Little, Brown.

BARNARD, CHESTER I. 1947. *The Functions of the Executive.* Cambridge, Mass.: Harvard University Press.

BARNES, SAMUEL. 1967. *Party Democracy: Politics in an Italian Socialist Federation.* New Haven, Conn.: Yale University Press.

BARNES, SAMUEL H. 1971. "Left, Right, and the Italian Voter," *Comparative Political Studies*, vol. 4 (July), 157–175.

———. 1972. "The Legacy of Fascism: Generational Differences in Italian Political Attitudes and Behavior," *Comparative Political Studies*, vol. 5 (April), 41–57.

BARNES, SAMUEL H. and BARBARA FARAH. 1972. "National Representatives and Constituency Attitudes in Germany and Italy." Paper read at the Sixty-eighth Annual Meeting of the American Political Science Association, Washington, D.C., September.

BARNETT, A. DOAK. 1967a. *China After Mao, with Selected Documents.* Princeton, N.J.: Princeton University Press.

———. 1967b. *Cadres, Bureaucracy, and Political Power in Communist China.* New York: Columbia University Press.

BARTON, ALLEN H. 1969. "A Model of National Opinion-Making Processes" (unpublished manuscript).

———. 1973. "Determinants of Leadership Attitudes in a Socialist Society," in *Opinion-Making*

Elites in Yugoslavia, ed. Allen H. Barton, Bogdan Denitch, and Charles Kadushin. New York: Praeger, pp. 220–262.

_____. 1974-1975. "Consensus and Conflict Among American Leaders," *Public Opinion Quarterly*, vol. 38 (Winter), 507–530.

BARTON, ALLEN H., BOGDAN DENITCH, and CHARLES KADUSHIN. 1973. *Opinion-Making Elites in Yugoslavia*. New York: Praeger.

BAUER, RAYMOND A., ITHIEL DE SOLA POOL, and LEWIS ANTHONY DEXTER. 1963. *American Business and Public Policy: The Politics of Foreign Trade*. New York: Atherton.

BAUMAN, ZYGMUNT. 1964. "Economic Growth, Social Structure, Elite Formation: The Case of Poland," *International Social Science Journal*, vol. 14, 203–216, as reprinted in *Class, Status, and Power*, 2nd ed., ed. Reinhard Bendix and Seymour Martin Lipset. New York: The Free Press, 1966, pp. 534–540.

BAYLIS, THOMAS A. 1973. "Elites and the Idea of Post-Industrial Society in the Two Germanies." Paper read at the Sixty-ninth Annual Meeting of the American Political Science Association, New Orleans, Louisiana, September 1973.

_____. 1974. *The Technical Intelligentsia and the East German Elite*. Berkeley: University of California Press.

BECK, CARL. 1970. "Career Characteristics of East European Leadership," in *Political Leadership in Eastern Europe and the Soviet Union*, ed. R. Barry Farrell. Chicago: Aldine, pp. 157–194.

_____. 1973. "Leadership Attributes in Eastern Europe: The Effects of Country and Time," in Carl Beck et al. *Comparative Communist Political Leadership*. New York: David McKay, pp. 86–153.

BECK, CARL, et al. 1973. *Comparative Communist Political Leadership*. New York: David McKay.

BEER, SAMUEL H. 1957. "The Representation of Interests in British Government: Historical Background," *American Political Science Review*, vol. 51 (September), 613–650.

BELL, CHARLES G. and CHARLES M. PRICE. 1969. "Pre-Legislative Sources of Representational Roles," *Midwest Journal of Political Science*, vol. 13 (May), 254–270.

BELL, DANIEL. 1973. *The Coming of Post-Industrial Society: A Venture in Social Forecasting*. New York: Basic Books.

BELL, WENDELL. 1964. *Jamaican Leaders: Political Attitudes in a New Nation*. Berkeley: University of California Press.

BELLISFIELD, GWEN MOORE. 1973. "Preliminary Notes on the Influence Structure of American Leaders," (unpublished manuscript).

BENDA, HARRY J. 1960. "Non-Western Intelligentsia as Political Elites," *Australian Journal of Politics and History*, vol. 6 (November), 205–218.

BENDIX, REINHARD. 1945. "Bureaucracy and the Problem of Power," *Public Administrative Review*, vol. 5, 194–209, reprinted in *Reader in Bureaucracy*, ed. Robert K. Merton et al. New York: Free Press, 1952, pp. 114–135.

_____. 1970. "Tradition and Modernity Reconsidered," in *Embattled Reason: Essays on Social Knowledge*. (New York: Oxford University Press.

BENNETT, STEPHEN EARL. 1973. "Consistency Among the Public's Social Welfare Policy Attitudes in the 1960's," *American Journal of Political Science*, vol. 17 (August), 544–570.

BERGER, PETER and THOMAS LUCKMANN. 1969. *The Social Construction of Reality*. London: Penguin.

BERLE, ADOLF A., JR., and GARDINER MEANS. 1933. *The Modern Corporation and Private Property*. New York: Macmillan.

BERRINGTON, HUGH. 1974. "The Fiery Chariot: British Prime Ministers and the Search for Love," *British Journal of Political Science*, vol. 4 (July), 345–369.

Biographical Directory of the American Congress, 1774–1961. House Document No. 442, 85th Congress, Second Session. Washington, D.C.: Government Printing Office, 1961.

BIRCH, ANTHONY H. 1964. *Representative and Responsible Government.* Toronto: University of Toronto Press.

———. 1971. *Representation.* London: Pall Mall.

BLACK, GORDON. 1970. "A Theory of Professionalization in Politics," *American Political Science Review,* vol. 64, no. 3 (September), 865–878.

BLACKWELL, ROBERT E., JR. 1972. "Elite Recruitment and Functional Change: An Analysis of the Soviet Obkom Elite 1950-1968," *Journal of Politics,* vol. 34 (February), 124–152.

BLANK, DAVID EUGENE. 1973. *Politics in Venezuela.* Boston: Little, Brown.

BLAU, PETER M. and OTIS DUDLEY DUNCAN. 1967. *The American Occupational Structure.* New York: John Wiley.

BLONDEL, JEAN. 1963. *Voters, Parties, and Leaders: The Social Fabric of British Politics.* Harmondsworth, England: Penguin Books.

———. 1973. *Comparative Legislatures.* Englewood Cliffs, N.J.: Prentice-Hall.

BONILLA, FRANK. 1970. *The Failure of Elites.* Cambridge, Mass.: M.I.T. Press.

BOTTOMORE, T. B. 1964. *Elites and Society.* New York: Basic Books.

BOYD, DAVID. 1973. *Elites and Their Education.* London: National Foundation for Educational Research.

BRADY, DAVID W. 1975. "Critical Elections, Congressional Parties, and Clusters of Policy Changes: A Comparison of the 1896 and 1932 Realignment Eras." Paper read at the Seventy-first Annual Meeting of the American Political Science Association, San Francisco, September.

BRADY, DAVID W., and NAOMI B. LYNN. 1973. "Switched-Seat Congressional Districts: Their Effect on Party Voting and Public Policy," *American Journal of Political Science,* vol. 17 (August), 528–543.

BRAND, JOHN A. 1972. "Councillors, Activists, and Electors: Democratic Relationships in Scottish Cities," in *Comparative Legislative Behavior: Frontiers of Research,* ed. Samuel C. Patterson and John C. Wahlke. New York: Wiley-Interscience, pp. 235–265.

BRAND, JACK. 1973. "Party Organization and the Recruitment of Councillors [Glasgow]," *British Journal of Political Science,* vol. 3 (October), 473–486.

BRANDENBURG, FRANK. 1964. *The Making of Modern Mexico.* Englewood Cliffs, N.J.: Prentice-Hall.

BRICHTA, AVRAHAM. 1974–1975. "Women in the Knesset: 1949–1969," *Parliamentary Affairs,* vol. 28 (Winter), 31–50.

BROUSSARD, J. A. 1956. "A Comparative Study of the Distribution of Social Power in One Hundred Preliterate Societies," Ph.D. dissertation, University of Washington, as cited in Robert M. Marsh, *Comparative Sociology.* New York: Harcourt, Brace & World, 1967, p. 399.

BROWNING, RUFUS P. 1968. "The Interaction of Personality and Political System in Decisions to Run for Office: Some Data and a Simulation Technique," *Journal of Social Issues,* vol. 24, (July), 93–110.

BROWNING, RUFUS P. and HERBERT JACOB. 1964. "Power Motivation and the Political Personality," *Public Opinion Quarterly,* vol. 28 (Spring), 75–90.

BRZEZINSKI, ZBIGNIEW, and SAMUEL P. HUNTINGTON. 1964. *Political Power: USA/USSR.* New York: Viking Press.

BUDGE, IAN. 1970. *Agreement and the Stability of Democracy.* Chicago: Markham.

BUDGE, IAN, J. A. BRAND, MICHAEL MARGOLIS, and A. L. M. SMITH. 1972. *Political Stratification and Democracy.* Toronto: University of Toronto Press.

BUNCE, VALERIE. 1976. "Elite Succession, Petrification, and Policy Innovation in Communist States: An Empirical Assessment," *Comparative Political Studies,* vol. 9 (April, forthcoming).

BURKS, R. V. 1961. *The Dynamics of Communism in Eastern Europe.* Princeton, N.J.: Princeton University Press.

BURNHAM, JAMES. 1941. *The Managerial Revolution.* New York: John Day.

BURNHAM, WALTER DEAN. 1965. "The Changing Shape of the American Political Universe," *American Political Science Review,* vol. 59 (March), 7–28.

_____. 1970. *Critical Elections and the Mainsprings of American Politics.* New York: Norton.

_____. 1974. "Theory and Voting Research: Some Reflections on Converse's 'Change in the American Electorate,'" *American Political Science Review,* vol. 68 (September), 1002–1023.

BUTLER, DAVID E., and MICHAEL PINTO-DUSCHINSKY. 1971. *The British General Election of 1970.* London: Macmillan.

CAMPBELL, DAVID, and JOE R. FEAGIN. 1975. "Black Politics in the South: A Descriptive Analysis," *Journal of Politics,* vol. 37 (February), 129–159.

CARDOSO, FERNANDO H. 1967. "The Industrial Elite," in *Elites in Latin America,* ed. Seymour Martin Lipset and Aldo Solari. New York: Oxford University Press, pp. 94–114.

CAVALA, BILL, and AARON WILDAVSKY. 1970. "The Political Feasibility of Income by Right," *Public Policy,* vol. 18 (Spring), 321–354.

CHARLOT, JEAN. 1973. "Les élites politiques en France de la IIIe à la Ve République," *Archives Européenes de Sociologie,* vol. 14, 78–92.

CHAU, PAHN THIEN. 1972. "Leadership in the Viet Nam Workers Party: The Process of Transition," *Asian Survey,* vol. 12 (September), 772–782.

CHENG, PETER. 1974. "The Japanese Cabinets, 1885-1973: An Elite Analysis," *Asian Survey,* vol. 14 (December), 1055–1071.

CHILDS, DAVID. 1966. *From Schumacher to Brandt: The Story of German Socialism 1945-1965.* London: Pergamon Press.

CHOWDHRY, KAMLA, and T. M. NEWCOMB. 1965. "The Relative Abilities of Leaders and Non-Leaders to Estimate Opinions of their own Groups," in *Small Groups: Studies in Social Interaction,* rev. ed., ed. A. Paul Hare, E. F. Borgatta, and Robert F. Bales. New York: Alfred A. Knopf, pp. 206–216.

CIBOSKI, KENNETH N. 1974. "Ambition Theory and Candidate Members of the Soviet Politburo," *Journal of Politics,* vol. 36 (February), 172–183.

CLARKE, HAROLD D., RICHARD G. PRICE, and ROBERT KRAUSE. 1975. "Ideological Self-Perceptions of Canadian Provincial Legislators: A Comparative Analysis," (unpublished manuscript, University of Windsor, Windsor, Ontario, 1975).

CLUBOK, ALFRED B., FORREST J. BERGHORN, and NORMAN WILENSKY. 1969. "Family Relationships, Congressional Recruitment, and Political Modernization," *Journal of Politics,* vol. 31 (November), 1035–1062.

COBB, ROGER W. 1973. "The Belief-Systems Perspective: An Assessment of a Framework," *Journal of Politics,* vol. 35 (February), 121–153.

COBB, ROGER W., and CHARLES D. ELDER. 1972. *Participation in American Politics: The Dynamics of Agenda-Building.* Boston: Allyn and Bacon.

COCHRANE, JAMES D. 1967. "Mexico's 'New Cientificos': The Diaz Ordaz Cabinet," *Inter-American Economic Affairs,* vol. 21 (Summer), 61–72.

COHAN, AL. 1972. *The Irish Political Elite.* Dublin: Gill and Macmillan.

COHAN, A. S. 1973. "Career Patterns in the Irish Political Elite," *British Journal of Political Science,* vol. 3 (April), 213–228.

COHEN, LENARD. 1973. "The Social Background and Recruitment of Yugoslav Political Elites, 1918-1948," in *Opinion-Making Elites in Yugoslavia,* ed. Allen H. Barton, Bogdan Denitch, and Charles Kadushin. New York: Praeger, pp. 25–68.

COLE, G. D. H. 1955. "Elites in British Society," in Cole, *Studies in Class Structure*. London: Routledge and Kegan Paul, pp. 101–146.

COMSTOCK, ALZADA. 1926. "Women Members of European Parliaments," *American Political Science Review*, vol. 20 (May), 379–384.

CONVERSE, PHILIP E. 1964. "The Nature of Belief Systems in Mass Publics," in *Ideology and Discontent*, ed. David E. Apter. New York: The Free Press, pp. 206–261.

CONVERSE, PHILIP E., AAGE R. CLAUSEN, and WARREN E. MILLER. 1965. "Electoral Myth and Reality: The 1964 Election," *American Political Science Review*, vol. 59 (June), 321–336.

CONVERSE, PHILIP E., WARREN E. MILLER, JERROLD G. RUSK, and ARTHUR C. WOLFE. 1969. "Continuity and Change in American Politics: Parties and Issues in the 1968 Election," *American Political Science Review*, vol. 63 (December), 1083–1105.

COSTANTINI, EDMOND. 1963. "Intraparty Attitude Conflict: Democratic Party Leadership in California," *Western Political Quarterly*, vol. 16 (December), 956–972.

COSTANTINI, EDMOND and KENNETH H. CRAIK. 1972. "Women as Politicians: The Social Background, Personality, and Political Careers of Female Party Leaders," *Journal of Social Issues*, vol. 28, no. 2, 217–236.

CRANE, ROBERT I. 1959. "The Leadership of the Congress Party," in *Leadership and Political Institutions in India*, ed. Richard L. Park and Irene Tinker. Princeton, N.J.: Princeton University Press, pp. 169–187.

CRENSON, MATTHEW A. 1971. *The Un-Politics of Air Pollution: A Study of Non-Decisionmaking in the Cities*. Baltimore: Johns Hopkins Press.

CZUDNOWSKI, MOSHE M. 1972. "Sociocultural Variables and Legislative Recruitment," *Comparative Politics*, vol. 4 (July), 561–587.

DAALDER, HANS. 1971. "On Building Consociational Nations: The Cases of the Netherlands and Switzerland," *International Social Science Journal*, vol. 23, 355–370.

————. 1974. "The Consociational Democracy Theme," *World Politics*, vol. 26 (July), 604–621.

DAALDER, HANS, and JERROLD G. RUSK. 1972. "Perceptions of Party in the Dutch Parliament," in *Comparative Legislative Behavior: Frontiers of Research*, ed. Samuel C. Patterson and John C. Wahlke. New York: Wiley-Interscience, pp. 143–198.

DAHL, ROBERT A. 1956. *A Preface to Democratic Theory*. Chicago: University of Chicago Press.

————. 1958. "A Critique of the Ruling Elite Model," *American Political Science Review*, vol. 52 (June), 463–469.

————. 1961. *Who Governs? Democracy and Power in an American City*. New Haven, Conn.: Yale University Press.

————, ed. 1966. *Political Oppositions in Western Democracies*. New Haven: Yale University Press.

————. 1968. "Power," *International Encyclopedia of the Social Sciences*. New York: Crowell Collier and Macmillan, vol. 12, 405–415.

————. 1971. *Polyarchy: Participation and Opposition*. New Haven, Conn.: Yale University Press.

DAHL, ROBERT A., and EDWARD R. TUFTE. 1973. *Size and Democracy*. Stanford, Calif.: Stanford University Press.

DAHLSTRÖM, EDMUND. 1971. *The Changing Roles of Men and Women*. Boston: Beacon Press.

DAHRENDORF, RALF. 1959. *Class and Class Conflict in Industrial Society*. Stanford, Calif.: Stanford University Press.

————. 1964. "Recent Changes in the Class Structure of European Societies," in *A New Europe?*, ed. Stephen R. Graubard. Boston: Houghton Mifflin, pp. 291–336.

————. 1969. *Society and Democracy in Germany*. Garden City, N.Y.: Doubleday.

DANIELS, ROBERT V. 1971. "Soviet Politics Since Khrushchev," in *The Soviet Union under Brezhnev and Kosygin*, ed. John W. Strong. New York: Van Nostrand-Reinhold, pp. 16–25.

DAVID, PAUL T., and ROSS POLLOCK. 1957. *Executives for Government*. Washington, D.C.: The Brookings Institution.

DAVIDSON, ROGER H. 1969. *The Role of the Congressman*. New York: Pegasus.

DEANE, PHYLLIS, and W. A. COLE. 1967. *British Economic Growth 1688–1959: Trends and Structure*, 2nd ed. Cambridge: Cambridge University Press.

DEKMEJIAN, R. H. 1971. *Egypt Under Nasser*. Albany: State University of New York Press.

———. 1975. *Patterns of Political Leadership: Lebanon, Israel, Egypt*. Albany: State University of New York Press.

DEUTSCH, KARL W. 1961. "Social Mobilization and Political Development," *American Political Science Review*, vol. 55 (September), 493–514.

———. 1966. *The Nerves of Government*. New York: Free Press.

———. 1968. *The Analysis of International Relations*. Englewood Cliffs, N.J.: Prentice-Hall.

DEUTSCH, KARL W. et al. 1967. *France, Germany, and the Western Alliance*. New York: Charles Scribner.

DEXTER, LEWIS ANTHONY. 1963. "The Representative and His District," in *New Perspectives on the House of Representatives*, ed. Robert L. Peabody and Nelson W. Polsby. Chicago: Rand McNally, pp. 3–29.

DI PALMA, GIUSEPPE. 1973. *The Study of Conflict in Western Society: A Critique of the End of Ideology*. Morristown, N.J.: General Learning Press.

DIRENZO, GORDON J. 1967. *Personality, Power, and Politics: A Social Psychological Analysis of the Italian Deputy and His Parliamentary System*. Notre Dame, Ind.: University of Notre Dame Press.

DJILAS, MILOVAN. 1957. *The New Class*. New York: Praeger.

DODD, C. H. 1965. "The Social and Educational Background of Turkish Officials," *Middle Eastern Studies*, vol. 1 (April), 268–276.

DOGAN, MATTEI. 1961. "Political Ascent in a Class Society: French Deputies 1870–1958," in *Political Decision-Makers*, ed. Dwaine Marvick. New York: Free Press, pp. 57–90.

———. 1967. "Les filières de la carrière politique," *Revue Française de Sociologie*, vol. 8 (October–December), 468–492.

DOGAN, MATTEI, and MARIA SCHEFFER-VAN DER VEEN. 1957–1958. "Le Personnel Ministeriel Hollandais (1848–1958), *L'Annee Sociologique*, 3rd ser., pp. 95–125.

DOMHOFF, G. WILLIAM. 1967. *Who Rules America?* Englewood Cliffs, N.J.: Prentice-Hall.

DOMHOFF, G. WILLIAM, and HOYT B. BALLARD, eds. 1968. *C. Wright Mills and the Power Elite*. Boston: Beacon Press.

DONALDSON, ROBERT H., and DEREK J. WALLER. 1970. *Stasis and Change in Revolutionary Elites: A Comparative Analysis of the 1956 Party Central Committees in China and the U.S.S.R.* Beverly Hills, Calif.: Sage Publications.

DOWNS, ANTHONY. 1957. *An Economic Theory of Democracy*. New York: Harper & Row.

DYE, THOMAS R. 1972. *Understanding Public Policy*. Englewood Cliffs, N.J.: Prentice-Hall.

DYE, THOMAS R., and JOHN W. PICKERING. 1974. "Governmental and Corporate Elites: Convergence and Differentiation," *Journal of Politics*, vol. 36 (November), 900–925.

DYE, THOMAS R., and L. HARMON ZEIGLER. 1972. *The Irony of Democracy*, 2nd ed. Belmont, Calif.: Wadsworth.

EASTON, DAVID A. 1965. *Systems Analysis of Political Life*. New York: Wiley.

ECKSTEIN, HARRY. 1966. *Division and Cohesion in Democracy.* Princeton, N.J.: Princeton University Press.

EDELMAN, MURRAY. 1964. *The Symbolic Uses of Politics.* Urbana: University of Illinois Press.

EDINGER, LEWIS J. 1960. "Post-Totalitarian Leadership: Élites in the German Federal Republic," *American Political Science Review,* vol. 54 (March), 58–82.

———. 1961. "Continuity and Change in the Background of German Decision-Makers," *Western Political Quarterly,* vol. 14 (March), 17–36.

———. 1964. "Political Science and Political Biography, II," *Journal of Politics,* vol. 26 (August), 648–676.

———. 1965. *Kurt Schumacher: A Study in Personality and Political Behavior.* Stanford, Calif.: Stanford University Press.

EDINGER, LEWIS J., and DONALD D. SEARING. 1967. "Social Background in Elite Analysis: A Methodological Inquiry," *American Political Science Review,* vol. 61 (June), 428–445.

EHRMANN, HENRY W. 1971. *Politics in France,* 2nd ed. Boston: Little Brown.

EISENSTEIN, JAMES. 1973. *Politics and the Legal Process.* New York: Harper & Row.

EMMERSON, DONALD K., ed. 1968. *Students and Politics in Developing Nations.* New York: Praeger.

ENCEL, SOLOMON. 1961. "The Political 'Elite' in Australia," *Political Studies,* vol. 9 (February), 16–36.

———. 1970. *Equality and Authority: A Study of Class, Status and Power in Australia.* London: Tavistock.

ENGELS, FREDERICK. 1939. *Herr Eugen Dühring's Revolution in Science,* trans. E. Burns. New York: International Publishers.

ERIKSON, ROBERT, and NORMAN LUTTBEG. 1973. *American Public Opinion: Its Origins, Content, and Impact.* New York: John Wiley.

ETHEREDGE, LLOYD S. 1974. "A World of Men: The Private Sources of American Foreign Policy," Ph.D. dissertation, Yale University.

EULAU, HEINZ, and KENNETH PREWITT. 1973. *Labyrinths of Democracy: Adaptations, Linkages, Representation, and Policies in Urban Politics.* New York: Bobbs-Merrill.

EULAU, HEINZ, and JOHN D. SPRAGUE. 1964. *Lawyers in Politics.* Indianapolis: Bobbs-Merrill.

FAINSOD, MERLE. 1963. *How Russia is Ruled,* rev. ed. Cambridge, Mass.: Harvard University Press.

FARRELL, R. BARRY. 1970a. "Top Political Leadership in Eastern Europe," in *Political Leadership in Eastern Europe and the Soviet Union,* ed. R. Barry Farrell. Chicago: Aldine, pp. 88–107.

FARRELL, R. BARRY, ed. 1970b. *Political Leadership in Eastern Europe and the Soviet Union.* Chicago: Aldine.

FEIN, LEONARD J. 1967. *Politics in Israel.* Boston: Little, Brown.

FELDMESSER, ROBERT A. 1966. "Toward the Classless Society?" in *Class, Status, and Power,* 2nd ed., ed. Reinhard Bendix and Seymour Martin Lipset. New York: Free Press, pp. 527–533.

FENNO, RICHARD F., JR. 1959. *The President's Cabinet.* New York: Vintage Books.

———. 1962. "The House Appropriations Committee as a Political System: The Problem of Integration," *American Political Science Review,* vol. 56 (June), 310–324.

FIELD, G. LOWELL, and JOHN HIGLEY. 1973. "Elites and Non-Elites: The Possibilities and Their Side Effects," Warner Modular Publications, Andover, Mass., Module 13, pp. 1–38.

FIELLIN, ALAN. 1967. "Recruitment and Legislative Role Conceptions: A Conceptual Scheme and a Case Study," *Western Political Quarterly,* vol. 20 (June), 271–287.

FIORINA, MORRIS P. 1974. *Representatives, Roll Calls, and Constituencies.* Lexington, Mass.: Lexington Books.

FISCHER, GEORGE. 1968. *The Soviet System and Modern Society.* New York: Atherton.

FISHEL, JEFF. 1972. "On the Transformation of Ideology in European Political Systems," *Comparative Political Studies,* vol. 4 (January), 406–437.

_____. 1973. *Party and Opposition: Congressional Challengers in American Politics.* New York: David McKay.

FLERON, FREDERIC J., JR. 1969. "Toward a Reconceptualization of Political Change in the Soviet Union: The Political Leadership System," in *Communist Studies and the Social Sciences,* ed. Frederic J. Fleron, Jr. Chicago: Rand McNally, pp. 222–243.

_____. 1970. "Representation of Career Types in Soviet Political Leadership," in *Political Leadership in Eastern Europe and the Soviet Union,* ed. R. Barry Farrell. Chicago: Aldine, pp. 108–139.

_____. 1973. "System Attributes and Career Attributes: The Soviet Leadership System, 1952 to 1965," in *Comparative Communist Political Leadership,* ed. Carl Beck et al. New York: David McKay, pp. 43–85.

FRANK, PETER. 1971. "The CPSU Obkom First Secretary: A Profile," *British Journal of Political Science,* vol. 1 (April), 173–190.

FRASURE, ROBERT C. 1971. "Constituency Racial Composition and the Attitude of British M.P.'s," *Comparative Politics,* vol. 3 (January), 201–210.

FREE, LLOYD A. 1959. *Six Allies and a Neutral.* Glencoe, Ill.: The Free Press.

FREY, FREDERICK W. 1963. "Political Development, Power, and Communications in Turkey," in *Communications and Political Development,* ed. Lucian W. Pye. Princeton, N.J.: Princeton University Press, pp. 298–326.

_____. 1965. *The Turkish Political Elite.* Cambridge, Mass.: M.I.T. Press.

_____. 1970 "The Determination and Location of Elites: A Critical Analysis." Paper read at the Sixty-sixth Annual Meeting of the American Political Science Association, Los Angeles, September 1970.

FRIEDRICH, CARL JOACHIM. 1937. *Constitutional Government and Politics.* New York: Harper.

_____. 1966. "An Introductory Note on Revolution," in *Revolution,* ed. Carl J. Friedrich. New York: Atherton, pp. 3–9.

GALBRAITH, JOHN KENNETH. 1969. *The New Industrial State.* Harmondsworth, England: Penguin Books. First published in 1967.

GALLI, GIORGIO, and ALFONSO PRANDI. 1970. *Patterns of Political Participation in Italy.* New Haven, Conn.: Yale University Press.

GALTUNG, JOHAN. 1964. "A Structural Theory of Aggression," *Journal of Peace Research,* vol. 1, no. 2, 95–119.

GANS, HERBERT J. 1964. *The Urban Villagers: Group and Class in the Life of Italian-Americans.* Glencoe, Ill.: Free Press.

GEERTZ, CLIFFORD. 1964. "Ideology as a Cultural System," in *Ideology and Discontent,* ed. David E. Apter. New York: Free Press, pp. 47–76.

GEHLEN, MICHAEL P. 1970. "The Soviet Apparatchiki," in *Political Leadership in Eastern Europe and the Soviet Union,* ed. R. Barry Farrell. Chicago: Aldine, pp. 140–156.

GEHLEN, MICHAEL P., and MICHAEL McBRIDE. 1968. "The Soviet Central Committee: An Elite Analysis," *American Political Science Review,* vol. 62 (December), 1234–1241.

GEORGE, ALEXANDER L. 1968. "Power as a Compensatory Value for Political Leaders," *Journal of Social Issues,* vol. 24, no. 3 (July), 29–50.

_____. 1969. "The 'Operational Code': A Neglected Approach to the Study of Political Leaders and Decision-Making," *International Studies Quarterly,* vol. 13 (June), 190–222.

———— 1974. "Assessing Presidential Character," *World Politics*, vol. 26 (January), 234–282.

GEORGE, ALEXANDER L., and JULIETTE L. GEORGE. 1964. *Woodrow Wilson and Colonial House: A Personality Study*, 2nd ed. New York: Dover.

GIDDENS, ANTHONY. 1972. "Elites in the British Class Structure," *Sociological Review*, vol. 20 (August), 345–372.

GILBERT, G. M. 1950. *Psychology of Dictatorship: Based on an Examination of the Leaders of Nazi Germany*. New York: Ronald Press.

GOLDTHORPE, JOHN H. 1964. "Social Stratification in Industrial Society," in *The Development of Industrial Societies*, ed. Paul Halmos. *Sociological Review*, Monograph no. 8, pp. 97–122. Reprinted in *Class, Status, and Power: Social Stratification in Comparative Perspective*, 2nd ed., ed. Reinhard Bendix and Seymour Martin Lipset. New York: Free Press, 1966, pp. 648–659.

GRANICK, DAVID. 1962. *The European Executive*. Garden City, N.Y.: Doubleday.

GRAZIANO, LUIGI. 1973. "Patron-Client Relationships in Southern Italy," *European Journal of Political Research*, vol. 1 (March), 3–34.

GREENSTEIN, FRED I. 1969. *Personality and Politics*. Chicago: Markham.

GREENSTEIN, FRED I. and MICHAEL LERNER, eds. 1971. *A Source Book for the Study of Personality and Politics*. Chicago: Markham.

GREGOR, A. JAMES. 1968. "Political Science and the Uses of Functionalist Analysis," *American Political Science Review*, vol. 62 (June), 425–439.

GROSSHOLTZ, JEAN. 1964. *Politics in the Philippines*. Boston: Little, Brown.

GROSSMAN, JOEL. 1967. "Social Background and Judicial Decisions: Notes for a Theory," *Journal of Politics*, vol. 29 (May), 334–351.

GRUBER, WILFRED. 1971. "Career Patterns of Mexico's Political Elite," *Western Political Quarterly*, vol. 24 (September), 467–482.

GURR, TED ROBERT. 1970. *Why Men Rebel*. Princeton, N.J.: Princeton University Press.

GUTTSMAN, W. L. 1951. "The Changing Social Structure of the British Political Elite, 1886–1935," *British Journal of Sociology*, vol. 2 (June), 122–134.

————. 1963. *The British Political Elite*. New York: Basic Books.

————. 1974. "The British Political Elite and the Class Structure," in *Elites and Power in British Society*, ed. Philip Stanworth and Anthony Giddens. London: Cambridge University Press, pp. 22–44.

HACKER, ANDREW. 1961. "The Elected and the Anointed: Two American Elites," *American Political Science Review*, vol. 55 (September), 539–549.

HAGEN, EVERETT E. 1962. *On the Theory of Social Change: How Economic Growth Begins*. Homewood, Ill.: Dorsey Press.

HALSEY, A. H., and I. M. CREWE. 1969. "Social Survey of the Civil Service," *The Civil Service: Surveys and Investigations*. London: Her Majesty's Stationery Office, vol. 3(1).

HAMILTON, RICHARD F. 1968. "Party Systems, Party Organizations, and the Politics of New Masses," in *Proceedings of the 3rd International Conference on Comparative Political Sociology*, ed. Otto Stammer. Berlin: Institut für Politische Wissenschaft an der Freien Universität.

HANBY, VICTOR J. 1974. "A Changing Labour Elite: The National Executive Committee of the Labour Party 1900–1972," in *British Political Sociology Yearbook*, vol. 1, ed. Ivor Crewe. London: Croom, Helm, pp. 126–158.

HANCOCK, M. DONALD. 1972. *Sweden: The Politics of Post-Industrial Change*. Hinsdale, Ill.: Dryden Press.

HANSEN, SUSAN BLACKALL. 1975. "Participation, Political Structure, and Concurrence," *American Political Science Review* (forthcoming).

HARASYMIW, BOHDAN. 1969. "Nomenklatura: The Soviet Communist Party's Leadership System," *Canadian Journal of Political Science*, vol. 2 (December), 493–512.

HARBISON, FREDERICK. 1959. "Management in Modern Egypt," in *Management in the Industrial World: An International Analysis*, ed. Frederick Harbison and Charles A. Myers. New York: McGraw-Hill, pp. 154–168.

HARDGRAVE, ROBERT L. 1970. *India: Government and Politics in a Developing Nation.* New York: Harcourt, Brace & World.

HARGROVE, ERWIN. 1969. "Values and Change: A Comparison of Young Elites in England and America," *Political Studies*, vol. 17 (September), 339–344.

HARRIS, P. M. G. 1969. "The Social Origins of American Leaders: The Demographic Foundations," in *Perspectives in American History*, vol. 3. Cambridge, Mass.: Charles Warren Center for Studies in American History, Harvard University, pp. 159–344.

HARRIS, JOHN S. and THOMAS V. GARCIA. 1966. "The Permanent Secretaries: Britain's Top Administrators," *Public Administration Review*, vol. 26 (March), 31–44.

HARTMANN, HEINZ. 1959. "Management in Germany," in *Management in the Industrial World: An International Analysis*, ed. Frederick Harbison and Charles A. Myers. New York: McGraw-Hill, pp. 265–284.

HECLO, HUGH. 1973. "Presidential and Prime Ministerial Selection," in *Perspectives on Presidential Selection*, ed. Donald R. Matthews. Washington, D.C.: Brookings Institution, pp. 19–48.

HEDLUND, RONALD D. 1973. "Psychological Predispositions: Political Representatives and the Public," *American Journal of Political Science*, vol. 17 (August), 489–505.

HEDLUND, RONALD D., and H. PAUL FRIESEMA. 1972. "Representatives' Perceptions of Constituency Opinion," *Journal of Politics*, vol. 34 (August), 730–752.

HEWITT, CHRISTOPHER J. 1974. "Policy-Making in Postwar Britain: a National-Level Test of Elitist and Pluralist Hypotheses," *British Journal of Political Science*, vol. 4 (April), 187–216.

HIRSCHMAN, ALBERT O. 1970. *Exit, Voice, and Loyalty.* Cambridge, Mass.: Harvard University Press.

HO, PING-TI. 1962. *The Ladder of Success in Imperial China: Aspects of Social Mobility, 1368–1911.* New York: Columbia University Press.

HODNETT, GREY. 1965. "The *Obkom* First Secretaries," *Slavic Review*, vol. 24 (December), 636–652.

HOFFERBERT, RICHARD I. 1972. "State and Community Policy Studies: A Review of Comparative Input-Output Analyses," in *Political Science Annual, III*, ed. James A. Robinson. Indianapolis: Bobbs-Merrill, pp. 3–72.

HOLMBERG, SÖREN. 1974. *Riksdagen Representerar Svenska Folket.* Lund, Sweden: Studentlitteratur.

HOMANS, GEORGE C. 1950. *The Human Group.* New York: Harcourt, Brace.

HOOGENBOOM, ARI. 1968. "Industrialism and Political Leadership: A Case Study of the United States Senate," in *The Age of Industrialism in America: Essays in Social Structure and Cultural Values*, ed. Frederic Cople Jaher. New York: Free Press, pp. 49–78.

HOPKINS, RAYMOND F. 1969. "Aggregate Data and the Study of Political Development," *Journal of Politics*, vol. 31 (February), 71–94.

HOSELITZ, BERT F. 1960. *Sociological Aspects of Economic Growth.* Glencoe, Ill.: Free Press of Glencoe.

HOUGH, JERRY. 1967a. "The Soviet Elite: I. Groups and Individuals," *Problems of Communism*, vol. 16, no. 1 (January–February), 28–35.

_____. 1967b. "The Soviet Elite: II. In Whose Hands the Future?" *Problems of Communism*, vol. 16, no. 2 (March–April), 18–25.

_____. 1969. *The Soviet Prefects: The Local Party Organs in Industrial Decision-Making.* Cambridge, Mass.: Harvard University Press.

_____. 1971. "The Party *Apparatchiki*," in *Interest Groups in Soviet Politics*, ed. Gordon Skilling and Franklyn Griffiths. Princeton, N.J.: Princeton University Press, pp. 47–92.

————. 1972. "The Soviet System: Petrification or Pluralism?" *Problems of Communism*, vol. 21, no. 2 (March–April), 25–45.

————. 1975. "The Soviet Experience and the Measurement of Power," *Journal of Politics*, vol. 37 (August), 685–710.

HUNT, WILLIAM H. 1969. "Legislative Roles and Ideological Orientations of French Deputies." Paper read at the Sixty-fifth Annual Meeting of American Political Science Association, New York, September, 1969.

HUNTER, FLOYD. 1953. *Community Power Structure: A Study of Decision Makers*. Chapel Hill: University of North Carolina Press.

————. 1959. *Top Leadership, U.S.A.* Chapel Hill: University of North Carolina Press.

HUNTINGTON, SAMUEL P. 1968. *Political Order in Changing Societies*. New Haven, Conn.: Yale University Press.

————. 1973. "Congressional Responses to the Twentieth Century," in *The Congress and America's Future*, 2nd ed., ed. David B. Truman. Englewood Cliffs, N.J.: Prentice-Hall, pp. 6–38.

IKE, NOBUTAKA. 1972. *Japanese Politics: Patron-Client Democracy*, 2nd ed. New York: Alfred A. Knopf.

IMAZ, JOSE LUIS DE. 1970. *Los Que Mandan (Those Who Rule)*, translated and with an introduction by Carlos A. Astiz. Albany: State University of New York Press, 1970. (Originally published in Spanish—Buenos Aires: Editorial Universitaria de Buenos Aires, 1964.)

International Studies of Values in Politics. 1971. Philip E. Jacob et al. *Values and the Active Community*. New York: Free Press.

IREMONGER, LUCILLE. 1970. *The Fiery Chariot: A Study of British Prime Ministers and the Search for Love*. London: Secker and Warburg.

JACKMAN, ROBERT W. 1972. "Political Elites, Mass Publics, and Support for Democratic Principles," *Journal of Politics*, vol. 34 (August), 753–773.

————. 1975. *Politics and Social Equality*. New York: Wiley-Interscience.

JACKSON, ROBERT H. 1970. "Social Structure and Political Change in Ethiopia and Liberia," *Comparative Political Studies*, vol. 3 (April), 36–62.

JAMES, RALPH C. 1959. "Management in the Soviet Union," in *Management in the Industrial World: An International Analysis*, ed. Frederick Harbison and Charles A. Myers. New York: McGraw-Hill, pp. 319–359.

JENNINGS, M. KENT, and HARMON ZEIGLER. 1971. "Response Styles and Politics: The Case of School Boards," *Midwest Journal of Political Science*, vol. 15 (May), 290–321.

JENNINGS, W. IVOR. 1940. *Parliament*. New York: Macmillan.

JOHNSON, KENNETH F. 1971. *Mexican Democracy: A Critical View*. Boston: Allyn and Bacon.

JOHNSON, LOCH. 1976. "Operational Codes and the Prediction of Leadership Behavior: Senator Frank Church at Mid Career" in *A Psychological Examination of Political Man*, ed. Margaret G. Hermann and Thomas W. Milburn. New York: Free Press (forthcoming).

JOHNSON, R. W. 1973. "The British Political Elite, 1955–1972," *Archives Européenes de Sociologie*, vol. 14, 35–77.

Joint Center for Political Studies. 1975. *National Roster of Black Elected Officials*. Washington, D.C.

JUDD, GERRIT P., IV. 1955. *Members of Parliament: 1734–1832*. New Haven, Conn.: Yale University Press.

KADUSHIN, CHARLES. 1968. "Power, Influence, and Social Circles: A New Methodology for Studying Opinion Makers," *American Sociological Review*, vol. 33 (October), 685–699.

KADUSHIN, CHARLES, and PETER ABRAMS. 1973. "Social Structure of Yugoslav Opinion-Makers: Part I, Informal Leadership," and "Part II, Formal and Informal Influences and Their Consequences for Opinion," in *Opinion-Making Elites in Yugoslavia*, ed. Allen H. Barton, Bogdan Denitch, and Charles Kadushin. New York: Praeger, pp. 155–219.

KATZ, ELIHU, and PAUL F. LAZARSFELD. 1955. *Personal Influence*. New York: Free Press.

KAU, YING-MAO. 1969. "The Urban Bureaucratic Elite in Communist China: A Case Study of Wuhan, 1949–1965," in *Chinese Communist Politics in Action*, ed. A. Doak Barnett. Seattle: University of Washington Press, pp. 216–269.

KAUFMAN, HERBERT. 1960. *The Forest Ranger*. Baltimore: Johns Hopkins Press.

KAUTSKY, JOHN H. 1968. *Communism and the Politics of Development: Persistent Myths and Changing Behavior*. New York: John Wiley.

———. 1969. "Revolutionary and Managerial Elites in Modernizing Regimes," *Comparative Politics*, vol. 1 (July), 441–467.

KAVANAGH, DENNIS. 1974. "Crisis, Charisma and British Political Leadership: Winston Churchill as the Outsider," Sage Professional Paper in Contemporary Political Sociology, 1, 06-001. Beverly Hills, Calif.: Sage Publications.

KELLER, SUZANNE I. 1963. *Beyond the Ruling Class: Strategic Elites in Modern Society*. New York: Random House.

KELSALL, R. K. 1955. *Higher Civil Servants in Britain from 1870 to the Present Day*. London: Routledge & Kegan Paul.

———. 1974. "Recruitment to the Higher Civil Service: How Has the Pattern Changed?" in *Elites and Power in British Society*, ed. Philip Stanworth and Anthony Giddens. London: Cambridge University Press, pp. 170–184.

KENWORTHY, ELDON. 1970. "Coalititions in the Political Development of Latin America," in *The Study of Coalition Behavior: Theoretical Perspectives and Cases from Four Continents*, ed. Sven Groennings, E. W. Kelley, and Michael Leiserson. New York: Holt, Reinhart and Winston, pp. 103–140.

KERR, CLARK, JOHN T. DUNLOP, FREDERICK H. HARBISON, and CHARLES A. MYERS. 1960. *Industrialism and Industrial Man*. Cambridge, Mass.: Harvard University Press.

KESSELMAN, MARK. 1973. "Recruitment of Rival Party Activists in France: Party Cleavages and Cultural Differentiation," *Journal of Politics*, vol. 35 (February), 2–44.

KEY, V. O., JR. 1961. *Public Opinion and American Democracy*. New York: Knopf.

KEYNES, JOHN MAYNARD. 1936. *The General Theory of Employment, Interest, and Money*. New York: Harcourt, Brace.

KIM, JAE-ON, NORMAN NIE, and SIDNEY VERBA. 1974. "The Amount and Concentration of Political Participation," *Political Methodology*, vol. 1 (Spring), 105–132.

KING, ANTHONY. 1973. "Ideas, Institutions, and the Policies of Governments: A Comparative Analysis," *British Journal of Political Science*, vol. 3 (July and October), 291–313, 409–423.

KING, MICHAEL R., and LESTER G. SELIGMAN. 1974. "Critical Elections, Congressional Recruitment, and Public Policy." Paper read at the Annual Convention of the Midwest Political Science Association, Chicago, April 1974.

KINGDON, JOHN W. 1967. "Politicians' Beliefs about Voters," *American Political Science Review*, vol. 61 (March), 137–145.

———. 1973. *Congressmen's Voting Decisions*. New York: Harper & Row.

KINGSLEY, J. DONALD. 1944. *Representative Bureaucracy: An Interpretation of the British Civil Service*. Yellow Springs, Ohio: Antioch Press.

KIRKPATRICK, JEANE J. 1974. *Political Woman*. New York: Basic Books.

———. 1975. "Representation in the American Political Conventions: The Case of 1972," *British Journal of Political Science*, vol. 5 (July), 403–459.

KISSINGER, HENRY A. 1968. "The White Revolutionary: Reflections on Bismarck," *Daedalus*, ("Philosophers and Kings: Studies in Leadership"), vol. 97, no. 3 (Summer), 888–924.

KLEIN, DONALD W. 1966. "The 'Next Generation' of Chinese Communist Leaders," in *China Under Mao: Politics Takes Command*, Roderick MacFarquhar. Cambridge, Mass.: M.I.T. Press, pp. 69–86.

KLEIN, OTA, and JINDRICH ZELENY. 1970. "The Dynamics of Change: Leadership, the Economy, Organizational Structure, and Society," in *Political Leadership in Eastern Europe and the Soviet Union*, ed. R. Barry Farrell. Chicago: Aldine, pp. 199–223.

KNIGHT, MAXWELL. 1952. *The German Executive, 1890–1933*. Stanford, Calif.: Stanford University Press.

KOCHANEK, STANLEY A. 1968. "The Relations Between Social Background and Attitudes of Indian Legislators," *Journal of Commonwealth Political Studies*, vol. 6 (March), 34–53.

KORNBERG, ALLAN. 1967. *Canadian Legislative Behavior*. New York: Holt, Rinehart and Winston.

KORNBERG, ALLAN, and ROBERT C. FRASURE. 1971. "Policy Differences in British Parliamentary Parties," *American Political Science Review*, vol. 65 (September), 694–703.

KORNBERG, ALLAN, WILLIAM MISHLER, and JOEL SMITH. 1975. "Political Elite and Mass Perceptions of Party Locations in Issue Space: Some Tests of Two Positions," *British Journal of Political Science*, vol. 5 (April), 161–185.

KORNBERG, ALLAN, and NORMAN THOMAS. 1965. "The Political Socialization of National Legislative Elites in the United States and Canada," *Journal of Politics*, vol. 27 (November), 761–775.

KORNBERG, ALLAN, and HAL H. WINSBOROUGH. 1968. "Recruitment of Candidates for the Canadian House of Commons," *American Political Science Review*, vol. 62 (December), 1242–1257.

KORNHAUSER, WILLIAM. 1959. *The Politics of Mass Society*. Glencoe, Ill.: Free Press.

KOSTROSKI, WARREN LEE. 1973. "Senatorial Accountability: Volunteerism and Vulnerability, 1920–1970." Paper read at the Sixty-ninth Annual Meeting of the American Political Science Association, New Orleans, Louisiana, September 1973.

KOTHARI, RAJNI. 1970. *Politics in India*. Boston: Little, Brown.

KOURVETARIS, GEORGE A., and BETTY A. DOBRATZ. 1973. "Social Recruitment and Political Orientations of the Officer Corps in a Comparative Perspective," *Pacific Sociological Review*, vol. 16 (April), 228–254.

KRISLOV, SAMUEL. 1974. *Representative Bureaucracy*. Englewood Cliffs, N.J.: Prentice-Hall.

KUBOTA, AKIRA. 1969. *Higher Civil Servants in Postwar Japan*. Princeton, N.J.: Princeton University Press.

KURODA, YASUMASA. 1974. "Successful Politicians in the Japanese House of Representatives, 1890–1972." Paper read at the Seventieth Annual Meeting of the American Political Science Association, Chicago, September 1974.

KURTZ, DONN M., II. 1971. "A Framework for the Analysis of Elite Integration." Paper prepared for the Annual Meeting of the Southern Political Science Association, Gatlinburg, Tennessee, November 1971.

LADD, EVERETT CARLL, JR., and SEYMOUR MARTIN LIPSET. 1972. "Politics of Academic Natural Scientists and Engineers," *Science*, vol. 176 (June 9), 1091–1100.

LAMB, ROBERT K. 1952. "Political Elites and the Process of Economic Development," in *The Progress of Underdeveloped Areas*, ed. Bert F. Hoselitz. Chicago: University of Chicago Press, pp. 30–53.

LANDÉ, CARL H. 1973. "Networks and Groups in Southeast Asia: Some Observations on the Group Theory of Politics," *American Political Science Review*, vol. 67 (March), 103–127.

LANE, DAVID. 1971. *The End of Inequality: Stratification Under State Socialism*. Harmondsworth, England: Penguin.

LANGDON, FRANK. 1967. *Politics in Japan*. Boston: Little, Brown.

LAPALOMBARA, JOSEPH. 1964. *Interest Groups in Italian Politics*. Princeton, N.J.: Princeton University Press.

_____. 1974. *Politics Within Nations.* Englewood Cliffs, N.J.: Prentice-Hall.

LAPIDUS, GAIL WARSHOFSKY. 1975. "Political Mobilization, Participation, and Leadership: Women in Soviet Politics," *Comparative Politics,* vol. 8 (October), 90–118.

LASKI, HAROLD J. 1928. "The Personnel of the English Cabinet, 1801–1924," *American Political Science Review,* vol. 22 (February), 12–31.

LASSWELL, HAROLD D. 1941. "The Garrison State," *American Journal of Sociology,* vol. 46 (January), 455–468.

_____. 1948. *Power and Personality.* New York: W. W. Norton.

_____. 1954. "The Selective Effect of Personality on Political Participation," *Studies in the Scope and Method of "The Authoritarian Personality,"* ed. Richard Christie and Marie Jahoda. Glencoe, Ill.: The Free Press, pp. 197–225.

_____. 1960. *Psychopathology and Politics.* New York: Viking Press. (First published in 1930 by the University of Chicago Press.)

_____. 1961. "Agenda for the Study of Political Elites," in *Political Decision-Makers,* ed. Dwaine Marvick. New York: Free Press, pp. 264–287.

_____. 1965. "Introduction: The Study of Political Elites," in *World Revolutionary Elites,* ed. Harold D. Lasswell and Daniel Lerner. Cambridge, Mass.: M.I.T. Press, pp. 3–28.

LASSWELL, HAROLD D., and ABRAHAM KAPLAN. 1950. *Power and Society: A Framework for Political Inquiry.* New Haven, Conn.: Yale University Press.

LASSWELL, HAROLD D., and DANIEL LERNER. 1965. *World Revolutionary Elites: Studies in Coercive Ideological Movements.* Cambridge, Mass.: M.I.T. Press.

LASSWELL, HAROLD D., DANIEL LERNER, and C. EASTON ROTHWELL. 1952. *The Comparative Study of Elites: An Introduction and Bibliography.* Stanford, Calif.: Stanford University Press.

LASSWELL, HAROLD D., with RENZO SERENO. 1965. "The Fascists: The Changing Italian Elite," in *World Revolutionary Elites: Studies in Coercive Ideological Movements,* ed. Harold D. Lasswell and Daniel Lerner. Cambridge, Mass.: M.I.T. Press, pp. 179–193. (Originally published in the *American Political Science Review,* vol. 31 (October 1937), pp. 914–929.

LEE, MING T. 1968. "The Founders of the Chinese Communist Party: A Study in Revolutionaries," *Civilisations,* vol. 18, 113–127.

LEE, RENSSELAER W., III. 1966. "The *Hsia Fang* System: Marxism and Modernization," *China Quarterly,* no. 28, (October–December), 40–62.

LEGG, KEITH R. 1969. *Politics in Modern Greece.* Stanford, Calif.: Stanford University Press.

_____. 1972. "Interpersonal Relationships and Comparative Politics: Political Clientelism in Industrial Society," *Politics,* vol. 7 (May), 1–11.

LEMARCHAND, RENE, and KEITH LEGG. 1972. "Political Clientelism and Development: A Preliminary Analysis," *Comparative Politics,* vol. 4 (January), 149–178.

LENIN, V. I. 1929. "What is to be Done? Burning Questions of our Movement," in *Collected Works of V. I. Lenin.* New York: International Publishers, vol. 4:2, 89–258.

LENSKI, GERHARD E. 1966. *Power and Privilege.* New York: McGraw-Hill.

LEONARDI, ROBERT. 1974. "Opinioni Politiche delle Correnti Democristiane in Emilia-Romagna," *Rivista Italiana di Scienza Politica,* vol. 4, 387–407.

LERNER, DANIEL, and MORTON GORDEN. 1969. *Euratlantica: Changing Perspectives of the European Elites.* Cambridge, Mass.: M.I.T. Press.

LERNER, DANIEL, with ITHIEL DE SOLA POOL and GEORGE K. SCHUELLER. 1965. "The Nazi Elite," in *World Revolutionary Elites,* ed. Harold D. Lasswell and Daniel Lerner. Cambridge, Mass.: M.I.T. Press, pp. 194–318. (Originally published separately by Stanford University Press in 1951.)

LEVINE, DANIEL H. 1973. *Conflict and Political Change in Venezuela.* Princeton, N.J.: Princeton University Press.

LEWIS, JOHN W. 1968. "Leader, Commissar, and Bureaucrat: The Chinese Political System in the Last Days of the Revolution," in *China in Crisis*, ed. Ping-ti Ho and Tang Tsou. Chicago: University of Chicago Press, vol. 1, bk. 2, 449–481.

LEWIS, PAUL H. 1972. "The Spanish Ministerial Elite, 1938–1969," *Comparative Politics*, vol. 5 (October), 83–106.

LEWYTZKYJ, BORYS. 1967. "Generations in Conflict," *Problems of Communism*, vol. 16, no. 1 (January–February), 36–40.

LIJPHART, AREND. 1968a. *The Politics of Accommodation: Pluralism and Democracy in the Netherlands*. Berkeley: University of California Press.

———. 1968b. "Typologies of Democratic Systems," *Comparative Political Studies*, vol. 1 (April), 3–44.

———. 1969. "Consociational Democracy," *World Politics*, vol. 21 (January), 207–225.

LIPSKY, MICHAEL. 1968. "Protest as a Political Resource," *American Political Science Review*, vol. 62 (December), 1144–1158.

LODGE, MILTON. 1969. *Soviet Elite Attitudes Since Stalin*. Columbus, Ohio: Charles E. Merrill.

———. 1973. "Attitudinal Cleavages Within the Soviet Political Leadership," in *Comparative Communist Political Leadership*, ed. Carl Becket et al. New York: David McKay, pp. 202–225.

LOEWENBERG, GERHARD. 1967. *Parliament in the German Political System*. Ithaca, N.Y.: Cornell University Press.

LOWI, THEODORE J. 1964a. *At the Pleasure of the Mayor: Patronage and Power in New York City, 1898–1958*. New York: Free Press.

———. 1964b. "American Business, Public Policy Case-Studies, and Political Theory," *World Politics*, vol. 16 (July), 677–715.

LUDZ, PETER C. 1972. *The Changing Party Elite in East Germany*. Cambridge, Mass.: M.I.T. Press.

LUPTON, TOM, and C. SHIRLEY WILSON. 1959. "The Social Background and Connections of 'Top Decision Makers,' " *Manchester School of Economic and Social Studies*, vol. 27 (January), 30–51.

LUTTBEG, NORMAN R. 1968. *Public Opinion and Public Policy: Models of Political Linkage*. Homewood, Ill.: Dorsey Press.

MCALISTER, JOHN T., JR. 1969. *Viet Nam: The Origins of Revolution*. New York: Alfred A. Knopf.

MCCLOSKY, HERBERT. 1964. "Consensus and Ideology in American Politics," *American Political Science Review*, vol. 58 (June), 361–382.

MCCLOSKY, HERBERT, PAUL J. HOFFMANN, and ROSEMARY O'HARA. 1960. "Issue Conflict and Consensus among Party Leaders and Followers," *American Political Science Review*, vol. 54 (June), 406–427.

MCCONAUGHY, JOHN. 1950. "Certain Personality Factors of State Legislators in South Carolina," *American Political Science Review*, vol. 44 (December), 897–903.

MCCONAUGHY, JOHN B., and J. DAVID PALMER. 1971. "Personality Traits and Attitudes of Regional Federal Executives." Paper read at the Sixty-seventh Annual Meeting of the American Political Science Association, Chicago, September.

MCFARLAND, ANDREW S. 1969. *Power and Leadership in Pluralist Systems*. Stanford, Calif.: Stanford University Press.

MCGOWAN, PATRICK, and PATRICK BOLLAND. 1971. *The Political and Social Elite of Tanzania*. Syracuse, N.Y.: Syracuse University Program of East African Studies.

MCGREGOR, EUGENE B., JR. 1974. "Politics and the Career Mobility of Bureaucrats," *American Political Science Review*, vol. 68 (March), 18–26.

MCGUIRE, WILLIAM J. 1969. "The Nature of Attitudes and Attitude Change," in *The Handbook of*

Social Psychology, 2nd ed., ed. Gardner Lindzey and Elliot Aronson. Menlo Park, Calif.: Addison-Wesley, vol. 3, 136–314.

McQUAIL, DENIS, L. O'SULLIVAN, and W. G. QUINE. 1968. "Elite Education and Political Values," *Political Studies,* vol. 16 (June), 257–265.

MACRAE, DUNCAN, JR. 1967. *Parliament, Parties, and Society in France, 1946–1958.* New York: St. Martin's Press.

MANLEY, JOHN F. 1965. "The House Committee on Ways and Means: Conflict Management in a Congressional Committee," *American Political Science Review,* vol. 59 (December), 927–939.

MANNHEIM, KARL. 1952. "The Problem of Generations," in Mannheim, *Essays on the Sociology of Knowledge,* ed. Paul Kecskmeti. New York: Oxford University Press, pp. 276–322.

MAO TSE-TUNG. 1965. "Some Questions Concerning Methods of Leadership," in *Selected Works of Mao Tse-Tung.* Peking: Foreign Languages Press, vol. 3, 117–122.

MARCUS, GEORGE E. 1969. "Psychopathology and Political Recruitment," *Journal of Politics,* vol. 31 (November), 913–931.

MARSH, ROBERT M. 1961. *The Mandarins: The Circulation of Elites in China, 1600–1900.* Glencoe, Ill.: The Free Press.

MARTIN, PENNY GILL. 1972. "Administrative and Partisan Experience in the Career Patterns of Norwegian Labor Party Leaders." Paper read at the Sixty-eighth Annual Meeting of the American Political Science Association, Washington, D.C., September.

MARVICK, DWAINE. 1968a. "Political Recruitment and Careers," *International Encyclopedia of the Social Sciences.* New York: Crowell Collier and Macmillan, vol. 12, 273–282.

_____. 1968b. "The Middlemen of Politics," in *Approaches to the Study of Party Organization,* ed. William J. Crotty. Boston: Allyn and Bacon, pp. 341–374.

MATTHEWS, DONALD R. 1954. *The Social Background of Political Decision-Makers.* New York: Random House.

_____. 1960. *U.S. Senators and Their World.* New York: Vintage Books.

_____. 1967. "The Senators in the U.S.A.," in *Decisions and Decision-Makers in the Modern State.* Paris: UNESCO.

MAY, JOHN D. 1973. "Opinion Structure of Political Parties: The Special Law of Curvilinear Disparity," *Political Studies,* vol. 21 (June), 135–151.

MAYHEW, DAVID R. 1974. *Congress: The Electoral Connection.* New Haven, Conn.: Yale University Press.

MEANS, INGUNN NORDERVAL. 1972. "Political Recruitment of Women in Norway," *Western Political Quarterly,* vol. 25 (September), 491–521.

MEDDING, PETER Y. 1972. *Mapai in Israel: Political Organization and Government in a New Society.* Cambridge: Cambridge University Press.

MEIER, KENNETH JOHN. 1975. "Representative Bureaucracy," *American Political Science Review,* vol. 69 (June), 526–542.

MEIER, KENNETH JOHN, and LLOYD G. NIGRO. 1975. "Representative Bureaucracy and Policy Preferences: A Study in the Attitudes of Federal Executives." Paper read at the Seventy-first Annual Meeting of the American Political Science Association, San Francisco, September.

MEISEL, JAMES H. 1962. *The Myth of the Ruling Class: Gaetano Mosca and the "Elite".* Ann Arbor: University of Michigan Press.

MENNIS, BERNARD. 1971. *American Foreign Policy Officials: Who They Are and What They Believe Regarding International Politics.* Columbus: Ohio State University Press.

MEYER, ALFRED G. 1970. "Theories of Convergence," in *Change in Communist Systems,* ed. Chalmers Johnson. Stanford, Calif.: Stanford University Press.

MEYNAUD, JEAN. 1969. *Technocracy*, trans. Paul Barnes. New York: The Free Press.

MICHELS, ROBERT. 1959. *Political Parties: A Sociological Study of the Oligarchical Tendencies of Modern Democracy.* New York: Dover. (First published in German in 1911.)

MICKIEWICZ, ELLEN. 1973. *Handbook of Soviet Social Science Data.* New York: Free Press.

MILBRATH, LESTER W. 1963. *The Washington Lobbyists.* Chicago: Rand McNally.

————. 1965. *Political Participation.* Chicago: Rand McNally.

MILIBAND, RALPH. 1969. *The State in Capitalist Society.* New York: Basic Books.

MILL, JOHN STUART. 1962. *Considerations on Representative Government.* Chicago: Henry Regnery. (First published in 1882.)

MILLER, WARREN E. 1970. "Majority Rule and the Representative System of Government," in *Mass Politics: Studies in Political Sociology*, ed. Erik Allardt and Stein Rokkan. New York: Free Press, pp. 284–311.

MILLER, WARREN E., and DONALD E. STOKES. 1963. "Constituency Influence in Congress," *American Political Science Review*, vol. 57 (March), 45–56.

MILLS, C. WRIGHT. 1956. *The Power Elite.* New York: Oxford University Press.

MITCHELL, BRIAN R., and PHYLLIS DEANE. 1962. *Abstract of British Historical Statistics.* Cambridge: Cambridge University Press.

MOORE, CLEMENT HENRY. 1970. *Politics in North Africa: Algeria, Morocco, and Tunisia.* Boston: Little, Brown.

MOSCA, GAETANO. 1939. *The Ruling Class*, ed. and rev. by Arthur Livingston, trans. Hannah D. Kahn. New York: McGraw-Hill.

MOSKOS, CHARLES C., JR. 1965. "From Monarchy to Communism: The Social Transformation of the Albanian Elite," in *Social Change in Developing Areas: A Reinterpretation of Evolutionary Theory*, ed. H. R. Barringer et al. Cambridge: Schenkman, pp. 205–221.

MUELLER, DENNIS C., ROBERT TOLLISON, and THOMAS D. WILLETT. 1972. "Representative Democracy via Random Selection," *Public Choice*, vol. 12 (Spring), pp. 57–68.

MUSSEN, PAUL H., and ANNE B. WARREN. 1952. "Personality and Political Participation," *Human Relations*, vol. 5 (February), 65–82.

MYERS, CHARLES A. 1959. "Management in Sweden," in *Management in the Industrial World: An International Analysis*, ed. Frederick Harbison and Charles A. Myers. New York: McGraw-Hill, pp. 285–300.

NADEL, S. F. 1956. "The Concept of Social Elites," *International Social Science Bulletin*, vol. 8, no. 3, 419–431.

NAGLE, JOHN D. 1973a. "The Soviet Political Elite, 1917–1971: Application of a Generational Model of Social Change." Paper read at the Sixty-ninth Annual Meeting of the American Political Science Association, New Orleans, Louisiana, September 1973.

————. 1973b. "System and Succession: A Generational Analysis of Elite Turnover in Four Nations." Paper read at the Annual Meeting of the Southern Political Science Association, Atlanta, Georgia, November 1973.

————. 1975. "A New Look at the Soviet Elite: A Generational Model of the Soviet System," *Journal of Political and Military Sociology*, vol. 3 (Spring), 1–13.

NAKANE, CHIE. 1970. *Japanese Society.* Berkeley: University of California Press.

NANDA, KRISHAN. 1973. "Issue Consensus and Dissensus Among Indian Legislators," *Asian Survey*, vol. 13 (August), 740–749.

NATHAN, ANDREW J. 1973. "A Factionalism Model for CCP Politics," *China Quarterly*, no. 53 (January–March), 34–66.

NETTL, J. P. 1967. *Political Mobilization: A Sociological Analysis of Methods and Concepts.* New York: Basic Books.

NEUMANN, HELGA, and BÄRBEL STEINKEMPER. 1973. "Consensus or Dissensus among Elites in the Federal Republic of Germany." Paper read at the Ninth Meeting of the International Political Science Association, Montreal, Canada, August 1973.

NEUSTADT, RICHARD E. 1966. "White House and Whitehall," *The Public Interest*, no. 2 (Winter), 55–69.

NEWCOMER, MABEL. 1955. *The Big Business Executive*. New York: Columbia University Press.

———. 1965. *The Big Business Executive/1964* New York: Scientific American.

NICHOLSON, NORMAN K. 1975. "Integrative Strategies of a National Elite: Career Patterns in the Indian Council of Ministers," *Comparative Politics*, vol. 7 (July), 533–557.

NIE, NORMAN H., G. BINGHAM POWELL, JR., and KENNETH PREWITT. 1969. "Social Structure and Political Participation: Developmental Relationships, Part II," *American Political Science Review*, vol. 63 (September), 808–832.

NIE, NORMAN H., with KRISTI ANDERSEN. 1974. "Mass Belief Systems Revisited: Political Change and Attitude Structure," *Journal of Politics*, vol. 36 (August), 540–591.

NIGHTINGALE, R. T. 1930. "The Personnel of the British Foreign Office and Diplomatic Service, 1851–1929," *American Political Science Review*, vol. 24 (May), 310–331.

NORDLINGER, ERIC A. 1976. *The Praetorian Soldier*. Englewood Cliffs, N.J.: Prentice-Hall.

NORTH, ROBERT C., with ITHIEL DE SOLA POOL. 1965. "Kuomintang and Chinese Communist Elites," in *World Revolutionary Elites: Studies in Coercive Ideological Movements*, ed. Harold D. Lasswell and Daniel Lerner. Cambridge, Mass.: M.I.T. Press, pp. 376–402. (Originally published separately by Stanford University Press in 1952.)

OBREGON, ANÍBAL QUIJANO. 1967. "Contemporary Peasant Movements," in *Elites in Latin America*, ed. Seymour Martin Lipset and Aldo Solari. New York: Oxford University Press, pp. 301–340.

OKSENBERG, MICHEL. 1969. "Local Leaders in Rural China, 1962–65," in *Chinese Communist Politics in Action*, ed. A. Doak Barnett. Seattle: University of Washington Press, pp. 155–215.

ORWELL, GEORGE. 1953. *Shooting an Elephant and Other Essays*. London: Secker and Warburg.

PAHL, R. E., and WINKLER, J. T. 1974. "The Economic Elite: Theory and Practice," in *Elites and Power in British Society*, ed. Philip Stanworth and Anthony Giddens. London: Cambridge University Press, pp. 102–122.

PANTIC, DRAGAN. 1971. "Some Values, Attitudes and Opinions of Opinion Makers" (unpublished manuscript).

PARETO, VILFREDO. 1966. *Vilfredo Pareto: Sociological Writings*, selected and introduced by S. E. Finer, trans. Derick Mirfin. New York: Praeger.

PARK, ROBERT E. 1950. *Race and Culture*. Glencoe, Ill.: The Free Press.

PARKIN, FRANK. 1971. *Class, Inequality, and Political Order: Social Stratification in Capitalist and Communist Societies*. New York: Praeger.

PARRY, GERAINT. 1969. *Political Elites*. New York: Praeger.

PARRY, VERNON J. 1969. "Elite Elements in the Ottoman Empire," in *Governing Elites: Studies in Training and Selection*, ed. Rupert Wilkinson. New York: Oxford University Press, pp. 50–73.

PARSONS, R. WAYNE, and ALLEN H. BARTON. 1974. "Social Background and Policy Attitudes of American Leaders." Paper read at the Seventieth Annual Meeting of the American Political Science Association, Chicago, September 1974.

PAYNE, JAMES L. 1965. *Labor and Politics in Peru*. New Haven: Yale University Press.

———. 1972. *Incentive Theory and Political Process: Motivation and Leadership in the Dominican Republic*. Lexington, Mass.: Lexington Books.

PAYNE, JAMES L., and OLIVER H. WOSHINSKY. 1972. "Incentives for Political Participation," *World Politics*, vol. 24, no. 4 (July), 518–546.

PEDERSEN, MOGENS N. 1972. "Lawyers in Politics: The Danish Folketing and United States Legislatures," in *Comparative Legislative Behavior: Frontiers of Research*, ed. Samuel C. Patterson and John C. Wahlke. New York: Wiley-Interscience, pp. 26–63.

PFEFFER, RICHARD M. 1972. "Serving the People and Continuing the Revolution," *China Quarterly*, no. 52 (October–December), 620–653.

PIERCE, ROY. 1973. *French Politics and Political Institutions*, 2nd ed. New York: Harper & Row.

PIRENNE, HENRI. 1966. "The States in the Social History of Capitalism," *American Historical Review* (1914), pp. 494–515, as reprinted in *Class, Status, and Power: Social Stratification in Comparative Perspective*, 2nd ed., ed. Reinhard Bendix and Seymour Martin Lipset. New York: The Free Press, pp. 97–107.

PITKIN, HANNA FENICHEL. 1967. *The Concept of Representation*. Berkeley: University of California Press.

POLSBY, NELSON W. 1963. *Community Power and Political Theory*. New Haven, Conn.: Yale University Press.

———. 1968. "Community: The Study of Community Power," in *International Encyclopedia of the Social Sciences*. New York: Crowell, Collier and Macmillan, vol. 3, 157–163.

POLSBY, NELSON W., MIRIAM GALLAHER, and BARRY SPENCER RUNDQUIST. 1969. "The Growth of the Seniority System in the U.S. House of Representatives," *American Political Science Review*, vol. 63 (September), 787–807.

POMPER, GERALD M. 1968. *Elections in America: Control and Influence in Democratic Politics*. New York: Dodd, Mead.

———. 1969. "Controls and Influence in American Elections (Even 1968)," *American Behavioral Scientist*, vol. 13 (November–December), 215–230.

PORTER, JOHN A. 1965. *The Vertical Mosaic: An Analysis of Social Class and Power in Canada*. Toronto: University of Toronto Press.

POWELL, G. BINGHAM, JR. 1970. *Social Fragmentation and Political Hostility: An Austrian Case Study*. Stanford, Calif.: Stanford University Press.

———. 1974. "Citizen-Elite Linkages in Austrian Communities: Degree, Structure, and Process of Opinion Representation." Paper read at the Seventieth Annual Meeting of the American Political Science Association, Chicago, September.

———. 1975. "Cultural and Strategic Explanations of Conflict Behavior: Partisan Elites in Austrian Communities." Paper read at the Seventy-first Annual Meeting of the American Political Science Association, San Francisco, September.

POWELL, JOHN DUNCAN. 1970. "Peasant Society and Clientelist Politics," *American Political Science Review*, vol. 64 (June), 411–425.

PRESTHUS, ROBERT. 1964. *Men at the Top: A Study in Community Power*. New York: Oxford University Press.

PREWITT, KENNETH. 1965. "Political Socialization and Leadership Selection," *The Annals of the American Academy of Political and Social Science*, vol. 361 (September), 96–111.

———. 1970. *The Recruitment of Political Leaders: A Study of Citizen-Politicians*. New York: Bobbs-Merrill.

PREWITT, KENNETH, and HEINZ EULAU. 1969. "Political Matrix and Political Representation: Prolegomenon to a New Departure from an Old Problem," *American Political Science Review*, vol. 63 (June), 427–441.

———. 1971. "Social Bias in Leadership Selection, Political Recruitment, and Electoral Context," *Journal of Politics*, vol. 33 (May), 293–315.

PREWITT, KENNETH, HEINZ EULAU, and BETTY ZISK. 1966–1967. "Political Socialization and Political Roles," *Public Opinion Quarterly*, vol. 30, no. 4 (Winter), 569–582.

PREWITT, KENNETH, and WILLIAM G. NOWLIN. 1969. "Political Ambitions and the Behavior of Incumbent Politicians," *Western Political Quarterly*, vol. 22 (June), 298–308.

PREWITT, KENNETH, and ALAN STONE. 1973. *The Ruling Elites: Elite Theory, Power, and American Democracy.* New York: Harper & Row.

PRICE, JOHN W. 1957. "Education and the Civil Service in Europe," *Western Political Quarterly*, vol. 10 (December), 817–832.

PUTNAM, ROBERT D. 1973a. *The Beliefs of Politicians: Ideology, Conflict, and Democracy in Britain and Italy.* New Haven, Conn.: Yale University Press.

———. 1973b. "The Political Attitudes of Senior Civil Servants in Western Europe: a Preliminary Report," *British Journal of Political Science*, vol. 3 (July), 257–290.

———. 1975. "The Italian Communist Politician," in *Communism in France and Italy*, ed. Donald L. M. Blacker and Sidney Tarrow. Princeton, N.J.: Princeton University Press.

QUANDT, WILLIAM B. 1969. *Revolution and Political Leadership: Algeria, 1954–1968.* Cambridge, Mass.: M.I.T. Press.

———. 1970. *The Comparative Study of Political Elites.* Beverly Hills, Calif.: Sage Professional Papers in Comparative Politics, vol. 1, no. 01–004.

———. 1972. "Palestinian and Algerian Revolutionary Elites: A Comparative Study of Structures and Strategies." Paper read at the Sixty-eighth Annual Meeting of the American Political Science Association, Washington, D.C., September 1972.

QUINT, JULES V., and BIANCA R. CODY. 1970. "Preeminence and Mortality: Longevity of Prominent Men," *American Journal of Public Health*, vol. 60 (June), 1118–1124.

RANNEY, AUSTIN. 1965. *Pathways to Parliament: Candidate Selection in Britain.* Madison: University of Wisconsin Press.

———. 1972. "Turnout and Representation in Presidential Primary Elections," *American Political Science Review*, vol. 66 (March), 21–37.

RANNEY, AUSTIN, and WILLMOORE KENDALL. 1956. *Democracy and the American Party System.* New York: Harcourt, Brace.

REJAI, MOSTAFA. 1969. "Toward the Comparative Study of Political Decision-Makers," *Comparative Political Studies*, vol. 2 (October), 349–360.

———. 1973. *The Strategy of Revolution.* Garden City, N.Y.: Doubleday.

REX, JOHN. 1972. "Power," *New Society*, vol. 22, no. 522 (October 5), 25

———. 1974. "Capitalism, Elites, and the Ruling Class," in *Elites and Power in British Society*, ed. Philip Stanworth and Anthony Giddens. London: Cambridge University Press, pp. 208–219.

RIDLEY, F. F. 1966. "French Technocracy and Comparative Government," *Political Studies*, vol. 14 (February), 34–52.

RIGBY, T. H. 1968. *Communist Party Membership in the U.S.S.R., 1917–1967.* Princeton, N.J.: Princeton University Press.

———. 1970. "The CPSU Elite: Turnover and Rejuvenation from Lenin to Khrushchev," *Australian Journal of Politics and History*, vol. 16 (April), 11–23.

———. 1971. "The Soviet Political Elite 1917–1922," *British Journal of Political Science*, vol. 1 (October), 415–436.

———. 1972. "The Soviet Politburo: A Comparative Profile 1951–71," *Soviet Studies*, vol. 24 (July), 3–23.

RIGBY, T. H., and L. G. CHURCHWARD. 1962. *Policymaking in the U.S.S.R., 1953–1961: Two Views.* Melbourne: Landsdowne Press.

RINTALA, MARVIN. 1968. "Two Compromises: Victorian and Bismarckian," *Government and Opposition*, vol. 3 (Spring), 207–221.

RISKIN, CARL. 1971. "Homo Economicus vs. Homo Sinicus: A Discussion of Work Motivation in China." Paper read at the Conference on New Perspectives for the Study of Contemporary China, Montreal, 1971.

ROBINS, ROBERT S. 1975. *Political Institutionalization and the Integration of Elites.* Beverly Hills, Calif.: Sage Publications.

ROGOW, ARNOLD A., and HAROLD D. LASSWELL. 1963. *Power, Corruption and Rectitude.* Englewood Cliffs, N.J.: Prentice-Hall.

ROOS, LESLIE L., JR., and NORALOU P. ROOS. 1971. *Managers of Modernization: Organizations and Elites in Turkey (1950–1969).* Cambridge, Mass.: Harvard University Press.

ROSE, ARNOLD M. 1967. *The Power Structure: Political Process in American Society.* New York: Oxford University Press.

ROSE, RICHARD. 1962. "The Political Ideas of English Party Activists," *American Political Science Review,* vol. 56 (June), 360–371.

———. 1969. "The Variability of Party Government: A Theoretical and Empirical Critique," *Political Studies,* vol. 17 (December), 413–415.

———. 1974. *Politics in England,* 2nd ed. Boston: Little, Brown.

ROSE, RICHARD, and HARVE MOSSAWIR. 1967. "Voting and Elections: A Functional Analysis," *Political Studies,* vol. 15 (June), 173–201.

ROSENAU, JAMES N. 1963. *National Leadership and Foreign Policy.* Princeton, N.J.: Princeton University Press.

ROSENTHAL, DONALD B. 1970. "Deurbanization, Elite Displacement, and Political Change in India," *Comparative Politics,* vol. 2 (January), 169–201.

ROSS, J. F. S. 1955. *Elections and Electors: Studies in Democratic Representation.* London: Eyre & Spottiswoode.

ROUSSEAU, JEAN JACQUES. 1913. *The Social Contract and Discourses,* trans. G. D. H. Cole. London: Dent.

ROYKO, MICHAEL. 1971. *Boss: Richard J. Daley of Chicago.* New York: Dutton.

RUBINSTEIN, W. D. 1974. "Men of Property: Some Aspects of Occupation, Inheritance and Power among Top British Wealthholders," in *Elites and Power in British Society,* ed. Philip Stanworth and Anthony Giddens. London: Cambridge University Press, pp. 144–169.

RUDOLPH, LLOYD I. 1959. "The Eighteenth Century Mob in America and Europe," *American Quarterly,* vol. 11, 447–469.

RUDOLPH, SUSANNE HOEBER, and LLOYD I. RUDOLPH. 1974. "Bureaucratic Lineages in Princely India: The Patrimonial Politics of Authoritarian Regimes." Paper read at the Seventieth Annual Meeting of the American Political Science Association, Chicago, September 1974.

RUIN, OLOF. 1974. "Participatory Democracy and Corporativism: The Case of Sweden," *Scandinavian Political Studies,* vol. 9, 171–184.

RUNCIMAN, W. G. 1963. "Charismatic Legitimacy and One-Party Rule in Ghana," *Archives Européennes de Sociologie,* vol. 4, 148–165.

RUSH, MICHAEL. 1969. *The Selection of Parliamentary Candidates.* London: Thomas Nelson.

RUSH, MYRON. 1974. *How Communist States Change Their Rulers.* Ithaca, N.Y.: Cornell University Press.

RUSSETT, BRUCE M., and ELIZABETH C. HANSON. 1975. *Interest and Ideology: The Foreign Policy Beliefs of American Businessmen.* San Francisco: W. H. Freeman.

RUSSETT, BRUCE M., HAYWARD R. ALKER, JR., KARL W. DEUTSCH, and HAROLD D. LASSWELL. 1964. *World Handbook of Political and Social Indicators.* New Haven, Conn.: Yale University Press.

RUSTOW, DANKWART A. 1968. "Atatürk as Founder of a State," *Daedalus*, ("Philosophers and Kings: Studies in Leadership"), vol. 97, no. 3 (Summer), 795–828.

RUTHERFORD, BRENT. 1966. "Psychopathology, Decision-Making, and Political Involvement," *Journal of Conflict Resolution*, vol. 10 (December), 387–407.

SAINT-SIMON, HENRI COMTE DE. 1952. *Selected Writings*, ed. F. M. H. Markham. Oxford: Basil Blackwell.

SALAMON, LESTER M. 1973. "Leadership and Modernization: The Emerging Black Political Elite in the American South," *Journal of Politics*, vol. 35 (August), 615–646.

SALISBURY, ROBERT. 1965–1966. "The Urban Party Organization Members," *Public Opinion Quarterly*, vol. 29 (Winter), 550–564.

SAMPSON, ANTHONY. 1965. *The Anatomy of Britain Today*. New York: Harper & Row.

———. 1971. *The New Anatomy of Britain*. London: Hodder and Stoughton.

SARTORI, GIOVANNI. 1963. *Il Parliamento Italiano: 1946–1963*. Naples: Edizioni Scientifiche Italiane.

———. 1967. "Italy: Members of Parliament," in *Decisions and Decision-Makers in the Modern State*. Paris: UNESCO, pp. 156–173.

SCALAPINO, ROBERT A. 1972. "The Transition in Chinese Party Leadership: A Comparison of the Eighth and Ninth Central Committees," in *Elites in the People's Republic of China*, ed. Robert A. Scalapino. Seattle: University of Washington Press, pp. 67–148.

SCHATTSCHNEIDER, ELMER E. 1960. *The Semisovereign People*. New York: Holt, Rinehart and Winston.

SCHLESINGER, JOSEPH A. 1965. "Political Party Organization," in *Handbook of Organizations*, ed. James G. March. Chicago: Rand McNally, pp. 764–801.

———. 1966. *Ambition and Politics: Political Careers in the United States*. Chicago: Rand McNally.

———. 1967. "Political Careers and Party Leadership," in *Political Leadership in Industrialized Societies*, ed. Lewis J. Edinger. New York: John Wiley, pp. 266–293.

SCHLETH, UWE. 1971. "Once Again: Does It Pay to Study Social Background in Elite Analysis," in *Sozialwissenschaftliches Jahrbuch für Politik*, ed. Rudolf Wildenmann. Munich: Günter Olzog Verlag.

SCHMIDT, HANNELORE. 1963. "Die Deutsche Exekutive 1949–1960," *Archives Européennes de Sociologie*, vol. 4, 166–176.

SCHRAM, STUART R. 1973. "Introduction: the Cultural Revolution in Historical Perspective," in *Authority, Participation and Cultural Change in China*, ed. Stuart R. Schram. Cambridge: Cambridge University Press, pp. 1–108.

SCHUELLER, GEORGE K. 1965. "The Politburo," in *World Revolutionary Elites: Studies in Coercive Ideological Movements*, ed. Harold D. Lasswell and Daniel Lerner. Cambridge, Mass.: M.I.T. Press, pp. 97–178. (Originally published separately by Stanford University Press in 1951.)

SCHUMPETER, JOSEPH A. 1950. *Capitalism, Socialism and Democracy*, 3rd ed. New York: Harper & Row.

———. 1951. *Imperialism and Social Classes*, ed. Paul M. Sweezy, trans. Heinz Norden. New York: Augustus M. Kelley.

SCHURMAN, FRANZ. 1965. *Ideology and Organization in Communist China*. Berkeley: University of California Press.

SCHWARTZ, DAVID C. 1969. "Toward a Theory of Political Recruitment," *Western Political Quarterly*, vol. 22 (September), 552–571.

SCHWARZ, JOHN E. 1975. "The Impact of Constituency on the Behavior of British Conservative MPs," *Comparative Political Studies*, vol. 8, no. 1 (April), 75–89.

SCOTFORD-MORTON (ARCHER), MARGARET. 1969. "Higher Education and Recruitment of Higher Civil Servants," report prepared for the Working Party "Relation between University Attainment and Employment Requirements of Administrative and Executive Posts" of the International Social Science Council, ISSC/ED/69 W.P. 3 (April).

SCOTT, JAMES C. 1968. *Political Ideology in Malaysia.* New Haven, Conn.: Yale University Press.

―――. 1969. "Corruption, Machine Politics, and Political Change," *American Political Science Review,* vol. 63 (December), 1142–1158.

SCOTT, ROBERT E. 1964. *Mexican Government in Transition,* rev. ed., Urbana: University of Illinois Press.

―――. 1967. "Political Elites and Modernization: The Crisis of Transition," in *Elites in Latin America,* ed. Seymour Martin Lipset and Aldo Solari. New York: Oxford University Press, pp. 117–145.

SEARING, DONALD D. 1969. "The Comparative Study of Elite Socialization," *Comparative Political Studies,* vol. 1 (January), 471–500.

―――. 1971. "Two Theories of Elite Consensus: Tests with West German Data," *Midwest Journal of Political Science,* vol. 15 (August), 442–474.

―――. 1974. "Measuring Values in Elite Research: Development and Administration of a Rank Order Technique." Paper read at the Seventieth Annual Meeting of the American Political Science Association, Chicago, September 1974.

SELIGMAN, LESTER G. 1964. *Leadership in a New Nation: Political Development in Israel.* New York: Atherton Press.

―――. 1971. *Recruiting Political Elites.* New York: General Learning Press.

SELIGMAN, LESTER G., and MICHAEL KING. 1970. "Continuities and Discontinuities in the Recruitment of the U.S. Congress: 1870–1970: Critical Elections, Political Generations, and Legislation" paper read at the Eighth Meeting of the International Political Science Association, Munich, West Germany, August.

SHAFFER, WILLIAM R., RONALD E. WEBER, and ROBERT S. MONTJOY. 1973. "Mass and Political Elite Beliefs about the Policies of the Regime." Paper read at the Sixty-ninth Annual Meeting of the American Political Science Association, New Orleans, Louisiana, September 1973.

SHEEHAN, JAMES J. 1968. "Political Leadership in the German *Reichstag,* 1871–1918," *American Historical Review,* vol. 74 (December), 511–528.

SHILS, EDWARD. 1960. "The Intellectual in the Political Development of the New States," *World Politics,* vol. 12 (April), 329–368.

―――. 1961. "Influence and Withdrawal: The Intellectuals in Indian Political Development," in *Political Decision-Makers,* ed. Dwaine Marvick. New York: The Free Press, pp. 29–56.

―――. 1962. *Political Development in the New States.* The Hague: Mouton.

SHIMSHONI, DANIEL. 1975. "The Extent of the Disadvantage of [Israelis] of Asian and African Origin." (unpublished manuscript). Stanford, Calif.: Center for Advanced Study in the Behavioral Sciences.

SILBERMAN, BERNARD S. 1964. *Ministers of Modernization: Elite Mobility in the Meiji Restoration 1868–1873.* Tucson: University of Arizona Press.

SINGER, MARSHALL R. 1964. *The Emerging Elite: A Study of Political Leadership in Ceylon.* Cambridge, Mass.: M.I.T. Press.

SKILLING, H. GORDON, and FRANKLYN GRIFFITHS, eds. 1971. *Interest Groups in Soviet Politics.* Princeton, N.J.: Princeton University Press.

SMITH, PETER H. 1973. "Continuity and Turnover within the Mexican Political Elite." Paper read at the IV International Congress of Mexican Studies, Santa Monica, Calif., October 1973.

———. 1974. "Making It in Mexico: Aspects of Political Mobility Since 1946." Paper read at the Seventieth Annual Meeting of the American Political Science Association, Chicago, September 1974.

SNIDERMAN, PAUL M. 1975. *Personality and Democratic Politics.* Berkeley: University of California Press.

SNOWISS, LEO M. 1966. "Congressional Recruitment and Representation," *American Political Science Review,* vol. 60 (September), 627–639.

SOLOMON, RICHARD H. 1969. "On Activism and Activists: Maoist Conceptions of Motivation and Political Role Linking State to Society," *China Quarterly,* no. 39 (July–September), 76–114.

———. 1971. *Mao's Revolution and the Chinese Political Culture.* Berkeley: University of California Press.

SOULE, JOHN W. 1969. "Future Political Ambitions and the Behavior of Incumbent State Legislators," *Midwest Journal of Political Science,* vol. 13 (August), 439–454.

SOULE, JOHN W., and JAMES W. CLARKE. 1970. "Amateurs and Professionals: A Study of Delegates to the 1968 Democratic National Convention," *American Political Science Review,* vol. 64 (September), 388–398.

STANLEY, DAVID T., DEAN E. MANN, and JAMESON W. DOIG. 1967. *Men Who Govern: A Biographical Profile of Federal Political Executives.* Washington, D.C.: Brookings Institution.

STANWORTH, PHILIP, and ANTHONY GIDDENS. 1974. "An Economic Elite: Company Chairmen," in *Elites and Power in British Society,* ed. Philip Stanworth and Anthony Giddens. London: Cambridge University Press, pp. 81–101.

STASSEN, GLEN H. 1972. "Individual Preference versus Role-Constraint in Policy-Making: Senatorial Response to Secretaries Acheson and Dulles," *World Politics,* vol. 25 (October), 96–119.

STEINER, JÜRG, and ROBERT G. LEHNEN. 1974. "Political Status and Norms of Decision-Making," *Comparative Political Studies,* vol. 7 (April), 84–106.

STEINER, KURT. 1972. *Politics in Austria.* Boston: Little, Brown.

STERN, ALAN J., SIDNEY TARROW, and MARY FRASE WILLIAMS. 1971. "Factions and Opinion Groups in European Mass Parties," *Comparative Politics,* vol. 3 (July), 529–559.

STEWART, PHILIP D., et al. 1972. "Political Mobility and the Soviet Political Process: A Partial Test of Two Models," *American Political Science Review,* vol. 66 (December), 1269–1290.

STIEFBOLD, RODNEY P. 1974. "Segmented Pluralism and Consociational Democracy in Austria: Problems of Political Stability and Change," in *Politics in Europe: Structures and Processes in Some Post-Industrial Democracies,* ed. Martin O. Heisler. New York: David McKay, pp. 117–177.

STIEHM, JUDITH, and RUTH SCOTT. 1974. "Female and Male: Voluntary and Chosen Participation: Sex, SES, and Participation." Paper read at the Seventieth Annual Meeting of the American Political Science Association, Chicago, September 1974.

STINCHCOMBE, ARTHUR L. 1968. *Constructing Social Theories.* New York: Harcourt, Brace & World.

SUBRAMANIAM, V. 1967. "Representative Bureaucracy: A Reassessment," *American Political Science Review,* vol. 61 (December), 1010–1019.

SULEIMAN, EZRA H. 1974. *Politics, Power, and Bureaucracy in France: The Administrative Elite.* Princeton, N.J.: Princeton University Press.

SULEIMAN, MICHAEL W. 1973. "Attitudes of the Arab Elite Toward Palestine and Israel," *American Political Science Review,* vol. 67 (June), 482–489.

SULLIVAN, JOHN L., and ROBERT E. O'CONNOR. 1972. "Electoral Choice and Popular Control of Public Policy," *American Political Science Review,* vol. 66 (December), 1256–1268.

SZYLIOWICZ, JOSEPH S. 1971. "Elite Recruitment in Turkey: The Role of the Mülkiye," *World Politics,* vol. 23 (April), 371–398.

TACHAU, FRANK, with MARY-JO D. GOOD. 1973. "The Anatomy of Political and Social Change: Turkish Parties, Parliaments, and Elections," *Comparative Politics*, vol. 5 (July), 551–573.

THOMAS, J. A. 1939. *The House of Commons: 1832–1901: A Study of its Economic and Functional Character.* Cardiff: University of Wales Press Board.

———. 1958. *The House of Commons 1906–1911: An Analysis of its Economic and Social Character.* Cardiff: University of Wales Press.

THOMPSON, KENNETH. 1974. "Church of England Bishops as an Elite," in *Elites and Power in British Society,* ed. Philip Stanworth and Anthony Giddens. London: Cambridge University Press, pp. 198–207.

The Times Guide to the House of Commons 1966 and 1970. 1967 and 1970. London: Times Publishing Company.

TOTTEN, GEORGE O., and TAMIO KAWAKAMI, 1965. "The Functions of Factionalism in Japanese Politics," *Pacific Affairs*, vol. 38 (Summer), 109–122.

TOWNSEND, JAMES R. 1967. *Political Participation in Communist China.* Berkeley: University of California Press.

———. 1974. *Politics in China.* Boston: Little, Brown.

TROTSKY, LEON. 1932. *The History of the Russian Revolution,* vol. 1, *The Overthrow of Tzarism,* trans. Max Eastman, New York: Simon and Schuster.

TRUMAN, DAVID B. 1951. *The Governmental Process.* New York: Alfred A. Knopf.

TUCKER, ROBERT C. 1965. "The Dictator and Totalitarianism," *World Politics,* vol. 17 (July), 555–583.

TUFTE, EDWARD R. 1974. "The Political Manipulation of the Economy: Influence of the Electoral Cycle on Macroeconomic Performance and Policy" (unpublished manuscript).

TUOHY, WILLIAM, and DAVID RONFELDT. 1969. "Political Control and the Recruitment of Middle-Level Elites in Mexico: An Example from Agrarian Pol·tics," *Western Political Quarterly,* vol. 22 (June), 365–374.

TURNER, RALPH H. 1960. "Sponsored and Contest Mobility and the School System," *American Sociological Review,* vol. 25 (December), 855–867.

URRY, JOHN, and JOHN WAKEFORD, eds. 1973. *Power in Britain.* London: Heinemann.

VALEN, HENRY. 1966. "The Recruitment of Parliamentary Nominees in Norway," *Scandinavian Political Studies,* vol. 1, 1966. New York: Columbia University Press, 121–166.

VALENZUELA, ARTURO. 1976. *Center-Local Linkages in Chile: Local Government in a Centralized Polity.* Durham, N. Car.: Duke University Press.

VAUGHAN, MICHALINA. 1969. "The Grandes Ecoles," in *Governing Elites: Studies in Training and Selection,* ed. Rupert Wilkinson. New York: Oxford University Press, pp. 74–107.

VERBA, SIDNEY, and NORMAN H. NIE. 1972. *Participation in America: Political Democracy and Social Equality.* New York: Harper & Row.

VERBA, SIDNEY, NORMAN H. NIE, and NAE-ON KIM. 1971. *The Modes of Democratic Participation: A Cross-National Comparison.* Beverly Hills, Calif.: Sage Publications.

VERBA, SIDNEY et al. 1973. "The Modes of Participation: Continuities in Research," *Comparative Studies,* vol. 6 (July), 235–250.

VON BEYME, KLAUS. 1971. *Die Politische Elite in der Bundesrepublik Deutschland* [The Political Elite in the Federal Republic of Germany]. Munich: R. Piper.

VON DER MEHDEN, FRED R. 1969. *Politics of the Developing Nations,* 2nd ed. Englewood Cliffs, N.J.: Prentice-Hall.

WAHLKE, JOHN C. 1971. "Policy Demands and System Support: The Role of the Represented," *British Journal of Political Science,* vol. 1 (July), 271–290.

WALLER, DEREK J. 1973a. "The Chinese Communist Political Elite: Continuity and Innovation," in *Comparative Communist Political Leadership*, Carl Beck et al. New York: David McKay, pp. 154–201.

———. 1973b. "Elite Composition and Revolutionary Change in China: 1965–1969." Asian Studies Occasional Paper Series, no. 7, Southern Illinois University at Edwardsville.

WALTZ, KENNETH N. 1967. *Foreign Policy and Democratic Politics*. Boston: Little, Brown.

WARNER, W. LLOYD. 1963. *The American Federal Executive*. New Haven, Conn.: Yale University Press.

WATERBURY, JOHN. 1970. *The Commander of the Faithful: The Moroccan Political Elite: A Study of Segmented Politics*. New York: Columbia University Press.

WEBER, MAX. 1947. *The Theory of Social and Economic Organization*, ed. Talcott Parsons. New York: Oxford University Press.

———. 1954. *Max Weber on Law in Economy and Society*, ed. M. Rheinstein. Cambridge, Mass.: Harvard University Press.

———. 1958. *From Max Weber: Essays in Sociology*, ed. H. H. Gerth and C. Wright Mills. New York: Oxford University Press.

WEINBERG, IAN. 1967. *The English Public Schools*. New York: Atherton Press.

WEINER, MYRON. 1965a. "India: Two Political Cultures," in *Political Culture and Political Development*, ed. Lucian W. Pye and Sidney Verba. Princeton, N.J.: Princeton University Press, pp. 199–244.

———. 1965b. "Political Integration and Political Development," *Annals of the American Academy of Political and Social Science*, no. 358 (March), 52–64.

WELLHOFER, E. SPENCER. 1974. "Political Parties as 'Communities of Fate': Tests with Argentine Party Elites," *American Journal of Political Science*, vol. 18 (May), 347–363.

WELSH, WILLIAM A. 1969. "Toward a Multiple-Strategy Approach to Research on Comparative Communist Political Elites: Empirical and Quantitative Problems," in *Communist Studies and the Social Sciences*, ed. Frederic J. Fleron, Jr. Chicago: Rand McNally, pp. 318–356.

———. 1973. "Introduction: The Comparative Study of Political Leadership in Communist Systems," in *Comparative Communist Political Leadership*, Carl Beck et al. New York: David McKay, pp. 1–42.

WENCES, RASALIO. 1969. "Electoral Participation and Occupational Composition of Cabinets and Parliaments," *American Journal of Sociology*, vol. 75 (September), 181–192.

WHITSON, WILLIAM W. 1972. "Organizational Perspectives and Decision-Making in the Chinese Communist High Command," in *Elites in the People's Republic of China*, ed. Robert A. Scalapino. Seattle: University of Washington Press, pp. 384–400.

WILDENMANN, RUDOLF. 1968. "Eliten in der Bundesrepublik" (unpublished manuscript).

———. 1971. "Germany 1930/1970: The Empirical Findings," in *Sozialwissenschaftliches Jahrbuch Für Politik*, ed. Rudolf Wildenmann, vol. 2. Munich: Günter Olzog.

———. 1973. "Towards a Socio-Political Model of the German Federal Republic." Paper read at the Ninth Meeting of the International Political Science Association, Montreal, Canada, August 1973.

WILKINSON, RUPERT. 1970. "Political Leadership and the Late Victorian Public School," *British Journal of Sociology*, vol. 13 (1962), pp. 320–330, reprinted in *Learning About Politics: A Reader in Political Socialization*, ed. Roberta S. Sigel. New York: Random House, pp. 337–346.

———. 1964. *Gentlemanly Power: British Leadership and the Public School Tradition*. New York: Oxford University Press.

————, ed. 1969. *Governing Elites: Studies in Training and Selection.* New York: Oxford University Press.

WILLNER, ANN RUTH. 1968. *Charismatic Political Leadership: A Theory.* Princeton, N.J.: Center of International Studies, Princeton University.

WINDER, R. BAYLY. 1962. "Syrian Deputies and Cabinet Ministers, 1919–59, Part I," *Middle East Journal,* vol. 16 (Autumn), 407–429.

WITTE, JOHN F. 1972. "Paths to Power: Recruitment of U.S. Cabinet Secretaries 1789–1972" (unpublished manuscript).

WOLFENSTEIN, E. VICTOR. 1967a. "Some Psychological Aspects of Crisis Leaders," *Political Leadership in Industrialized Societies,* ed. Lewis J. Edinger. New York: John Wiley, pp. 155–181.

————. 1967b. *The Revolutionary Personality: Lenin, Trotsky, Gandhi.* Princeton, N.J.: Princeton University Press.

————. 1969. *Personality and Politics.* Belmont, Calif.: Dickenson.

WOO, BYUNG-KYU, and CHONG LIM KIM. 1971. "Intra-Elite Cleavages in the Korean National Assembly," *Asian Survey,* vol. 11 (June), 544–561.

WOOD, ROBERT C. 1964. "Scientists and Politics: The Rise of an Apolitical Elite," in *Scientists and National Policy-Making,* ed. Robert Gilpin and Christopher Wright. New York: Columbia University Press, pp. 41–72.

WOOTTON, GRAHAM. 1970. *Interest-Groups.* Englewood Cliffs, N.J.: Prentice-Hall.

WOSHINSKY, OLIVER. 1973. *The French Deputy: Incentives and Behavior in the National Assembly.* Lexington, Mass.: D. C. Heath.

ZANINOVICH, M. GEORGE. 1970. "Party and Non-Party Attitudes on Social Change," in *Political Leadership in Eastern Europe and the Soviet Union,* ed. R. Barry Farrell. Chicago: Aldine.

————. 1973. "Elites and Citizenry in Yugoslav Society: A Study of Value Differentiation," in *Comparative Communist Political Leadership,* Carl Beck et al. New York: David McKay, pp. 226–297.

ZAPF, WOLFGANG. 1965. *Wandlungen der Deutschen Elite: Ein Zirkulationsmodell Deutscher Führungsgruppen 1919–1961* [Changes in the German Elite: A Circulation Model of German Leadership Groups, 1919–1961]. Munich: Piper.

ZARTMAN, I. WILLIAM. 1976. "Toward a Theory of Elite Circulation," in *The Study of Political Elites in the Middle East,* ed. I. William Zartman. Princeton, N.J.: Princeton University Press, forthcoming.

ZIDON, ASHER. 1967. *Knesset: Parliament of Israel.* New York: Herzl Press.

ZOLBERG, ARISTIDE R. 1966. *Creating Political Order: The Party-States of West Africa.* Chicago: Rand McNally.

ZONIS, MARVIN. 1968. "Political Elites and Political Cynicism in Iran," *Comparative Political Studies,* vol. 1 (October), 351–371.

————. 1971. *The Political Elite of Iran.* Princeton, N.J.: Princeton University Press.

ZUCKERMAN, ALAN. 1975. *Political Clienteles in Power: Party Factions and Cabinet Coalitions in Italy.* Beverly Hills, Calif.: Sage Publications.

INDEX